The Houses of
Philip Johnson

The Houses of Philip Johnson

Stover Jenkins and David Mohney

Afterword by Neil Levine

Photographs by Steven Brooke

Abbeville Press Publishers   New York London

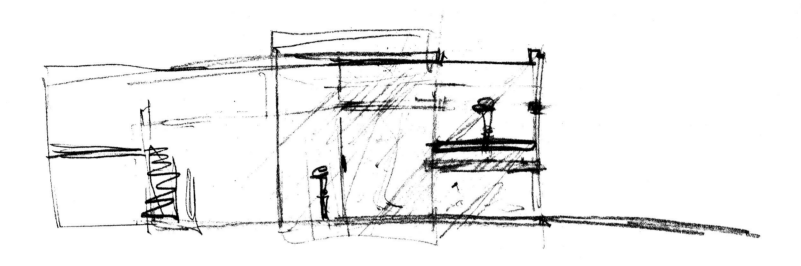

For John Manley and Landis Gores

For Joan Won Yee Chan

Front cover
Eric and Sylvie Boissonnas House
Cap Bénat, France
1958–64. View from central court

Back cover
Philip Johnson Residence (Glass House)
1945–49. View from base of promontory

Frontispiece
Eric and Sylvie Boissonnas House
New Canaan, Connecticut
1954–56. Exterior of garden terrace

This page
Joseph H. Hirshhorn House (project)
1955. Sectional sketch

Editor: Christopher Lyon
Art Director: Julietta Cheung
Designer: Scott Santoro/Worksight
Production Editor: Ashley Benning
Production Manager: Maria Pia Gramaglia

First edition
10 9 8 7 6 5 4 3 2 1

Library of Congress Cataloging-in-Publication Data
Jenkins, Stover, 1953–
    The houses of Philip Johnson / Stover Jenkins and David Mohney;
    afterword by Neil Levine; photography by Steven Brooke—1st ed.
    Includes bibliographical references and index.
    ISBN 0-7892-0114-3 (alk. paper)
        1. Johnson, Philip, 1906---Criticism and interpretation.
        2. Johnson, Philip. 1906---Catalogs. 3. Architect-designed houses.
        I. Mohney, David. II Johnson, Philip, 1906– III. Title.

NA737.J6 M64 2001
728'.092—dc21   2001022396

Contents

Introduction

Surely the two great lives in twentieth-century American architecture belong to Frank Lloyd Wright and Philip Johnson. Like rival stage actors, their mutual respect and antagonism for each other is legendary. Johnson once described Wright as "that great American that perhaps we can admire at the same time that we dislike him as much as I do."[1] Wright, on the other hand, could refer publicly to Johnson as "little Philip," mock his seminal Glass House as a little house left "out in the rain," and still maintain a professional relationship with Johnson over three decades.[2] Yet, despite apparent antagonism, their public careers show notable similarities. Both practiced into their twilight years; Wright was active until his death at the age of ninety-one, and at this writing Johnson is still working as he approaches his ninety-fifth birthday. Both were completely comfortable in a public role, able to use a sharp, even caustic intellect and wit to create significant public personas. Both earned the antipathy of professional counterparts, often because their criticism was directed at their peers. Most importantly, both designed major works that defined American architecture at certain periods in the century.

Here the resemblance falters. Even as most historians and practicing architects would recognize individual works like Wright's Unity Temple and Johnson's Glass House as among the best buildings in America, Wright's entire body of work is known, comprehensively, to a much greater degree than Johnson's. Certainly one reason is that more than forty years have passed since Wright's death, while Johnson continues with a career remarkable not least for its longevity. Scholars and historians have had a head start, so to speak, with Wright. But even with this consideration, Johnson has had less attention in the course of his career than Wright during his. For example, there is nothing on Johnson's achievement comparable to Henry-Russell Hitchcock's comprehensive review of Wright's career through the early 1940s, *In the Nature of Materials*.

Johnson came to the practice of architecture later than most, and from a privileged position as a critic and curator. After earning a degree in philosophy from Harvard College in 1930, he spent several years as head of the Department of Architecture at the fledgling Museum of Modern Art. In that role, he devoted himself to the cause of promoting modern design and

1 (left) Philip Johnson installing the exhibition *Machine Art*, 1934
2 (right) Le Corbusier section of *Modern Architecture: International Exhibition*, 1932, showing photographs and a model of the Villa Savoye (1928–29)

Ludwig Mies van der Rohe
Apartment for Philip Johnson, 1930
3 View of study

architecture in America. His first and most substantial effort was to organize (with Hitchcock) the 1932 *Modern Architecture: International Exhibition*, a groundbreaking effort that today is generally known by the title of a publication by Johnson and Hitchcock that accompanied the show, *The International Style: Architecture Since 1922*. The exhibition included key works of modern architecture such as Ludwig Mies van der Rohe's Barcelona Pavilion (1929; fig. 4) and Le Corbusier's Villa Savoye (1928–29; fig. 2). Johnson traveled extensively in Europe during the two years preceding the exhibition, inspecting outstanding recent projects and meeting with their architects. These leading advocates and practitioners of modernism would become recognized as the heroic first generation of modern architects, among them Mies, Walter Gropius, Le Corbusier, J. J. Oud, and, of course, Frank Lloyd Wright. Another pioneering exhibition was *Machine Art* of 1934, which brought together industrially manufactured objects in the first show of its kind in an American art museum (fig. 1).

Following a five-year period of political involvement, Johnson decided to pursue a career as a practicing architect and enrolled in Harvard's Graduate School of Design in 1940. He finished the program two

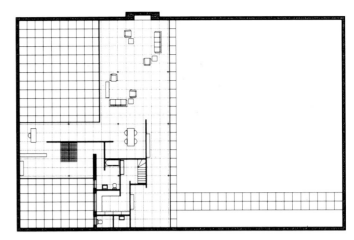

Ludwig Mies van der Rohe
German Pavilion, Barcelona, 1928–29
4 (above) View from the street

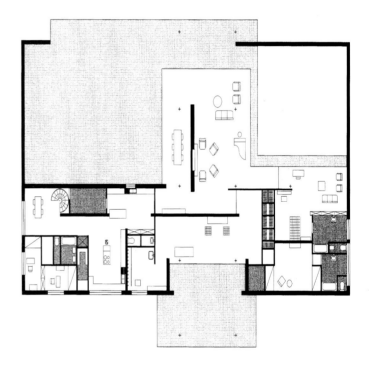

Ludwig Mies van der Rohe
House with three courts (project), 1934
5 (top) Plan

Hubbe House (project), 1935
6 (bottom) Plan

years later. Yet even with a professional degree in hand, he devoted significant time in the first decade of his practice to architectural interests outside those that normally engage a working architect. Thus, to this day, Johnson has seemed to be an architect and something else: museum curator, collector, benefactor, critic, and so forth. His involvement with architectural discourse unrelated to his own projects has allowed others, including Wright, to question his commitment to being an architect. While Wright's life was tempestuous at certain moments, one must consider him to have been an architect first and foremost. In contrast to Wright, Johnson has had a multifaceted life that has at times seemed to overshadow his built work.

A voracious appetite for architecture has nevertheless been a constant in Johnson's multiple careers. As a curator and critic, he has continually sought out and promoted discussion about the leading ideas and practitioners. Whether in the galleries of The Museum of Modern Art or at an impromptu weekend salon for architecture students at the Glass House, Johnson has always embraced the advancement of architecture. His activities have assumed a significant role in defining contemporary trends in architecture, and in furthering the careers of architects associated with those trends. Indeed, Johnson has at times played kingmaker.

His approach towards architectural discourse combines the sometimes conflicting positions of the detached museum professional and the passionate advocate. Perhaps because of his academic background

Philip Johnson Apartment
7 View from balcony

Ludwig Mies van der Rohe
Resor House (project), 1938
8 *(opposite)* Model

and early experience as a curator, Johnson has always attempted to contribute to a broader understanding of contemporary architecture. The exhibitions he has organized at The Museum of Modern Art over a forty-year period have done much to advance public discourse about architecture. Yet this sometimes resulted in Johnson's embrace of contradictory positions. At the height of the postmodern movement, just after Johnson's AT&T Building in New York was completed, critic Kurt Andersen quipped that Johnson should be recognized not only for leading America into the world of modern architecture but for leading it back out again.[3]

Johnson has sometimes benefited professionally and personally from his advocacy of a movement and the architect associated with it. His relationship with Ludwig Mies van der Rohe and Mies's work is the outstanding example of this. Throughout Mies's career, Johnson was his most effective advocate. Mies's work was a major component in the International Style exhibition, which introduced the German's work to an American audience. In 1947 he organized a major retrospective of Mies's work for The Museum of Modern Art that is still regarded as one of the seminal architectural exhibitions of the century. In the mid-1950s he

successfully promoted Mies for the Seagram Building commission.

Johnson gained in a variety of ways from his support of Mies. The renovation of Johnson's New York apartment was Mies's first built project in the United States (fig. 3). In 1934, Johnson himself designed a duplex apartment which prominently incorporated Mies's furniture (fig. 7). Johnson's student designs and early speculative projects were based on the broad ideas expressed in Mies's work as well as particular commissions that Mies had undertaken, such as the Barcelona Pavilion (fig. 4), the court-house projects of the 1930s (figs. 5 and 6), the Resor House project (fig. 8), and the projects for glass skyscrapers. Even Johnson's Glass House may owe its origins to a sketch by Mies for a glass house on a slope as well as to the house Mies designed for Dr. Edith Farnsworth in Plano, Illinois (fig. 75). Johnson gained in other ways from Mies's professional success; certainly the most prominent example is his collaboration with Mies on the design of the Seagram Building. Both the cause of modern architecture and Johnson's own place within it benefited from this engagement.

Johnson's strong advocacy of Mies should not obscure his study of the work of other great modern architects: Marcel Breuer, Le Corbusier,

Louis Kahn, and Frank Lloyd Wright. The association of Johnson's architecture with Wright may seem especially disconcerting. In the course of numerous interviews for this book, Johnson seemed reluctant to discuss Wright's architecture (in contrast to his eagerness to acknowledge Mies's designs as models for his own). When one examines the projects Johnson undertook, however, one senses the presence of the work of many architects. It is impossible, for example, to discuss Johnson's 1952 design of a house for Mr. and Mrs. John Lucas on Nantucket without considering Frank Lloyd Wright's Ralph Jester House of 1938. It is equally impossible to omit some discussion of historical sources, ranging from sixteenth-century Italian Renaissance villas to the work of eighteenth-century French architect Claude Nicolas Ledoux, when considering projects such as the two houses for Sylvie and Eric Boissonnas (see pages 152 and 172).

Johnson's willingness to openly embrace at least some of these sources, especially the historical ones, runs counter to the idea of invention that is such a strong undercurrent of modern architecture. It has thrown several generations of critics into uncertain waters. From the publication of Johnson's own assessment of his Glass House in *Architectural Review* (see Neil Levine's afterword, page 269, for a detailed analysis of that article), critics have shifted uncomfortably as Johnson readily acknowledged his sources. They have largely accepted it when he has claimed first-generation modern architects, artists, and theorists as his inspiration, and extended acceptance to the classical antecedents of high modernism. However, when Johnson turned to other, less obviously "modern" sources, critics soured. Johnson's subversion of the tradition of invention, and his embrace of unusual sources, have called his motivations into question. The fact that he possessed the design abilities to shape these precedents and ideas to a level of refinement that often surpasses the original work merely exacerbates the question. Like Wright, Johnson makes a tantalizing target but somehow dances out of the reach of his critics.

The fact that Johnson's most important building, his own Glass House in New Canaan, Connecticut, came so early in his career intensifies the critics' problem. In some respects, the remarkable accomplishment of that building was recognized so immediately that it precluded looking beyond it to other residential work. Furthermore, the Glass House has remained prominently in the architectural spotlight. As Johnson has added a series of structures to the estate during the half-century since its completion, he has reintroduced the Glass House to successive generations of architects and historians. Given its initial and enduring success, one might ask, What could he possibly do for an encore?

This certainly is the dilemma faced by critics and scholars examining the rest of Johnson's residential work. While some of the houses were published in journals and books through the 1950s and 1960s, many were not. Even those that were published, as interesting and remarkable as they might have been, could not compare with the Glass House, in all its Miesian splendor. Thus extensive examination of other projects, especially those that depart from the Miesian idiom, rarely happened. Those achievements were obscured, ironically enough, by the transparent pavilion in New Canaan and the multifaceted career of its designer.

Thus the full presentation, much less a complete understanding, of Philip Johnson's residential work has been lacking to date. The work, we believe, is remarkable, and in many respects unexpected in its range and diversity. To comprehend the entirety of Johnson's accomplishment, it is necessary to start by considering the unconventional beginnings of his architectural practice. Even as a student, he could garner the attention of the professional press with a project that set a high standard for the rest of his career.

Architect in Training

1940–1943

1

Philip Johnson House (Ash Street House)
9 View of courtyard and façade

In the fall of 1940, ten years after he graduated from Harvard College, Philip Johnson returned to his alma mater to study at the Graduate School of Design, intent on becoming a practicing architect. Ironies abound regarding his decision. In many respects, he fit the role of teacher more than student (fig. 10). First of all, he was thirty-four years old—older than not only his fellow students, but even a few of his professors. Secondly, in all likelihood he was far better acquainted with contemporary developments in architecture than were many of the faculty. Since graduating from Harvard College, he had served as head of the Department of Architecture at The Museum of Modern Art. In 1932, as noted earlier, he had organized *Modern Architecture: International Exhibition* and co-authored its accompanying book, *The International Style: Architecture since 1922* (see fig. 2).

In the course of preparing the book and exhibition, Johnson had developed first-hand relationships with many of the major modern architects of the early twentieth century: Ludwig Mies van der Rohe, Le Corbusier, Frank Lloyd Wright, and Walter Gropius, among others. Johnson was uniquely familiar with the composition, materials, and ideas behind this new architecture. Moreover, his collaboration and travels with Alfred H. Barr, Jr., the director of The Museum of Modern Art, and with Henry-Russell Hitchcock, an architectural historian whose time at Harvard had overlapped a year with Johnson's, had heightened and refined his visual sensibilities and understanding of modern art and architecture.

The arrival of modern architecture in the academic milieu, certainly spurred on by the International Style exhibition, was confirmed at the end of the 1930s by two significant appointments: Walter Gropius as chair of the Department of Architecture at Harvard's Graduate School of Design, and Mies van der Rohe as director of the Armour Institute of Technology in Chicago (later the Illinois Institute of Technology). Gropius's charge at Harvard was to transform the Beaux-Arts method of educating architects into one based on modern architecture and the culture that produced it. Because of his age, experience, and familiarity with this new way of thinking about architecture, Johnson must have felt very confident as an architecture student. He would later recall being excused from a required history class, since *The International Style: Architecture Since 1922* was a primary text for the course.[4]

10 Philip Johnson as an architecture student at Harvard University, 1941

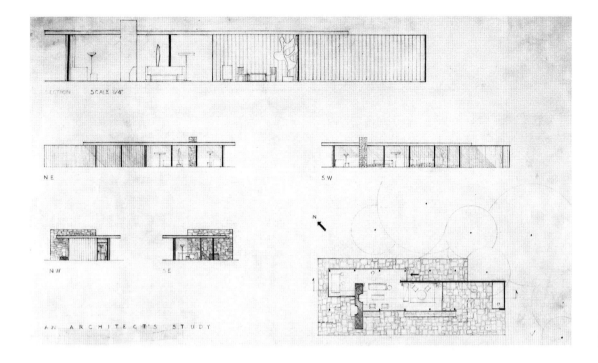

An Architect's Study (project)
11 Elevations and plan ("Oct 4")

An Architect's Study (project), 1940

Johnson was almost immediately recognized by both students and faculty for his unusual talent and his background in contemporary architecture.[5] His profound understanding of the vocabulary and application of modern architecture served him well and his social graces and bravado helped to establish him as a leader among his peers. For example, Johnson remembers organizing the students in one studio to standardize their presentation techniques for all their final projects, the better to impress their professor.[6] Yet it was in his design projects that Johnson made his strongest statement. In them he drew on the ideas of the design faculty at the Graduate School of Design—for example, Breuer's binuclear planning strategy, which appears in the row houses and freestanding house schemes discussed below. Ideas developed in these and other projects would appear repeatedly in the course of his entire professional career.

Two of Johnson's student projects are especially noteworthy for the degree to which they foreshadow his career, both in terms of their designs and the confidence with which he executed them. Interestingly, they are the first and last projects he carried out at Harvard. The final one, discussed below, was the built design for his house in Cambridge. The first, for an architect's study, was assigned in October 1940 (fig. 11). Its simple program, calling only for working and social spaces, is resolved into a pavilion made mostly of glass. Set on a stone terrace flush with the ground, the pavilion is dominated by a large masonry mass that incorporates two fireplaces facing opposite directions—one inside the pavilion, one outside. Though it is a student project, the architect's study is a remarkable precursor for much of Johnson's later domestic work. It was the first of many houses Johnson would design over the course of his career in which a glass pavilion is the central feature—his own Glass House, in New Canaan, Connecticut, being the paramount example of this theme in his work.

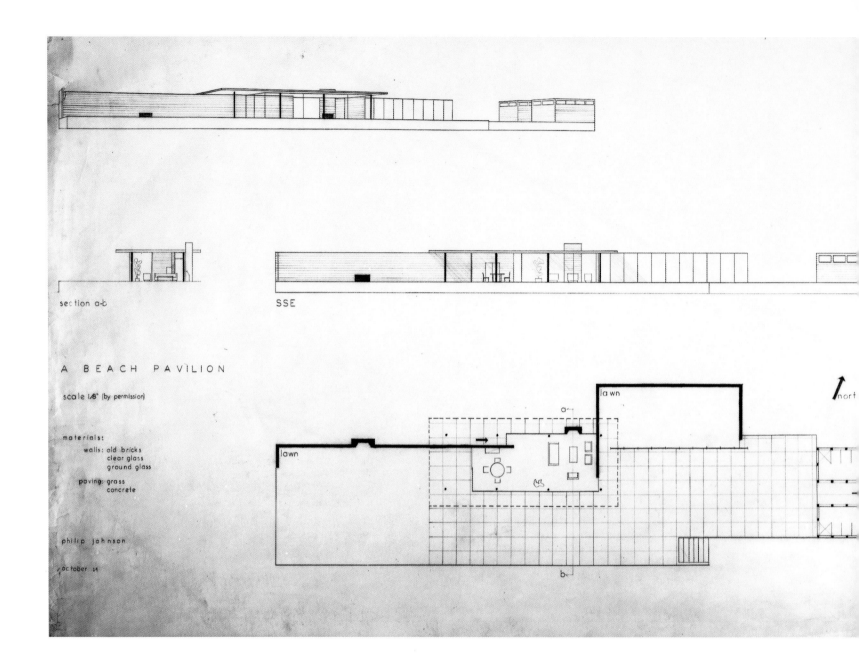

section a-b   SSE

A BEACH PAVILION

scale 1/8" (by permission)

materials:
    walls: old bricks
           clear glass
           ground glass

    paving: grass
            concrete

philip johnson

october 14

lawn   a   lawn   north   b

A Beach Pavilion (project), 1940

Another early design project, probably his second assignment in architecture school, affirms his fluency. The task was to design "a beach pavilion." Johnson's solution was thoroughly modern in character: a long podium serves as the base for a glass-walled pavilion located at the center of the composition and facing the water, which would be used for social activities. A pair of smaller structures at the east end of the podium provide changing rooms and showers. The roofs of all three buildings are flat, that of the pavilion being cantilevered far beyond the grid of column supports, while the edges of the service building roofs are defined by the perimeters of their bearing walls (fig. 12). Two sides of the pavilion are partially enclosed by walls of "old brick" that extend beyond the pavilion to the west and north, each enclosing from the rear a section of the area defined by the podium. These walls also define the view to the rear (northward) from within the pavilion.

A Beach Pavilion (project)
12 Plan and elevations ("Oct 14")

The podium's gridded surface of concrete pavers is flanked on the west and north by areas of lawn. The long wall behind the western section incorporates an outdoor fireplace. The other grass parterre is enclosed by masonry walls on three sides and a freestanding glass wall at its southern edge, creating a nearly private exterior space open to the elements yet almost completely enclosed.

Within the pavilion there are two areas for social activity: at one end a table for dining, and at the other a grouping of chairs and a sofa centered on an interior fireplace, which is engaged in a glass, not masonry, wall. The south and west walls, and most of the north one, are large sheets of glass. Contrasting in materials as well as function, the service pavilions are designed with masonry walls on all sides, to provide privacy for changing and showering, and clerestory windows running the length of three sides to allow natural illumination.

The composition and materials of the beach pavilion clearly derive from Mies van der Rohe's work, particularly the Barcelona Pavilion of 1928–29 (fig. 4).[7] A podium, large expanses of glass, and running masonry walls were defining features of Mies's project, which Johnson had featured in the International Style exhibition. The presentation drawing for the beach pavilion is interesting for several reasons. Johnson has never considered himself much of a draftsman, and the drawing quality is amateurish, as one might expect of a beginning student.[8] In the title block, the scale is noted as "⅛" by permission." Clearly the drawing was at some variance from the expectations of the studio teacher, and unusual in the culture of architectural education where presentation requirements are well-established. But the enormous size of the podium in Johnson's design must have made it necessary to reduce the scale by half, from a standard 1:48 to 1:96, in order to render the drawing at a reasonable size. Even so, Johnson remembered that his presentation was so much bigger than those of his classmates that his instructor was speechless: "This wasn't the kind of thing he'd ever seen in his lifetime, anyhow!"[9]

Looking carefully at the three structures, one notices a telling distinction. While the pavilion owes a clear debt to Mies, there is a nascent classicism evident in the pair of changing rooms, whose symmetrical relationship is defined by a central axis. These twin structures offer a dramatic contrast with the open, flowing space of the pavilion. Thus, the physical and programmatic separation of this pair of service buildings from the rest of the composition is accentuated by stylistic differences as well: open, asymmetrical modern space and new materials are opposed by contained, regularly ordered spaces built of traditional materials. This juxtaposition of disparate styles foreshadows a significant theme of Johnson's domestic architecture.

Row Houses and Freestanding House (projects), 1941

Recalling his days as an architecture student, Johnson has noted that the programs he was assigned were all houses. In fact, the student projects included an equal number of non-residential projects, including an office building and an airport in brick, steel, and glass. Among the residential projects were one for row houses

(figs. 13–14) and one for a freestanding house (figs. 15–17). In both he clearly differentiates public and private functions. The row house scheme uses an enclosed courtyard as a means of creating separate zones; the court would have also provided a striking backdrop as one entered each house. The street wall is brick, punctuated only by small bedroom windows. The rear walls, facing a garden area, are large panels of sliding glass (fig. 13). One of the goals of the modern movement, evident in the row house design, was efficient use of materials and spaces. While employing the spare, modern architectural language, Johnson's design is nevertheless generous in its allocations of space, especially the sizable living area and the enclosed courtyard. Reviewing the project late in his career, Johnson remarked that it "wasn't very cheap [to build], was it?"[10]

The freestanding house shows the clear influence of Marcel Breuer, who assigned the program. Johnson had gravitated to Breuer, entering his advanced class in 1941.[11] Here Johnson employs Breuer's concept of the binuclear house and assigns family activities and individual functions to separate blocks, connected only by a glass walkway (fig. 17). As in the plan of the row houses, this design is largely closed to the street, with only two clerestory windows on the front elevation (fig. 15). On the garden side, however, the design opens

Row Houses (project)
13 Perspective sketch

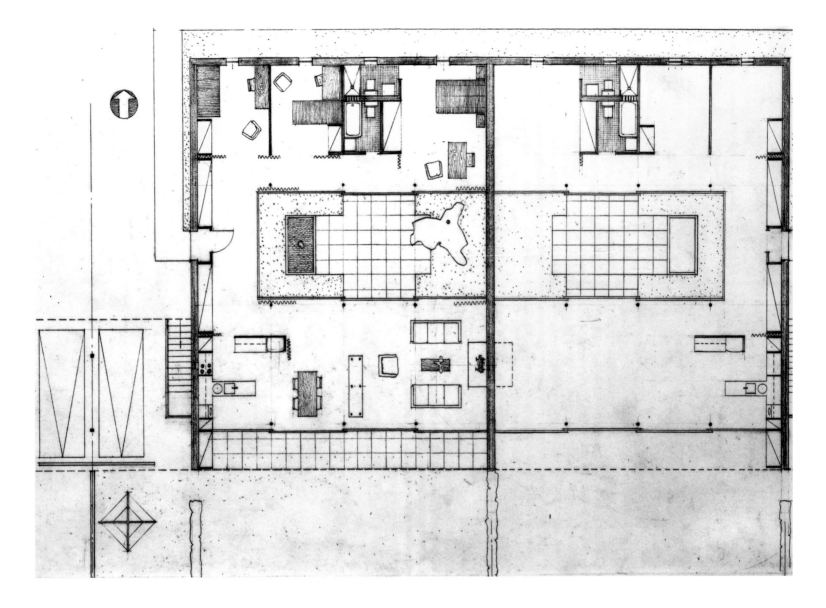

Row Houses (project)
14 Plan

up through the extensive use of large sheets of glass as walls (fig. 16). The orientation of the blocks—not aligned, but pushed to either side of the site in a pinwheel fashion—defines exterior spaces on opposing corners of the site. One, dedicated to private activity, is a terrace off the family area whose paving encloses a grass parterre with a sculpture. The other area, the service side of the building, is largely occupied by a carport.

The presentations of these two projects are more sophisticated than that for the beach pavilion. His perspectival sketches convey a sense of materials (though not specified, we can assume the exterior walls would have been brick). The plans are refined, with spatial, landscape, and furnishing elements clearly indicated at a variety of scales. In short, his presentation technique was catching up to his knowledge and abilities.

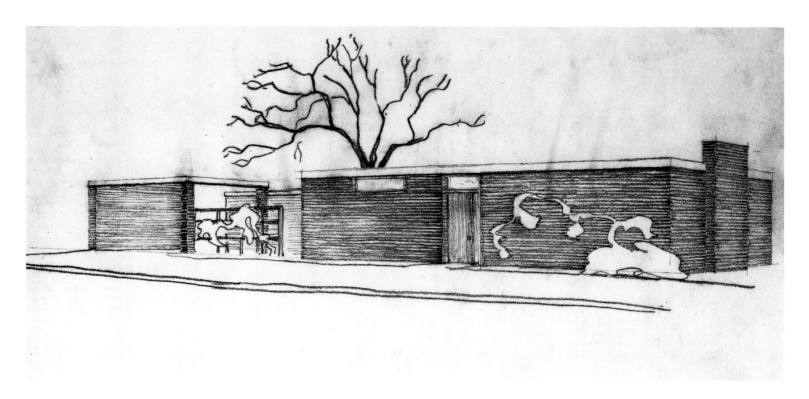

Freestanding House (project)
15 and 16 Perspective sketches

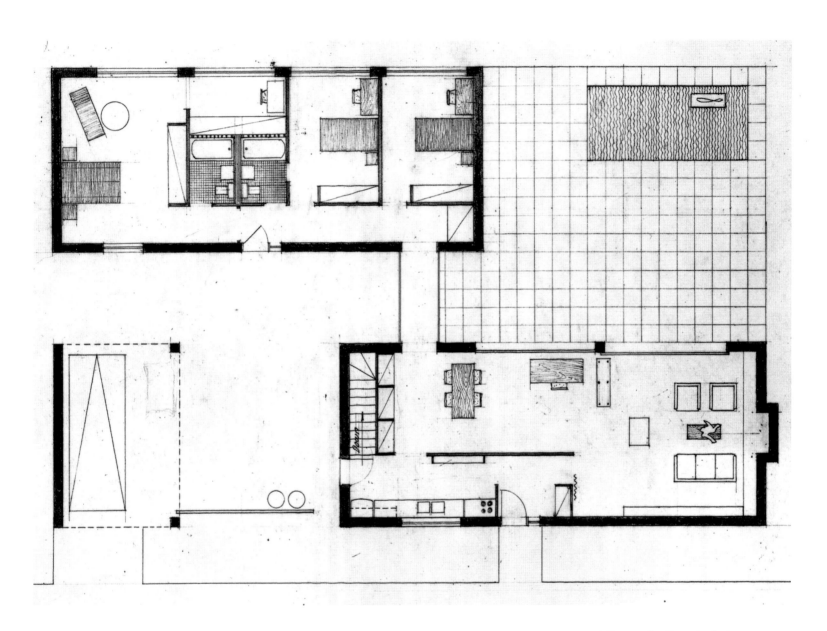

Freestanding House (project)

17 Plan

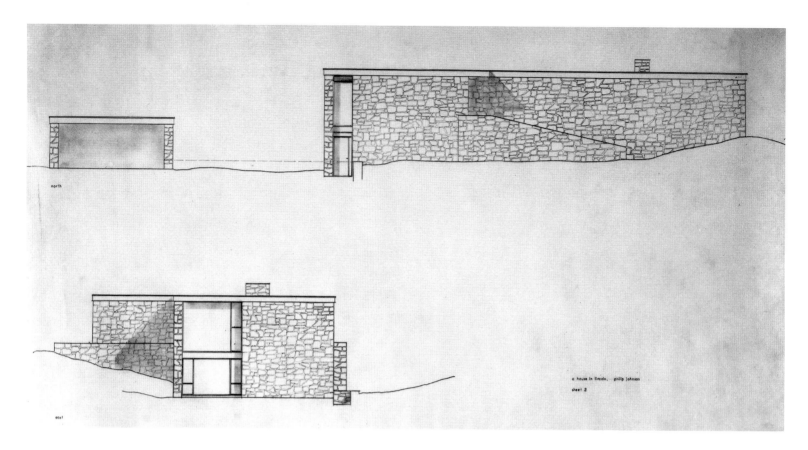

A House in Lincoln (project), 1941

The project for a house in Lincoln, Massachusetts, like that for an architect's study, described above, demonstrates his awareness of the work of Le Corbusier, specifically in the use of heavy masonry construction. Corbusier had published a number of house designs, such as that for the Maison de Mandrot of 1929–32, in which he turned away from the building materials of his early villas, chosen to emphasize their machinelike, abstract forms, in favor of traditional masonry construction (fig. 19). The later houses remained quite open spatially, however, allowing Corbusier to make a time-honored building method both frame and contrast with a modern sense of space.

Johnson followed Le Corbusier's example in this student project for a house and in the architect's study. The drawings for the Lincoln house even went so far as to include an interior perspective rendered in the same style as Le Corbusier's perspectives (fig. 20). Yet the basic composition remains Miesian, with a clear debt to Mies's court-house projects of the 1930s (see fig. 5). A number of different systems—column grids, planes of glass used as enclosures, and heavy masonry walls—interact spatially to define the interior and exterior spaces of the Mies court-houses.

The interplay between the very different aesthetic sensibilities of Mies and Corbusier would have been experienced in a heightened way by a visitor to the Lincoln house (fig. 18). A visitor would have first encoun-

A House in Lincoln (project)
18 (top) North and east elevations

Le Corbusier and Pierre Jeanneret
Maison de Mandrot, Le Pradet, France, 1929–32
19 (above) Exterior

A House in Lincoln (project)
20 Interior perspective

tered a nearly blank wall of stone on the north side of the house, with only a slender pair of windows—one above the other at one corner of the structure—to provide a sense of the scale of the house. A short ramp would have led to the entrance door, perpendicular to the façade. Beside the door a section of the stone wall would have terminated, offering a clear perception of the thickness of that traditional masonry construction. Entering the house, however, one would have seen an entirely modern space, dominated largely by the views through the south wall, built all of glass, across the room from the entrance. The roof would have extended beyond the glass wall to three columns, creating a covered area adjacent to the house, and this sheltered area would have then opened onto a large terrace, overlooking the sloping site. At either end of the building, bedrooms and service areas would have flanked the public space.

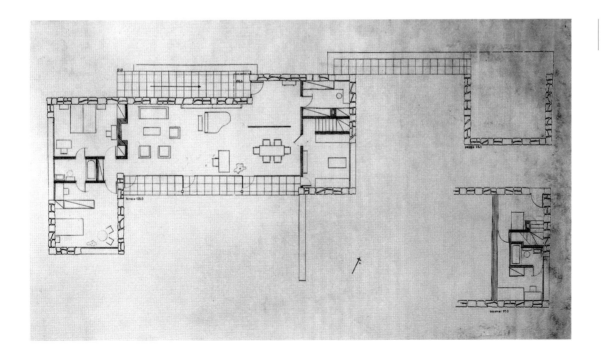

A House in Lincoln (project)
21 Plan

Philip Johnson House (Ash Street House), 1941–42

Surely the most audacious display of Johnson's unusual and privileged standing in school was his decision to build his own house in Cambridge and to propose the finished project as his final thesis, a proposal subsequently accepted by the dean of the Graduate School of Design. Known as the Ash Street House, this was Johnson's first free-standing built work, and it launched a lifelong dialogue both with professionals and the public about his architecture, an achievement that few—if any—students have ever matched.

The site was a small corner lot just off Brattle Street, a few blocks from Harvard Square, tucked in a largely residential neighborhood opposite buildings that were part of Radcliffe College. The design went through at least three different schemes. The first was an L-shaped form, with the house sited traditionally in the middle of the lot, with access to a carport at the rear (figs. 22–23). The bedroom and study were located in the ell, which came forward toward Ash Street; the main body of the house had an open living space at the front, behind three large glass windows, with a dining area and enclosed kitchen service spaces at the rear of the house. Johnson planned to build in brown Roman brick, "like Frank Lloyd Wright."[12] Henry-Russell Hitchcock reviewed the design and commented that the proposed brickwork was very fine, but "the house is so ordinary!"[13]

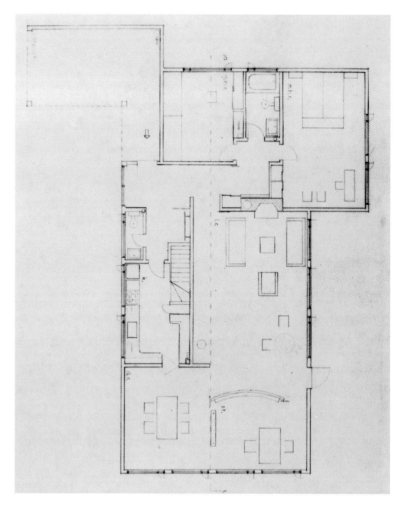

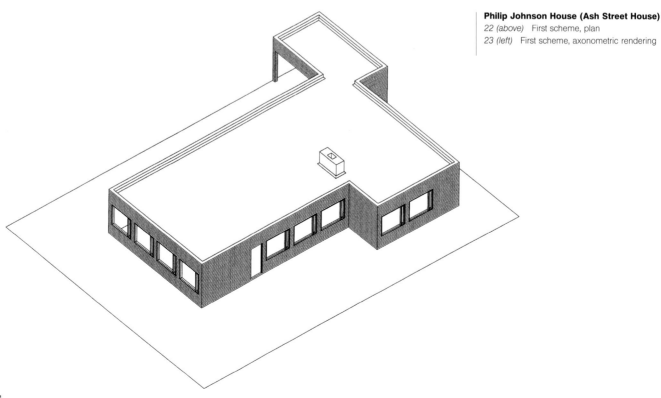

Philip Johnson House (Ash Street House)
22 (above) First scheme, plan
23 (left) First scheme, axonometric rendering

Johnson turned to the model of a Mies court-house for the second design (fig. 24). He used a similar organizing strategy for the plan, although he moved the fireplace mass to the back of the living room and pushed the entry to one side of the living room, closer to the bedroom. This had the effect of aligning the front door somewhat incongruously with the end of a major interior masonry wall dividing public and private areas of the house. But major changes were made to the structural system, materials, and exterior areas. A regular column grid and perimeter walls largely of glass, typical of Mies, are central features of the design. Two exterior courts, a public area with access from the living room and a private space off the bedroom, are defined by long horizontal walls which move from inside the house to the outside. The design was certainly an improvement from the earlier plan, but Johnson realized that neither of them fit the site well, and he moved on.[14]

In the final design for the Ash Street House, he simplified the plan dramatically (figs. 25–26). He omitted the study and reversed the locations of the living room and bedroom. Most importantly, he reduced the plan of the house to a single rectangle and pushed it to the back of the lot, putting a continuous flat roof over the entire structure. This siting created a large forecourt, enclosed by a nine-foot-high wall that matches the height of the interior walls and defines the perimeter of the lot. A single door, detailed to be perceived as a portion of the wall, opens from the court onto Ash Street (fig. 26). The awkwardness of the earlier designs was gone. Much later, Johnson would note that this was the only way one could do a house on this site.[15]

Most significantly, the wall between the house and the court was all glass: a continuous surface directly connecting activity inside and out (fig. 28). "The house became one big room," Johnson later commented. Space flowed, but not always "gracefully."[16] If this arrangement was a potent image of a new domestic architecture, it also had its ambiguities in terms of how the overlapping spaces were defined.

Due to a wartime shortage of materials, Johnson changed the wall construction from brick to striated plywood, which he used both outside and in. S. Clement Horsley, the draftsman he hired to prepare the construction documents for the house, assisted him with detailing these materials. Horsley, according to Johnson, had patented a system for plywood composition, and the Ash Street House offered a chance to utilize it.[17] Such a method of construction, based on inexpensive, standardized building elements, brought the issue of prefab-

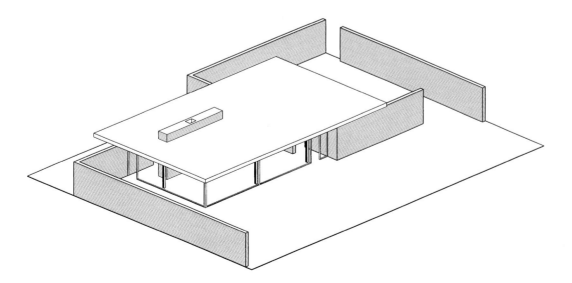

Philip Johnson House (Ash Street House)
24 Second scheme, axonometric rendering

rication into the design. This was a major topic within the architectural profession at this time, and it certainly would have been well-received within his department as a component of the thesis project.

The designs for the house were done in 1941, and construction was completed in mid-1942, less than two years after Johnson had begun architecture school. It was accepted as his final design project in anticipation of his architecture degree. He moved into the house and immediately began entertaining. It was a "great party house," he remembers. Classmates, coeds, and faculty from the Graduate School of Design all came to see it. The latter group, however, didn't like it much, according to Johnson: "It threatened them."[18] Johnson lived in the house for less than a year, leaving for military service in the spring of 1943. For a time, a housesitter cared for it, but he sold the house after he settled in New York.[19]

Despite the fact that Johnson lived in the house only for a short time, Ash Street was a prominent topic in architectural circles extending well beyond Harvard. *Architectural Forum* published the house in late 1943, noting that it represented the opportunity in modern architecture to "simplify, through standardization and repetition. . . . [I]n the hands of an accomplished artist and

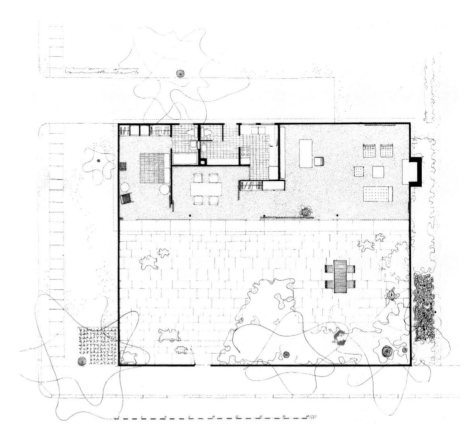

Philip Johnson House (Ash Street House)
25 (above) Final scheme, plan
26 (left) Final scheme, perspective

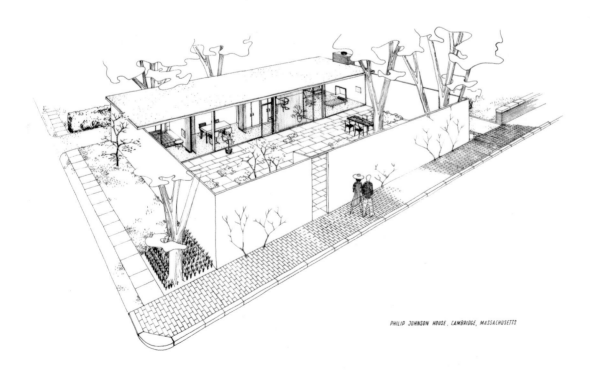

PHILIP JOHNSON HOUSE, CAMBRIDGE, MASSACHUSETTS

technician, such as Mies van der Rohe, the approach has produced buildings of remarkable quality. . . . This little house in Cambridge is probably the best example in America of the same attitude toward design."[20]

Johnson had long been fascinated with Mies van der Rohe's plans for courtyard houses, and the Ash Street House, like so many of his student projects, was clearly inspired by that precedent. How ironic—and indicative of the degree to which he would use examples from the work of other architects as inspiration for his own—that Johnson built a Mies courtyard house before Mies ever could. Yet the completion and publication of the Ash Street House clearly announced that Johnson's prominent position in the world of architecture had expanded beyond that of critic and curator to that of practicing architect.

Philip Johnson House (Ash Street House)
27 (above) View from courtyard
28 (pages 28–29) View of house interior and courtyard from entry

Starting a Practice

2

1944–1950

Mr. and Mrs. Eugene Farney House
29 View of façade

Unlike most architects at the beginnings of their careers, Philip Johnson was nearly forty when he began his professional practice, but he was propelled by a heady confidence arising from the critical recognition of his Ash Street House. Yet like many other new architects, his first years were erratic, both in the quantity and the quality of his work. Military service followed his studies at the Graduate School of Design, and Johnson lived in the environs of Washington, D.C. for most of this period. He was discharged in late 1944 and returned to New York early in 1945. There he began an architectural practice and assumed an unpaid position at The Museum of Modern Art, where he re-energized the Department of Architecture. As the war was ending, he invited his Harvard classmate Landis Gores to join his office.[21]

Both in Washington and in New York, Johnson was able to develop new relationships—most were through old friends—that led to a small number of private commissions. Johnson has explained of the projects of this period, "These houses were done mainly on spec: I didn't expect to get paid, and [the clients] didn't expect to build it."[22] This informal association with a potential clientele provided social benefits and may have buttressed the sense of a professional practice. Johnson's other responsibilities at the time included planning a major exhibition at MoMA on the architecture of Mies van der Rohe. Certainly the bar Johnson set for himself, by virtue of his associations with many of the finest architects, was very high. Thus, even his longstanding associate and friend Henry-Russell Hitchcock would write of Johnson during this period: "Because of, rather than despite, his age—and thanks also, doubtless, to the fact that he had so long been an observer rather than a maker of buildings—Philip Johnson was a timid designer."[23] In retrospect, Hitchcock appears to have conspicuously underestimated the achievement of these early works.

Mr. and Mrs. John Wiley House (project), 1944–45

If Johnson was not yet in a position to commit to designing buildings as a primary activity, it did not limit his inquisitiveness about what other architects were doing. Nowhere is this more evident than in a preliminary design he prepared for John Wiley, whom he met informally during his military service. Wiley was a career diplomat who served from 1944 to 1947 as ambassador to Colombia. He and his wife Irena were interested in a house for themselves in the vicinity of Washington, D.C. Gores remembers that it was to have been built "somewhere on the Virginia side of the Potomac."[24] The site seems to have been no more specific than that, allowing the new architect to speculate not only about the nature of a house appropriate to the career diplomat, but to create a site that would then serve the house. Unfortunately, only the plan for Johnson's design exists (fig. 30).

The house is both grand in scale, befitting an ambassador, and modern. Five separate pavilions are linked together in an S shape, arranged around two substantial courtyards. A pond or stream is sketched in at the southern edge of the house; in fact, the wing containing the master bedroom suite and study extends out over the water through the use of piers, or pilotis, which provide the structure to carry the pavilion. Short hall-like glass enclosures connect most of the pavilions, much as Johnson had connected the public and private areas of his freestanding house design done at the Graduate School of Design. The S-shaped plan allows the courtyards to become dominant elements in the architectural composition. Each courtyard is depicted with mature trees and other vegetation, and stone paths meandering through them. One court separates a pavilion primarily intended for service functions—carport, staff rooms, storeroom—from the more public areas of the house, which in turn form three sides of the other court. The latter court, however, is enhanced by the addition of a large swimming pool and paved terrace, which are closest to the pavilion encompassing the living room and reception hall. On the far side, past the master bedroom pavilion that projects over the water, is a final pavilion containing an informal entertaining area and an enclosed porch. The grand scale of the proposal was that of an estate or, perhaps more properly, an ambassador's residence: while the house provided just three bedrooms for family, there are four guest bedrooms and two staff bedrooms in separate pavilions.

In its overall conception, plan, and spatial arrangements, the Wiley House recalls a number of Frank Lloyd Wright's early houses. Johnson remembers that each pavilion was designed with a low pitched roof, such as Wright had used in many of his Prairie Style houses. The roofs cantilevered out beyond the walls of the pavilions and would have provided shaded walkways for circulation. Although the materials are merely suggested in the drawings, it is evident that Johnson intended to use a combination of masonry and glass. The horizontality of the house and the conscious intent to frame courtyards with portions of the building while preserving a direct relationship to the landscape are elements consistent with Wright's early domestic work.

Johnson recalls that the Wiley House was "just a sketch, a different way of looking at a house"—a departure from his approach at Harvard. Certainly the clustering of the hipped roofs varied greatly from the flat roofs of his student projects. But there is another emphasis in this house, one that extends and enhances the prominence of landscape elements that characterizes many of his Harvard designs. Johnson intentionally varied the pavilions in size and shape because he thought that equal pavilions would have been dull. Their sequential arrangement makes it difficult to take in the house at one glance; in Johnson's words, it is "not a single-image house." And that linear experience is further enhanced by the glass passages that would have connected the pavilions, especially those intended to pass over water. "How do you get distance quickly?" Johnson asked himself. "Go over water."[25] Thus Johnson's design combines simple pavilions in a complex arrangement that gives the impression of stretching out the house, making it seem like a substantial estate.

Mr. and Mrs. John Wiley House (project)
30 Plan

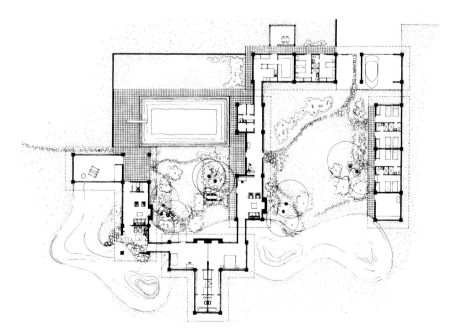

Townsend Farm Barn, 1944

In 1944, Johnson designed a small barn for his family's estate in New London, Ohio (fig. 31). This structure, so unlike a conventional barn of the Midwest, probably was inspired by the changing room buildings in Johnson's beach pavilion project from his first year in graduate school. The barn was built, but has deteriorated to the point where it is, as Johnson says, "a beautiful ruin."[26] It is rectangular in plan, built of cinder blocks, with a pair of garage doors on one side and a passage door on an adjacent side. The most striking feature is the fenestration: a regular pattern of windows around the entire perimeter of the structure makes a clerestory to provide light for the interior. Trusses behind the clerestory windows hold up a thin roof membrane. The symmetricality and clerestory fenestration are both elements of the beach pavilion service structures.

The Townsend Farm barn bears witness to Johnson's willingness to experiment in two somewhat paradoxical ways. First, he took a very traditional building type—the barn—and interpreted it in modern terms. Secondly, in realizing this modern design, he used the ordering systems of traditional, even classical, architecture. Its self-contained formality is at some distance from the free-plan spaces of modern architecture as taught at Harvard and practiced by notable modern architects of the period.

Townsend Farm Barn
31 View of exterior

"As Simple as That" House
Ladies' Home Journal, July 1945

Among his many activities in New York, Johnson was able to develop relationships with figures from the world of architectural journalism. Two competition designs he carried out for houses made their way into the pages of *Ladies' Home Journal* in the summer of 1945 and the spring of 1946. These houses helped reestablish his position with The Museum of Modern Art when a model made from the design was exhibited there in 1945. That project had its origins in a radio address Johnson had given about the state of housing in America. The design was presented in the July 1945 edition of the magazine in an article titled "As Simple As That" (fig. 32). The design was clearly intended to reap the benefits of prefabrication and functional technology: It could be assembled in "a single day," the article tells us, providing a "most livable layout, easy to manage and pleasant to occupy; not an inch of wasted space; not a chance for wasted work."[27]

The plan for the house is quite simple: a rectangle contains all of the basic functions of the house, with a wing coming forward to the street for a "car shelter" and laundry yard. As in many of his student projects, the street elevation is largely closed off, while the opposite side, facing a terrace and garden, is a glass wall. A combined living/dining area and three bedrooms all face onto the garden, with services—bath, kitchen, laundry, storage—on the opposite side of the plan. The effect was much like a more anonymous and simplified version of several of Frank Lloyd Wright's Usonian houses of the late 1930s and early 1940s. Johnson would largely dismiss the design quality of the first *Ladies' Home Journal* house later, noting that it was just a diagram, with "no architectural interest that I can see now."[28] Yet it did show his willingness to adapt to a new style of American living, or rather, American life as he believed it should be led: coming in from the garage, with the garden opening up from the interior. "It was a purely functionalist Harvard approach to design, hardly designed at all."[29]

"A House for a Millionaire with No Servants"
Ladies' Home Journal, April 1946

The second *Ladies' Home Journal* project, "A House for a Millionaire with No Servants," was far more elaborate in conception and execution (fig. 33). The magazine imposed no cost limitations, only a requirement that the house could be kept without any staff. Johnson's design shows four separate pavilions for sleeping, living, dining and the kitchen, and a garage with storage. The first three of these pavilions are linked by glazed passageways set back slightly from the main façade of the house. The four pavilions enclose an exterior space, which serves as the forecourt to the house. Dimensions are gracious but not generous. In the rear of the house are two small exterior courts, on either side of the living-room pavilion. The exterior materials are full-height windows and doors of clear or translucent glass, and the brick was to be set with vertical joints butted, a detail emphasizing horizontality.

Ladies' Home Journal **Houses**
32 (page 36) "As Simple as That"
33 (page 37) "A House For a Millionaire With No Servants"

Fixed glass panels alternate with glass-panel doors across the whole private sheltered side.

Simple planning makes for pleasantest living.

DRESSING ROOM OR DEN 11' X 10'6"

STOREROOM

ENTRY 6'9" X 8'6"

CAR SHELTER 22' X 11'

STORAGE 7'6" X 7'6"

LAUNDRY YARD

25'6" X 10'6"

LAUNDRY   KITCHEN

BEDROOM 11' X 14'   BEDROOM 10'6" X 14'   BEDROOM 10'6" X 14'   LIVING 33' X 14'   DINING

The first lesson in good community planning features here the semiprivate loop drive that serves each cluster of houses, all of which face away onto green and gardeny outlook. The first and third houses from the right in front are the house shown above. All the others have previously appeared in the JOURNAL.

BY RICHARD PRATT
Architectural Editor of the Journal

IT is my guess that the Greeks would have liked this house. They believed in the beauty of simple forms that came to life through the process of fine proportions. But for us today the simplicity of this house, both in plan and appearance, opens up possibilities of another very practical nature which couldn't have concerned the Greeks of old, who had no housing problem. We have—and its solution is vital to us all. We need better, less expensive houses, by the million. So let's see how a house like this can help the situation.

But first the floor plan, which, thanks in part to modern unfettered design and construction, hits a new high for livability through simplicity. See for yourself. Down the path, into the front door and an entry with elbow room. (Or in through the kitchen from either path or car shelter.) Look how the kitchen and laundry work together, with screenable dining close by at the faraway end of the living room. Then back off from the entry, three bedrooms in line, with a dressing room, study or guest room to spare; two baths, and a large daylit storage room at the handiest location in the house. And note with what directness the architect has created this most livable layout, easy to manage and pleasant to occupy; not an inch of wasted space; not a chance for wasted work.

And now, instead of being put together, piece by piece, with fifty thousand separate parts, like the average house, this house could be assembled in a single day with a mere few hundred fully finished panels, parts and units. Floor, roof, walls, windows, doors would come as properly sized panels, complete, from the factory, ready for fastening into place. Bathrooms, kitchen, laundry, closets, cupboards and fireplace would come as packaged units, ready for instant installation.

You can see what savings this would effect in time and labor at the site. But even bigger savings would have been effected before the panels, parts

and units arrived on the ground. These would be the savings effected by fully organized mass production, the benefits of which have been unavailable up to now. Unavailable because the home-building industry, vast as it is, has never been really co-ordinated. Also, the possibilities of greatly improved materials and much less expensive methods have never been fully explored. Home building, as a result, is frankly high in price, low in quality, when compared with what it could be if it were given a chance. And, as this is primarily your personal problem, here is what you can do about it.

You can urge your congressmen to get behind Federal legislation which would initiate and stimulate public and private research into materials, methods, industrial co-ordination, financing and community planning—all designed to make homes better, less expensive and more secure. For it is only fair that the fruits of victory should be ripened by the same kind of research which helped to hasten victory. If half a billion dollars' worth of research for military aviation has given us air supremacy in war, just think what a fraction of that would do for home improvement in peace.

There is something further you can do about better, less expensive living. You can help promote the well-planned community in which you want to live, whether city, town or countryside. This is more than a matter of civic pride; it is a matter of your own security. For no home is better than its neighborhood. Good neighborhoods, however, don't happen of their own accord, any more than good houses. But there is a simple pattern for the planning of both houses and communities which you can understand, if you will only try. So every month from now on, with every new house we show, we shall show how a good neighborhood grows—how life in a well-planned community can be happier, healthier, safer and less expensive—and how you can help to make all this happen.

PHOTO BY STUART

You drive up to the door or into the garage through the easily kept courtyard. Simplicity and purity of line and form give the house its elegance. Bricks laid with horizontal joints mortared, vertical joints butted, aluminum trim, and full-height doors of heavy clear or frosted glass give its modern design an ultraclean and classical distinction.

LIVING RM.
18' X 26'

DINING
TERRACE

6'X10' 10'X10'
L. K.

DINING ROOM
18'X16'

ENTRY
9'X18'

BEDROOM
12'X9'

BEDROOM
12'X9'

BEDROOM
12'X12'

BEDROOM
8'X12'

GARAGE 18'X18'

SHOP
8'X18'

STORAGE
10'X18'

Glazed passageways connect the three main blocks of the house: entry and living room center; bedrooms left; kitchen-dining right. Note a bath for each bedroom, and commodious work space and storage in the garage.

A House For a Millionaire With No Servants

★

A SELF-HELP HOUSE DE LUXE, STARRING BEAUTY, AND FEATURING EASE AND CONVENIENCE OF UPKEEP ★ **BY RICHARD PRATT**

Architectural Editor of the Journal

UP to now in our series of homes for tomorrow, we've kept the question of cost severely in mind. But here in this house we've let the designer consider what could be done if no expense were spared. Only one catch—it had to be a home that could be run without help. Fortunately, modern planning, materials, construction and equipment all conspire to produce not only a house with a high degree of taste, style and elegant simplicity, but reduce daily housework and yearly upkeep to a point that does away entirely with the servant problem. The clean directness of the floor plan indicates a house that is as easily cared for as it is pleasant to live in; for what the plan and the picture reveal is reflected within where the smooth unbroken surfaces of walls, floors, windows, doors offer no awkward corners, crevices, moldings or ledges so difficult to clean. Dusting is reduced to a minimum by the radiant heating which rises from the floor itself with no open ducts or draft-producing radiators, and the fully automatic gas-fired heater is out of sight and out of mind. The luxury, if you want to call it that, of a bath for every bedroom is one the self-helping family for this house can be allowed, along with a living room and dining room-study of really decent dimensions, not to mention a two-car garage with plenty of storage and work space. The work space would, of course, contain the most modern equipment for easing the kitchen and laundry jobs in a room so well arranged and lighted as to make operating there on your own a pleasure.

227

Mr. and Mrs. Richard E. Booth House, 1945–46

The two types of plan represented by the *Ladies' Home Journal* houses are seen in several other projects of

the mid- to late 1940s. The first type, a simple rectangle in plan, was realized in the Booth House of 1945–46,

built in Bedford Village, New York. Declaring it his "de Mandrot house," referring to Le Corbusier's Maison de

Mandrot, which he had drawn on for a student project (see fig. 19), Johnson planned a nearly square podium

on a sloping site. The main body of the house is set to the rear of the podium (recalling the siting of the Ash

Street House on its lot [fig. 36]), and a small pavilion—intended either as a guest bedroom, with bath, or a stu-

dio—was planned for the podium's front corner but was not built. The main house has two bedrooms separat-

ed from the public area by a utility core. A large brick fireplace separates the living area from the kitchen (fig.

37). This modest house, a mid–twentieth century realization of the American dream of owning a house in the

countryside, is the first house Johnson built for someone other than himself and a harbinger of the Glass House.

Mr. and Mrs. Richard E. Booth House
34 (above)   View of entrance façade
35 (opposite, above left)   Model
36 (opposite, above right)   Plan
37 (opposite, below)   View of interior

Mr. and Mrs. Eugene Farney House, 1945–46

The most successful variation on the court-house theme from this period of Johnson's work is a beach house begun in late 1945 in Sagaponack, Long Island, for Eugene Farney (fig. 29). The house drew both on Mies and on Le Corbusier. The site was at the edge of dunes overlooking the ocean. Johnson considered two different schemes to lift the house up to exploit the views. In the first scheme, the structure would have rested on a base of canted concrete walls containing the garage and storage (fig. 38). This approach, which proved uneconomical, was also adopted for the Ford House project (see below, pages 104–5).

The built scheme was a single-story structure carried on piers, a simple rectangle in plan, and although Johnson would later cite inspiration from both Le Corbusier (e.g., the pilotis) and Breuer (for the separation of plan elements), the strong influence of Mies's Resor House (fig. 8) is still evident. Echoing the Resor House, a glass-enclosed living room, open to the ocean and the opposite terrace, is set between two largely closed private areas: three bedrooms on one side and the kitchen and another bedroom on the other side (fig. 42). The scale is modest. A simple column grid carries through the public space only, helping to establish a lintel defining an exterior terrace facing north. A ramp to that terrace is the primary entrance to the house. The exterior is clad in cypress planks, laid vertically. Johnson calls this "a successful house," and he noted that subsequent houses of this period "follow from the Farney House." Even so, he has recently wondered if the first scheme, with its Usonian inspiration, might have been better.[30]

Mr. and Mrs. Eugene Farney House
38 (above) Perspective sketch (1945)
39 (opposite, top) First scheme, north and south elevations ("11-22-45")
40 (opposite, bottom) First scheme, plan ("11-22-45")

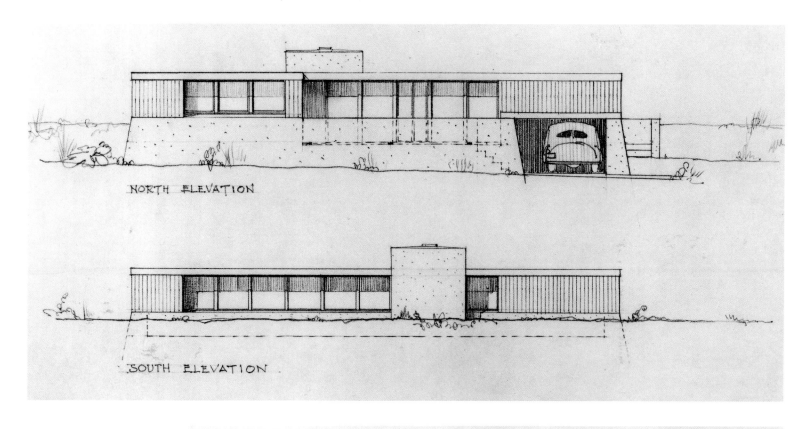

NORTH ELEVATION

SOUTH ELEVATION

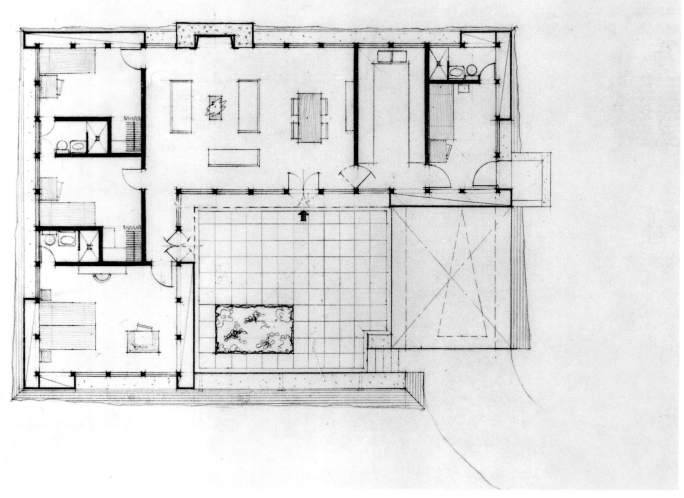

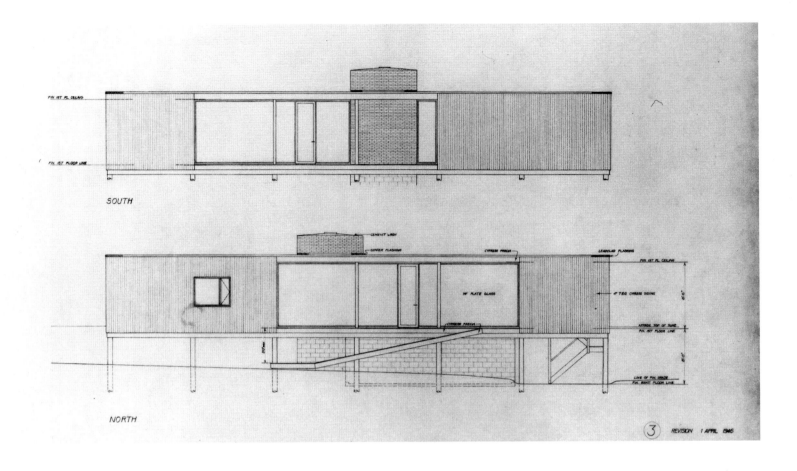

SOUTH

NORTH

③ REVISION 1 APRIL 1946

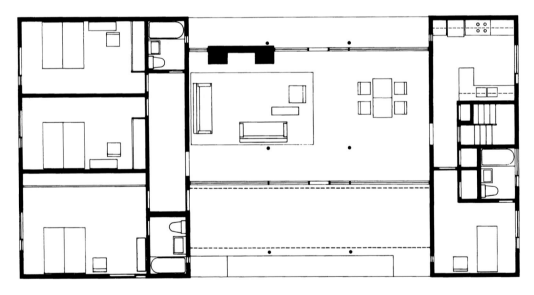

Mr. and Mrs. Eugene Farney House

41 (top) Final scheme, north (arrival) and south (ocean) elevations ("8 March 1946")

42 (bottom) Final scheme, plan

43 (opposite, top) Final scheme, west and east elevations ("8 March 1946")

44 (opposite, bottom) View of interior

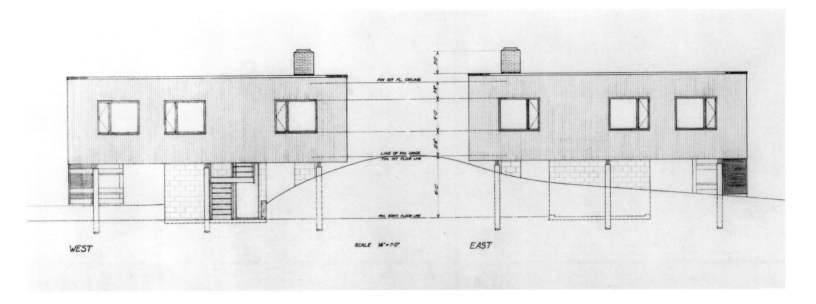

WEST   SCALE 1/4" = 1'-0"   EAST

Karl W. Schlubach House (project), 1946

The uncompromising directness of Mies's court-houses and Johnson's tentative exploration of other Miesian themes are evident in two schemes Johnson prepared in 1946 for Karl Schlubach, a Wall Street broker Johnson had met soon after his return to New York. It is unclear which design was executed first; however, the exterior-court scheme was developed further (figs. 47–48). The other, less fully-developed design (fig. 46) is nevertheless substantially more refined in its overall conception. Its plan is organized by overlapping rectangles. One is a perimeter wall of brick, enclosing two exterior courts on opposite ends of the house; the other rectangle represents the roof of the house. Two walls of the house itself align with the long sides of the brick perimeter wall. The sides of the house within the courts formed by the perimeter wall are expansive glass walls. The roof cantilevers far out from the brick walls to shelter and define the entry. Interior furnishings are spare: a few pieces of seating around a large masonry fireplace, a desk and cabinets in a study area, and a bed tucked behind the kitchenette and bathroom core.

Despite the apparent simplicity of the plan, the relationship between the interior and the exterior of the house is complex. The perimeter wall creates a strong sense of interior, private space, even though the two courtyards are open to the elements. The interior of the house, on the other hand, can be seen as an extension of the two courts, easily accessible through the broad glazed walls on either side of the house. Privacy within the house is minimal, as all the spaces are open to one another. Yet there is a feeling of seclusion since the brick perimeter is so dominant.

The more developed design for the Schlubach House called for a square court engaged on three sides by components of the house. A garage on one corner of the square ties into the long wall that closes the northern perimeter of the court and continues as the north wall of the living and dining area. That wall turns to make an alcove at the northeast corner of the house, but then stops. The remaining east wall is glazed, as is the opposing expanse looking out into the court. The third side of the court is held by a rectangular block of private and service functions: bedrooms, kitchen, and storage. A low wall and a driveway help define the fourth side of the court. As in the second *Ladies' Home Journal* house, the interior spaces are arranged around the exterior court. The court and the large open public space blend together, blurring the distinction between inside and outside.

Ludwig Mies van der Rohe
Project for a House with Three Courts, 1934
45 (top) Plan

Karl W. Schlubach House (project)
46 (bottom) Plan, less-developed scheme
("14 June 1946")

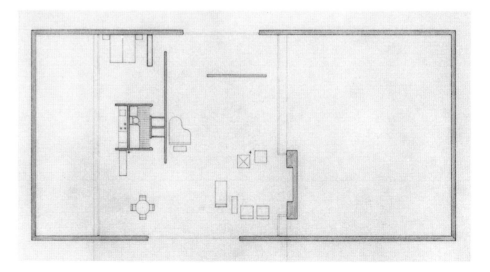

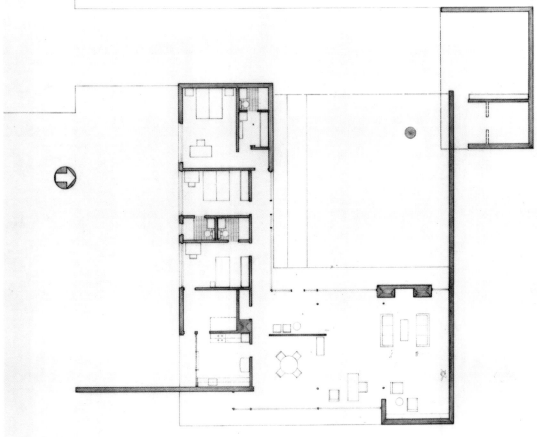

Karl W. Schlubach House (project)
47 (above) Model photograph
48 (below) Plan, second design

Mina Kirstein Curtiss House (project), 1946

Another design from 1946—for Mina Curtiss, a writer and the sister of Johnson's Harvard College friend Lincoln Kirstein—mediates between the two types of court-houses evident in the Schlubach designs. A masonry wall encloses the entire site, serving as the base for two roof planes that cover most, though not all, of the rectangular area. The largest portion of the roof shelters the entire rear half of the site, with the secondary portion set back only slightly from a side edge. This creates a large forecourt, with a pool and at least two major trees indicated in drawings and models.

The master bedroom is located off this court at one edge of the plan, while the garage, storage, and an additional bedroom are on the opposite side. This arrangement leaves a large open area, mostly in the center, for the primary public space of the house, recalling the plan of Mies's Resor House. Furthermore, this area is almost exactly the same size in plan as the forecourt. The dining portion of this public space is offset from the forecourt to give it a sense of seclusion. Large areas of glass interrupt the perimeter wall throughout, orienting the living room/dining room and master bedroom to the landscape outside, in contrast to the forecourt, which otherwise organizes the house. According to Johnson, he placed Mina Curtiss's writing desk in the only room to open directly on the forecourt as a gesture to her love of flowers.

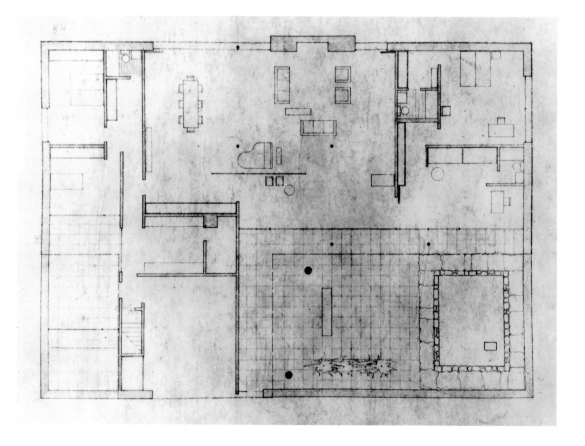

Mina Kirstein Curtiss House (project)
49 (above) Model photograph
50 (below) Plan

Joseph B. Bramlette House (project), 1947

Two projects from this period, one on Long Island and one in Maine (p. 49), do not conform to either of the types described previously. The former was to be a weekend house at Montauk for a Texas developer named Joseph Bramlette. Johnson took advantage of the sloping site to introduce a form having more to do with southern California than eastern New York (fig. 51). The proposed house is a glass prism, two stories in height at the lower, oceanfront side of the house, but entered from the opposite side, at the upper level. Thus one would have entered into an apparently one-story house, which would then have opened into a double-height space overlooking the ocean. Two masonry masses anchor the sides. The glass walls and pronounced horizontal overhang of the flat roof resonate with the work of Richard Neutra, but the plan's organization and the entry sequence have more similarities with Frank Lloyd Wright's Millard House, La Miniatura, in Pasadena. The mezzanine sleeping area is pulled back from the face of the surrounding glass walls, giving it a sense of being inserted within the vertical space.

Joseph B. Bramlette House (project)
51 (below) Elevation ("Sept. 5, 1947")
52 (below, left) Plan, upper (arrival) floor
53 (below, right) Plan, lower (living) floor

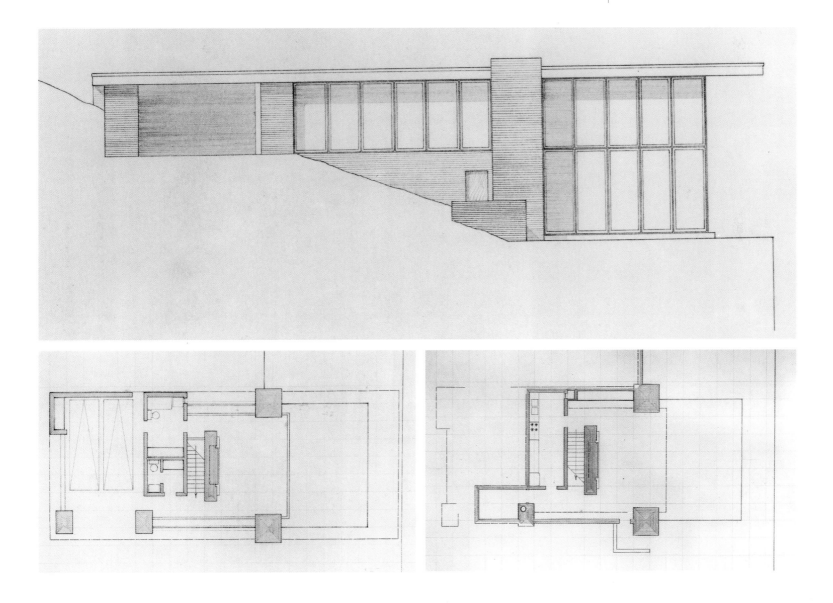

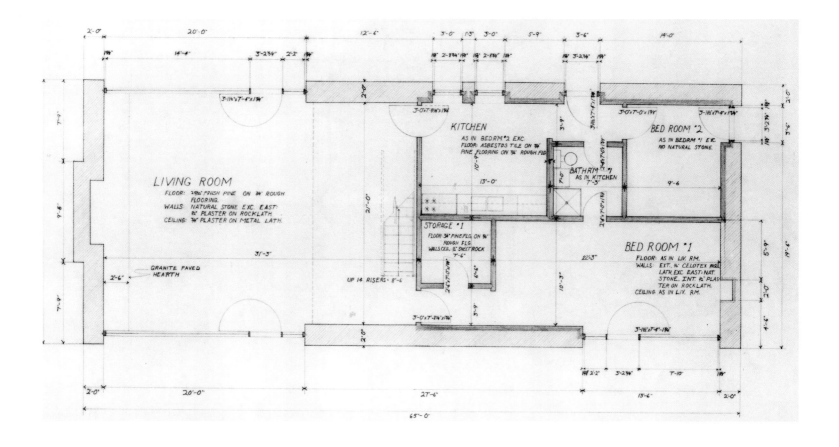

Mr. and Mrs. John E. Abbott House (project)

54 (top) Plan, first floor ("23 December 1947")
55 (bottom) Elevation ("23 December 1947")

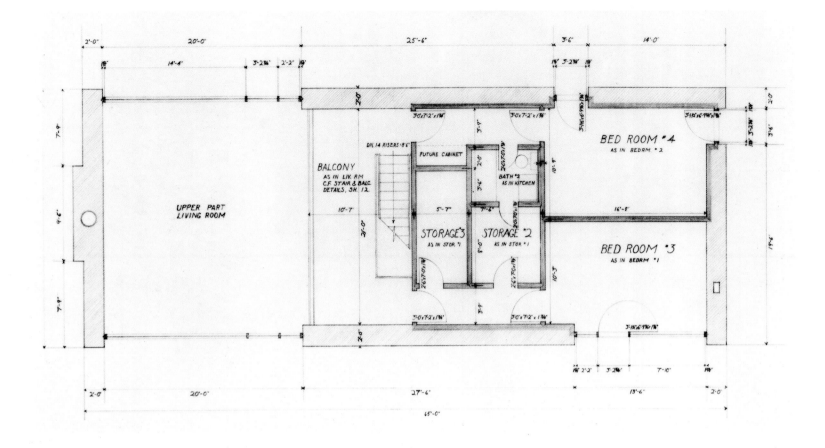

Mr. and Mrs. John E. Abbott House (project), 1947

An unbuilt house design for Mr. and Mrs. John E. Abbott, intended as a vacation retreat on Mount Desert Island, Maine, calls for a two-story rectangular bar with a double-height living room at one end and pairs of bedrooms at each level of the other end (figs. 54 and 56). Service functions occupy the middle of the house, separating the public and private zones. A straight-run stair would take occupants up to a balcony overlooking the living room. Like Johnson's student project for the house in Lincoln, Massachusetts, the exterior walls and interior living-room walls are natural stone, following the model of Le Corbusier's Villa le Sextant at La Palmyre les Mathes; Johnson called it "dressed stone." The east wall of the living room would have been, in effect, a massive freestanding fireplace. These two-foot-thick masonry walls are interrupted by large expanses of glass in the living room: the north and south walls would have been a pair of twenty-foot-wide glazed openings (fig. 55). Aside from the double-height living room, the spaces would have been tight and low.

Mr. and Mrs. Benjamin V. Wolf House, 1948–49

For the Wolf House, built on a sloping site in Newburgh, New York, Johnson used a brick ground floor containing service areas—garage, laundry, storage—as a podium for the cypress and glass main floor of the house (figs. 58–59). That volume cantilevers outward on all sides, giving the impression that it is floating (structural supports added later spoil this effect). The house looks out across the rolling terrain of the Hudson River valley north of New York City. Behind the large living area are a dining alcove and kitchen; a clerestory brings additional light into these areas. The remainder of the house is given over to two bedrooms, a study, and a small outdoor courtyard. One might enter the house through the garage (much like the first *Ladies' Home Journal* house) and then climb the stair in the center of the house to the main floor; or, more formally, one would enter a small court adjacent to that same stair and ascend to the living spaces.

Mr. and Mrs. Benjamin V. Wolf House
57 View of east façade

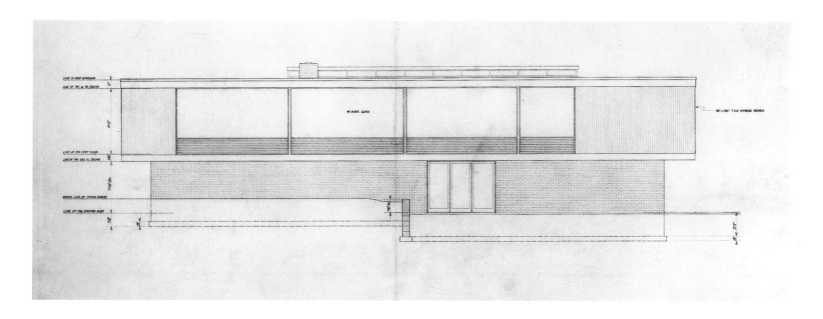

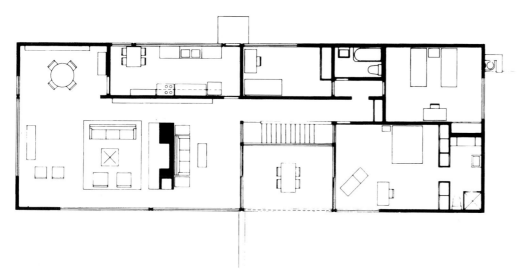

Mr. and Mrs. Benjamin V. Wolf House
58 (above) East elevation ("June 10 1948")
59 (left) Plans for main floor and ground floor

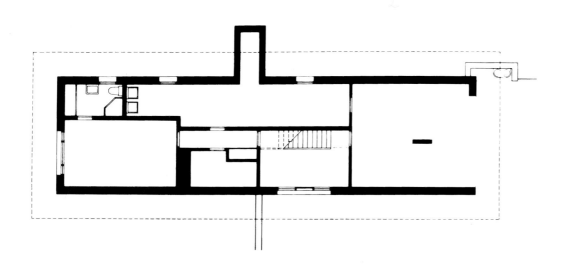

Mr. and Mrs. George E. Paine Jr. House, 1948–49

Located on the western shore of Lake Champlain, the Paine House is oriented toward the water and the view of Vermont across the lake (figs. 60–62). Both the Farney House and its inspiration, Mies's Resor House, served as models for it. But there are substantial differences between the Paine and Farney Houses. The Paine House consists of two structures, a main house and a summer wing, which contains six bedrooms to accommodate an extended family's use of the house for vacations. The structure seems to be an elaboration of a sleeping

Mr. and Mrs. George E. Paine Jr. House
60 (left) View of lake side, main house at left, summer wing at right
61 (below, left) View of entrance, looking through house to Lake Champlain
62 (below, right) View into living area from lake side

porch. The main house has a large, open public area between two relatively closed-in zones, one containing a kitchen and pantry and the other two bedrooms (fig. 63). Interior circulation in the Paine House occurs along an axis between the doorways to the closed end components; unfortunately, this line runs directly in front of the fireplace, interfering with the potential use of that area as social space. In the Farney House, this problem is avoided by routing circulation behind the fireplace seating area. A lonely pair of columns represents only a token effort to delineate a structural system in the Paine House, as opposed to the regular system evident in the Sagaponack project.

The arrival and entry sequence features a diagonal approach to the house. The public area is clearly visible through very large expanses of glass, but the view continues through the house to the water just beyond it. Thus the house acts as a frame for scenic views of Lake Champlain and its environs. The spatial relationship between the main house and the wing is unresolved, however, with just a narrow passage articulating their separation. Despite the extent to which he took advantage of the landscape, Johnson remembers the Paine House as being a relatively unsuccessful project, in part because of the ambiguous space between the two structures. In many ways the Paine House explored issues he was addressing far more successfully in his own house, then under construction.

Mr. and Mrs. George E. Paine Jr. House
63 Plan showing summer wing, left, and main body of house

Edwin Boysen House (project), 1948

A project with an even more expansive scale was sketched out in 1948 for Edwin Boysen, an acquaintance of Johnson's from his graduate years at Harvard.[31] Clearly based on Mies's Resor House, the plan calls for an exceptionally spacious living area flanked by two private zones (fig. 65). A large masonry fireplace mass loosely organizes the public space into a series of overlapping areas based on use: reception, sitting, and music. A freestanding shelving system and a glass wall define a dining area in one corner of the space, adjacent to a closed-in service block containing kitchen, staff quarters, storage, and washroom. Both the entry wall and its counterpart across the room make extensive use of glass. Thus the house seems far less private than Johnson's earlier court-house designs of this period, such as the Schlubach or Curtiss Houses. The elevations indicate just how visible the public spaces are from the exterior. That degree of openness is denied to the flanking areas of the house. One end contains two large bedrooms, separated by an enclosed zone with a bathroom for each bedroom. The bedrooms open out onto a large enclosed court, with the roof extending far enough beyond the bedroom walls to provide cover from the elements, as it does for the exterior walls of the living space.

The structural system for the Boysen project is unusual for this period: Johnson specified a combination of masonry walls, but ran an extensive column grid throughout the plan. This grid is so relentless that it even carries through the bedroom areas, resulting in a slightly awkward relationship to certain pieces of furniture. But the overall composition is intriguing, and expansive in its use of interior space. Most importantly, both the public and private qualities of the house are intensified. The social spaces are far more open, especially to the exterior, than those of other projects. At the same time, the private spaces would have been resolutely closed off from public scrutiny, either from within or from outside the house. All of the attributes one would desire for private living—a sense of spaciousness, contact with nature through the enclosed court—are there, but they would have been kept from public view. Only a single circular window on the rear façade, opening to the larger of the two bedrooms, would have compromised this privacy.

Edwin Boysen House (project)
64 Elevation
65 Plan

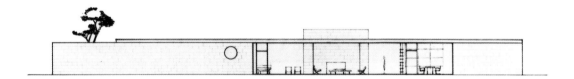

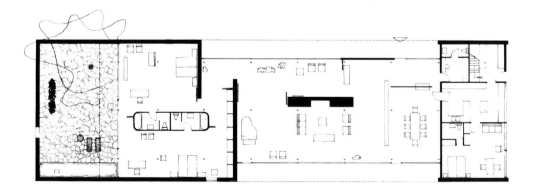

Mr. and Mrs. John de Menil House, 1949–50

The final house in this period was for John and Dominique de Menil, of Houston. The de Menils, part of the Schlumberger oil family, became important patrons of Johnson. The house had a complex program, which included serving as a gallery for the couple's collection of art, which would eventually become one of the nation's most significant. As pillars of the cultural community in Houston, and great supporters of the arts and education nationally, they hosted numerous parties and fundraising events.

The primary organizing feature of the house is an extremely long brick wall along the front or north side of the house (fig. 66). That wall, over 160 feet long, breaks only for three doors grouped as one unit and two pairs of small awning windows off the kitchen and laundry areas. Off the entrance hall (fig. 69) to the left is an open court, with the living room, almost exactly the same size, behind it (figs. 70–71). To the east of these are the master bedroom and a study. To the west of the entrance hall are the service spaces—kitchen, carport, staff rooms—and behind them is a separate wing with four children's bedrooms (fig. 67).

Johnson was beleaguered throughout the project by the extensive and ever-changing program: the transformation of the original dining room into a playroom—a change made well into the construction of the house—was one of these. It meant that the family had to pull a dining table into the entrance hall to have a

Mr. and Mrs. John de Menil House
66 Exterior showing arrival and entry

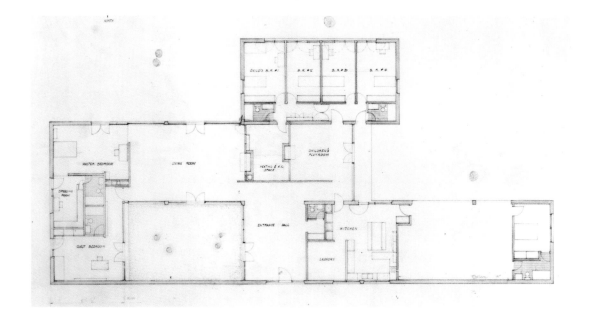

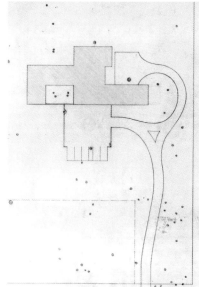

formal dinner. Interestingly, even as the children grew up and the playroom reverted to a dining room, the entry remained the formal dining area and the preferred location for serving large numbers of guests.

The design was crisply conceived in terms of the elevations. The front elevation would have been even more taut had Dominique de Menil not insisted that kitchen windows be added for the sake of the staff, even though Johnson had included a large skylight in the service area and there were views to the rear court. The plan, however, Johnson felt to be awkward. Despite the remarkable asset of major works of contemporary art, the design was vitiated by programmatic issues. Attempts to resolve questions of design and the role of art—

Mr. and Mrs. John de Menil House
67 (above, left) Plan
68 (above) Site plan
69 (left) View of foyer and enclosed court

Johnson's primary interests as a designer—were frustrated by the client's insistence on functional concerns. "This is what happens when you wrestle with clients," Johnson noted ruefully in a recent interview.[32] Fortunately, this experience did not set a precedent, for he carried out a number of notable projects, corporate as well as residential, for the extended Schlumberger family during his career.

At the same time he was struggling with the de Menil House, Johnson was basking in the attention his new Glass House, in New Canaan, was receiving. As his own client, he was able to resolve any issues arising between the relationship of design and function to his full satisfaction. The vastly different circumstances of these two projects brought Johnson to the conclusion that the only client he would have for any future domestic commissions would be himself. From that point on, only design would matter.

Mr. and Mrs. John de Menil House
70 (below) View of living area and garden terrace
71 (pages 58–59) View of living area with enclosed court to left and garden terrace to right

The Glass House

Philip Johnson Residence: Glass House and Guest House

New Canaan, Connecticut **1945–49**

3

Glass House
72   View from base of promontory

Glass House
73   View of Guest House from
Glass House

Philip Johnson's Glass House stands as one of the seminal buildings in the history of American architecture (figs. 72, 74). Ever since its completion in 1949, it has been recognized in the professional and public worlds as a defining work of modern architecture and contemporary culture. It has aroused intense interest—in the house itself and in its architect—throughout its history. From the 1950s through the early 1980s, Johnson conducted regular architectural salons at the Glass House for his students from Yale, professionals from New York, and visiting architectural dignitaries. A series of additional structures have been added to the property over the last half century; these later additions and the evolution of the compound are the subjects of chapter 8.

The Glass House's critical provocations have been part of its ongoing legacy. Soon after its completion, Johnson himself launched the first salvo, with a now-famous article in *Architectural Review* that defined an intellectual and formal lineage for the project (see Neil Levine's essay in this volume). In that article, Johnson tied the conception of the house not only to examples of modern art and architecture—the work of Le Corbusier, Mies van der Rohe, De Stijl artist Theo Van Doesburg, and Russian Suprematist Kasimir Malevitch—but to two architects, Karl Friedrich Schinkel and Claude Nicolas Ledoux, who redefined the conception of architecture at the beginning of the nineteenth century.

But it was to Mies that many critics—friend and foe—turned for precedents for the Glass House. After all, Mies had included drawings for a glass house as a part of the Museum of Modern Art exhibition in 1947, which Johnson had organized. Two years after the exhibition, and six months after completion of the Glass House, construction began on Mies's glass-walled house outside Chicago for Dr. Edith Farnsworth (fig. 75),

raising the question of originality. In what could be understood as a pre-emptive response to that question, Johnson fully acknowledged Mies's crucial role in the *Architectural Review* article:

Glass House
74 View of entry elevation

"The idea of a glass house comes from Mies van der Rohe. Mies had mentioned to me as early as 1945 how easy it would be to build a house entirely of large sheets of glass. I was sceptical at the time, and it was not until I had seen the sketches of the Farnsworth House that I started the three-year work of designing my glass house. My debt is therefore clear, in spite of the obvious difference in composition and relation to the ground."[33]

Nearly thirty years later, gathering together the writings of Johnson for publication, Robert A. M. Stern noted that the lineage of the Glass House as revealed in the process of its design was not nearly as direct as Johnson had maintained in his *Architectural Review* article. Stern reviewed many of the ninety-six drawings for the Glass House that Johnson had donated in 1976 to the Museum of Modern Art archives. Johnson had

Ludwig Mies van der Rohe
Farnsworth House (1949–51)
75   View of entrance façade

numbered the drawings in chronological sequence, using Roman numerals. Stern concluded that the two-year-long design effort was much more complicated than simply elaborating Mies's original idea for a house of glass.[34] Other historians and critics have reinforced Stern's conclusions and looked more closely at the preliminary drawings for the Glass House. In 1978, for example, the historian Kenneth Frampton analyzed the twenty-seven schemes Johnson identified. Frampton described the design process as one of balancing the inward and outward orientations of the promontory to resolve the "courthouse/belvedere conflict."[35] Johnson's assistant Landis Gores believed there could have been as many as seventy-nine "schemes and variations."[36]

The twenty-seven definitive schemes that have been preserved are fascinating to study, and not only for the light they shed on Johnson's process of arriving at the final design for the Glass House. Indeed, these studies afforded Johnson the opportunity to engage in an extended period of research about the nature of domestic architecture in America. Given the casual, often volunteer nature of the majority of his commissions of this period, the chance to engage in a long-term examination of a single domestic project for himself must have been gratifying. Several of the schemes were developed with great specificity; some even with construction documents. Johnson later remarked, "One wonders why I spent as much time as I did, but each scheme was a month in being drawn up."[37] The earliest design dates from late 1945, and the final plan was determined only in November 1947. Even after settling upon the version that would be built, additional possibilities were explored in December 1947. Thus, along with his other activities, Johnson devoted at least two full years to the definitive architectural design of his own residence.

The significance of the studies extends beyond the design of the Glass House. Johnson's career as an architect accelerated in the early 1950s after the completion of his house and its successful reception. As he began to explore design alternatives for this body of new work, the Glass House studies became a source for these projects. The linkages between specific drawings for the Glass House and later realized projects freshly illuminate his work in this period.

Johnson was drawn to the village of New Canaan in the first place because his teacher Marcel Breuer and his classmate Eliot Noyes were already living there. "There was a nucleus of architects, so you knew if you built a house here you wouldn't be laughed out of the town."[38] He chose the site for his house on Ponus Ridge Road in New Canaan primarily for the spectacular views from a promontory at some distance down a gentle hill from the road.[39] Initially a five-acre lot, the property has been added to incrementally, and it now covers forty acres. The added grounds afforded him room for his various additions to the compound over the years. The promontory was the focus of his attention as he considered the design of his house. A number of the early schemes took the changing grade of the promontory into account, while others adjusted it to make an even more prominent outcropping. The physical size of the area was an issue, often driving decisions about what was—and usually was not—possible. According to Johnson, the design for the Glass House was "worked out from the landscape point-of-view, which is something I always do. Take in nature, from all sides."[40]

Ironically enough, the preliminary schemes for the Glass House are, for the most part, not primarily glass. They can be categorized loosely into a limited number of organizational types, and it may be of some use to review these before looking in more depth at particular designs. The programmatic elements remain largely the same among the various schemes, and are the very spaces one would expect of a mid–twentieth century country house: informal social spaces, kitchen and dining areas, a master bedroom, bedrooms for guests, and bath and storage areas. Indeed, these elements were the program for many of Johnson's early house projects.

Among the building types evident in the preliminary schemes are a house composed of separate pavilions organized as a complex by a pergola, terrace, or court; a court-house (from the Mies type of the 1930s; see fig. 5); a house organized along a single wall; a masonry object on a podium; an object cantilevered off the slope (fig. 104); and, finally, a crystalline object on a podium. A general progression involving these types would start with schemes featuring a cluster of masonry buildings; move on to a single glass building; then to transparent versus solid elements; to a single masonry building; and then, finally, back to a single transparent object. Johnson has said that once he decided on using the site as a podium and the house as an object, everything fell into place.[41] Yet even after this realization, he spent almost two more years exploring and refining before beginning construction of the Glass House and Guest House.

Scheme I

The first scheme uses a loggia to loosely connect two separate rectangular structures around a court on a platform (figs. 77–78), recalling the Booth House, which Johnson was designing at this time. The larger house, clearly the main residence, is located near the edge of the slope (upper half of plan, fig. 78) to take advantage

Karl Friedrich Schinkel
Charlottenhof Palace, Potsdam, 1829–44
76 View of colonnaded pergola/loggia connecting house to landscape

of the views. The smaller house contains a guest bedroom, a service bedroom, and a garage. The loggia is handled awkwardly: it ties the two houses together tenuously as it follows a retaining wall near the edge of the promontory and does not provide direct access into the buildings. The court between the two structures is not developed at all, except for a set of three steps that one would ascend from the grade of the driveway. Johnson withheld the view out from the court until a visitor would have negotiated a twisting approach and ascended the steps past a low wall. Only then would the vista, framed by the buildings on either side and the pergola ahead, become visible. The intended experience was similar, according to Johnson, to that found at Karl Friedrich Schinkel's Casino and Charlottenhof Palace, near Potsdam, Germany (fig. 76).

Glass House
Scheme I
77 (opposite, top) Elevation
78 (opposite, bottom) Plan

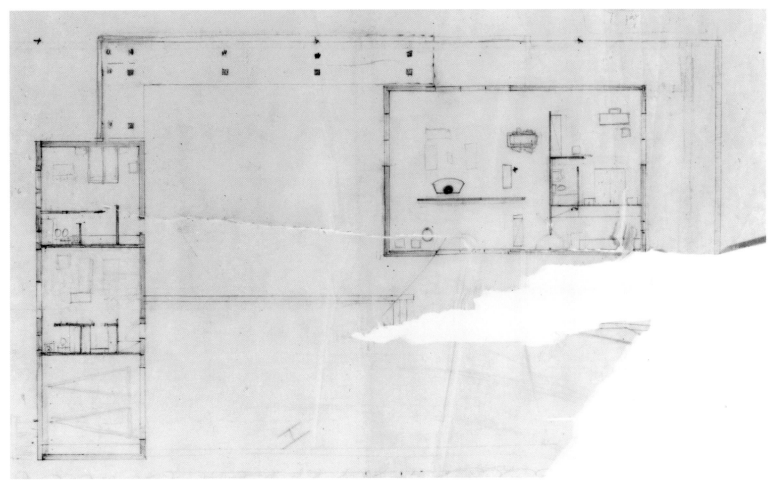

Schemes II and III

The sketches for Schemes II and III, from early 1946, increase the number of structures and the connections between them. Scheme III indicates three separate structures, with a loggia flanking one pavilion, presumably forming an overlook for the landscape, and another loggia, or perhaps a pergola, connecting the other two structures (figs. 79–80). The main block of the house is set squarely on the prow of the hill. A raised terrace would have been the primary arrival point for visitors. The elevation shows that both blocks have symmetrical façades. In its varying building heights, unique to this scheme, there is some similarity to Mies's Kröller-Müller House of 1912.[42]

Glass House
Scheme III
79 (left) Elevation
80 (below) Plan

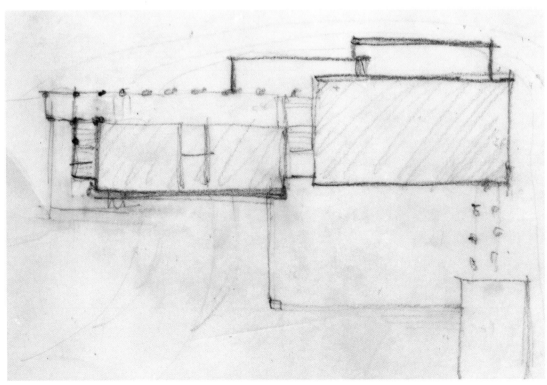

Scheme IV

Scheme IV, from roughly the same period, tightens up these elements so they become components around a more formalized raised court. Johnson experimented with differing orientations toward the landscape. In one variation (fig. 81), in which the loggia wraps around the interior of the court, he faces the court outward to the bluff. A second version (fig. 82) reverses this arrangement, showing a cloistered court facing the arrival side.

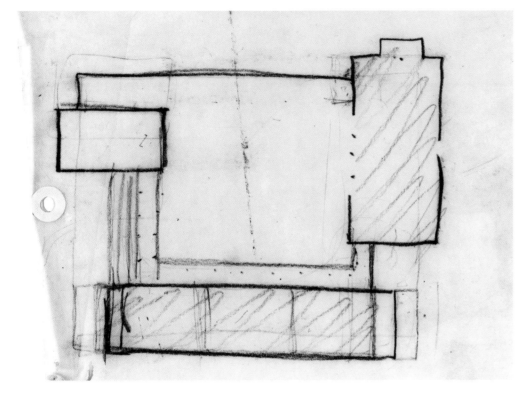

Glass House
Scheme IV
81 (left) Plan, first version
82 (below) Plan, second version

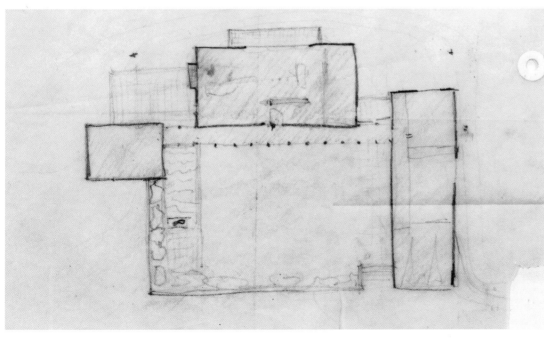

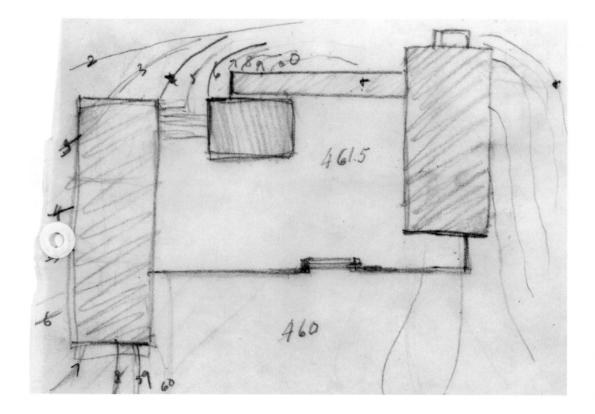

Scheme V

Scheme V, from February 1946, loosens the organization of the three pavilions and uses a larger court—terraced to follow the contours of the promontory—as a unifying feature (fig. 83). Programmatic functions are only marginally indicated. It can be surmised that a guest bedroom, servants' area, and parking are located on the lower level. One would have walked up to the court, past a small, centrally-located structure serving as Johnson's bedroom, to the largest pavilion, containing living and kitchen areas. Steps aligning with one edge of the court, on the arrival side, connect it to the land. In one variation (not shown), a large ceremonial gate structure frames these steps.

Schemes VI and VII

The last studies of this sequence of linked separate pavilions show narrow rectangles at the edge of a raised court, with steps ascending to the court. In Scheme VI, there are two pavilions, at the near edge of the court, on either side of a set of steps (fig. 84). This arrangement orients the arrival to the court and thus to the view. Specific activities within each pavilion are barely indicated: kitchen counters are sketched in one, along with partitions for bedrooms. In Scheme VII, dated February 1946, the two pavilions have been moved to the far edges of the court, and the steps are framed by the smaller pavilion and one of the walls that enclose the court and delineate the entry area (fig. 85). In both schemes, a separate pavilion for a garage is shown, but in different locations. Eventually Johnson would dispense with the garage altogether.

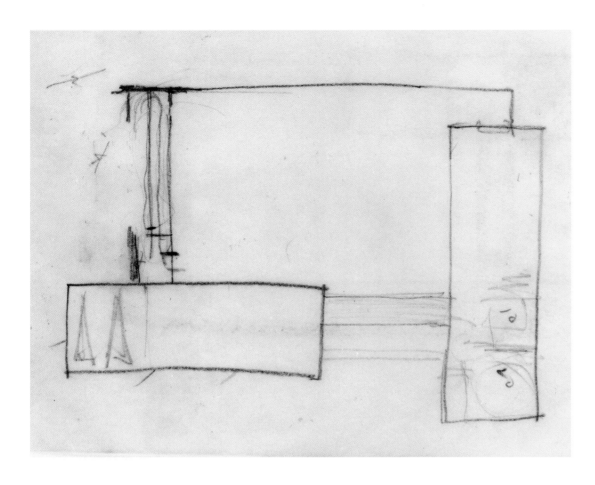

Glass House
Scheme VI
84 (left) Plan
Scheme VII
85 (below) Plan ("Feb. 1946")

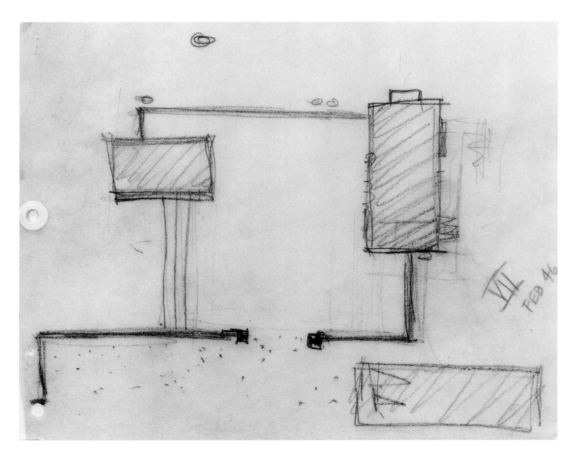

Schemes VIII and IX

All of these early schemes were to be of masonry construction. They also have in common a lack of development of specific programmatic ideas, and they pay relatively little attention to the site itself, beyond orienting the house to the scenic view. Shortly thereafter, however, Johnson developed another, more specific set of designs, dated March 1946 and designated Scheme IX (it is not known whether a representation of Scheme VIII is extant). In these designs, he clearly indicated not only the uses of various spaces but sketched furniture in them (fig. 86). They show a single structure toward one side of a reshaped promontory, which serves as a podium. For the first time, the walls seem to be entirely of glass, indicated by regular divisions at the perimeter of the structure in the plan. Two small sketches show the glass pavilion on a podium, with the hill falling away at its edge. Though the walls are transparent, the wide fireplace mass and interior partitions would limit the degree to which one could see through this structure. Yet the general disposition of spaces, with the living area to the south and bedrooms to the north, is that of the final design.

Glass House
Scheme IX
86 Plan ("Mar 46")

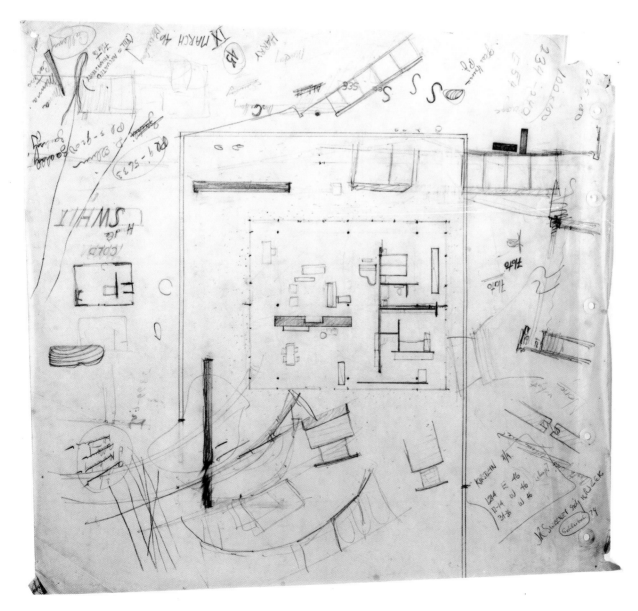

Scheme X

There was a hiatus in the production of design drawings until September 1946, when Scheme X appeared (figs. 87–88). These drawings are remarkable for the specificity of site development as well as of the architecture. The site is shaped with a clear edge on three sides (the side facing southwest has a slight cant in it); the land falls away steeply from those edges. The house is a rectangle, with no accoutrements like loggia, service structures, or an exterior fireplace. Unlike previous studies, which are sketches, the drawings for this plan are to scale and furnishings are indicated, so that the proportions of the spaces are clear. Roughly two-thirds of the plan is given over to living and dining spaces, while the remainder is taken up by a sleeping area and a study. Separating public and private functions is a spiral core that incorporates the bathroom in one end of the spiral and the kitchen in the other. Although materials are not specified, one can assume that the exterior walls are glass, while the spiral core is masonry. Elevations prepared for this scheme show symmetrical fenestration; a single door is set precisely in the middle of the front elevation.

Glass House
Scheme X
87 Plan ("Sept 46")

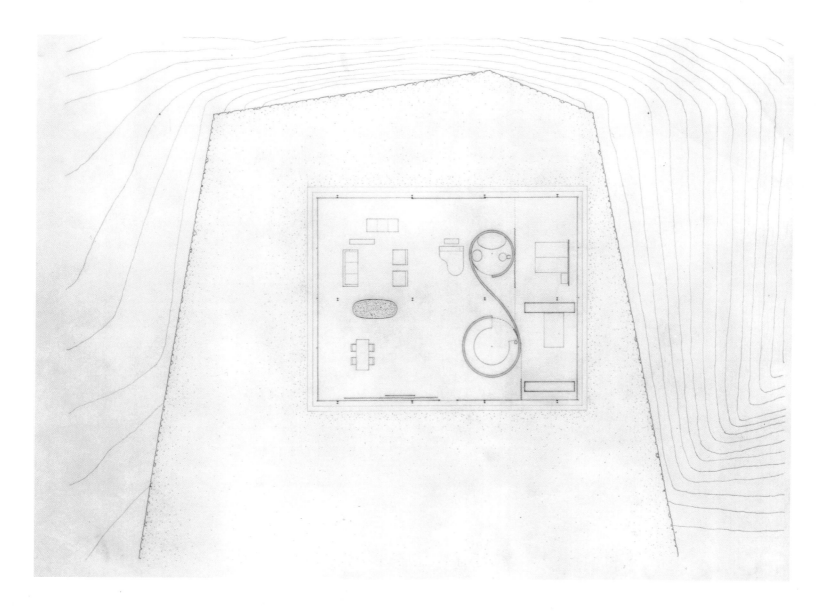

This building's proportions are not as slim as those of the final version, necessitating a third row of structural columns through the center of the plan. Although there is only one door, the stepped podium circumscribing the structure implies a notional openness: that the structure is not only transparent but that it can be entered at any point. This scheme defined the site conditions Johnson chose to follow, as well as the general strategy of a single pavilion, sitting up prominently on the site.

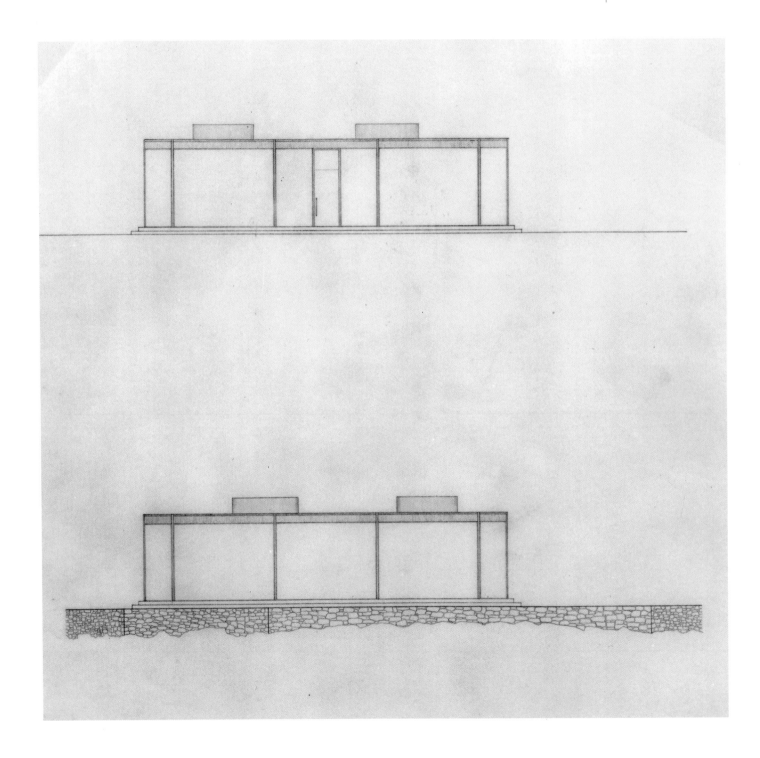

Scheme XI

The next scheme, from November 1946, represents an important development of the Glass House as a one-room pavilion (figs. 89–90). The site conditions remain the same, except that a stone wall separates the promontory from the approach down from the road. The wall also divides the slope down to the valley from the rest of the site; only by entering through a gap in the wall does one have access to the promontory and the house. The width of the house is reduced, and its proportions begin to approach those of the final version, allowing for a structural system of just two rows of columns at the perimeter. For the first time, there are four doors, symmetrically disposed, one in each façade.

While the structure has the same overall organization of public and private spaces, Johnson has transformed the core into three separate cylin-

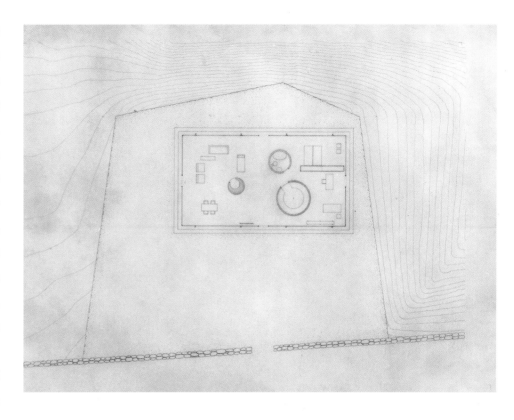

drical elements of differing sizes: the largest contains the kitchen, the middle-sized one houses the bathroom, and the smallest is a fireplace, located squarely in the middle of the public living spaces. The placement of the cylindrical cores does not relate directly to the rectilinear geometry of the perimeter of the house; instead, they seem to be abstract compositional elements within that rigid frame.

Glass House
Scheme XI
89 (above) Plan ("Nov. 1946")
Scheme XI
90 (below) Elevation ("Feb. 7, 1947")

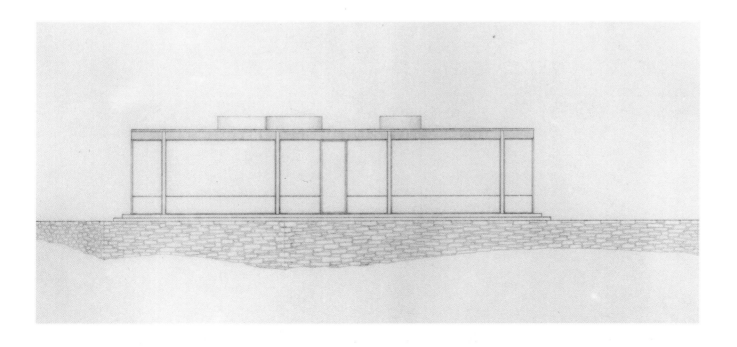

Scheme XII

Scheme XII, composed between January and April 1947 (figs. 91–92), refines the single-volume glass pavilion and adds a basement for storage and service areas. The uses for it are not specified, but it is enclosed by concrete foundation walls, making it most likely a storage and service area only. It is connected to the main floor by a stair contained in the largest cylindrical space (fig. 93). The stair emerges in the kitchen, which occupies just over half of the cylinder; the remainder is given over to a bathroom. A much smaller cylinder, for a fireplace, is in the diagonally opposite corner of the house. A single area for sleeping and a study are also indicated, and the furnishings are sparse compared with earlier schemes.

     The design for this scheme went quite far: Johnson developed dimensioned plans and detailed cabinet and interior elevations for the kitchen and bath. The steel columns that support the roof are expressed outside the face of the glass, and the end columns are pulled back from the corners, much as Mies intended for the Farnsworth House. This particular feature would be revised in the final design: the columns would be brought inside the house, leaving the exterior skin smooth and free of tectonic articulation and shadows.

Glass House
Scheme XII
91 Plan ("Jan 47")

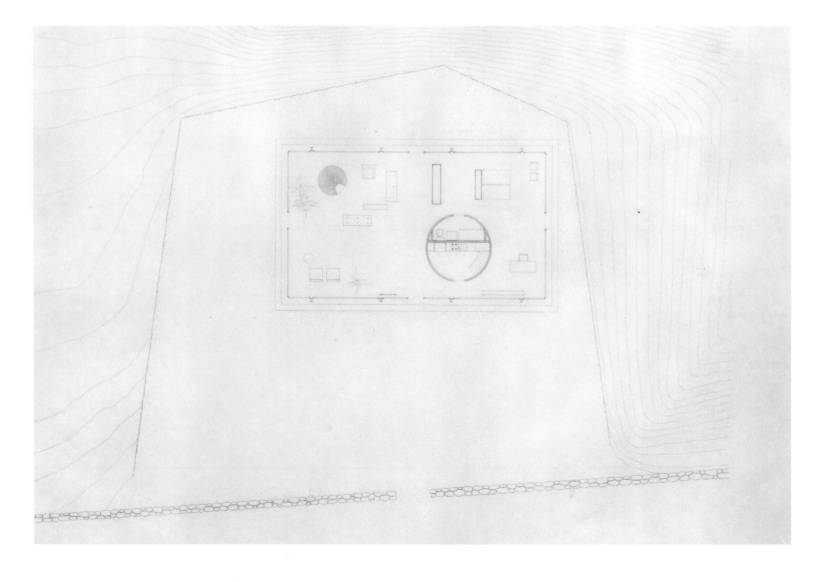

Glass House
Scheme XII
92 (above) Model photograph
93 (left) Details, kitchen and bath core

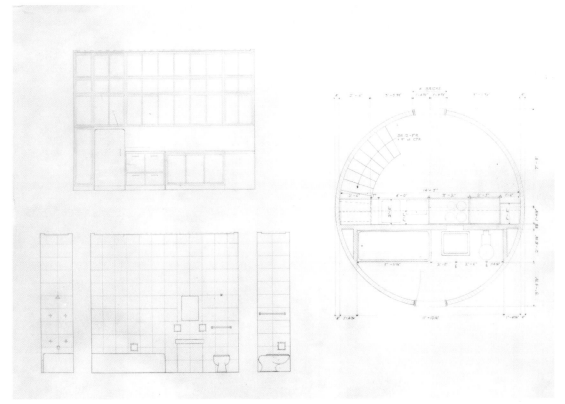

Scheme XIII

In May 1947, Johnson created one of his most intriguing designs. Scheme XIII depicts both the promontory and the structure sheared as if along the plane of a geologic fracture. The two unequal parts appear to have slid relative to each other along a plane represented by a masonry wall 120 feet in length (fig. 94). Inspired by Mies's 1922 project for a brick country house, Johnson extended the wall out from both ends of the house so that it descends each side of the promontory, which is smaller than in previous schemes.

In this design the promontory view is screened from the arrival side more completely than in any other scheme. The larger of only two openings in the brick wall is reached by an entryway, which also gives access to the kitchen and a guest bedroom. Passing through that opening, one would enter the living area, with Johnson's desk and sleeping area screened by cabinetry to the right and the view out over the promontory directly ahead. The wall is also indented to form a fireplace for the living area. Aside from the shared masonry wall, each block has three walls detailed in glass. Unfortunately, no elevations of this scheme exist. The design was one of Johnson's most experimental, and he did not explore it further in later schemes.

Glass House
Scheme XIII
94 Plan ("May 47")

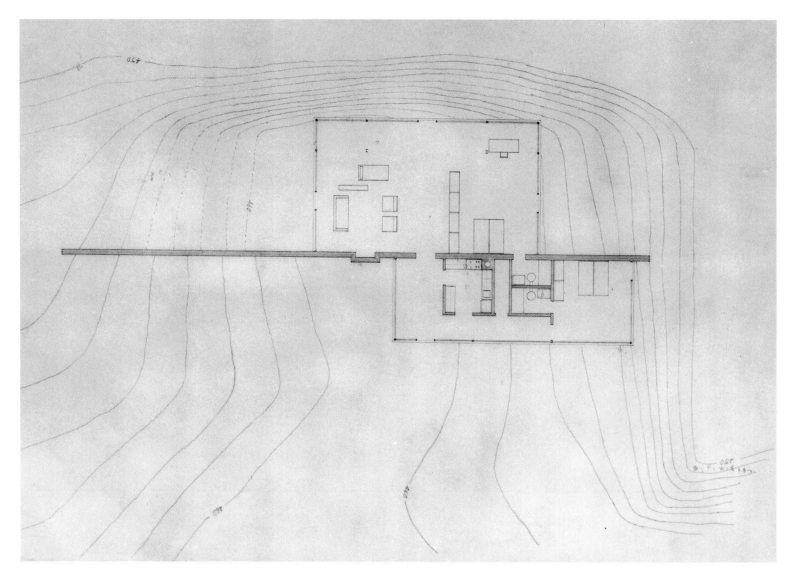

Schemes XIV and XV

Scheme XIV, from June of 1947, shows Johnson turning to the Resor House model of Mies (see fig. 8), which he had drawn on for a number of domestic projects for other clients (fig. 95). The site is not indicated in plan, and the house itself, while drawn mechanically, is at best a hard-lined sketch. A narrow rectangular wall of masonry is broken in two places, at opposite sides of the plan, by large areas of glass. The breaks in the wall would have defined the public spaces of the house, with the private and service activities taking place in the two flanking areas. A large, freestanding fireplace mass is set within the living room. Scheme XV (not illustrated) appears to be a variation on the elevation for this plan. It indicates that the house was sited with the long walls facing the arrival side and the valley. Johnson's Oneto House, begun in 1949, is strikingly similar to this scheme.

Glass House
Scheme XIV
95 Plan ("June 47")

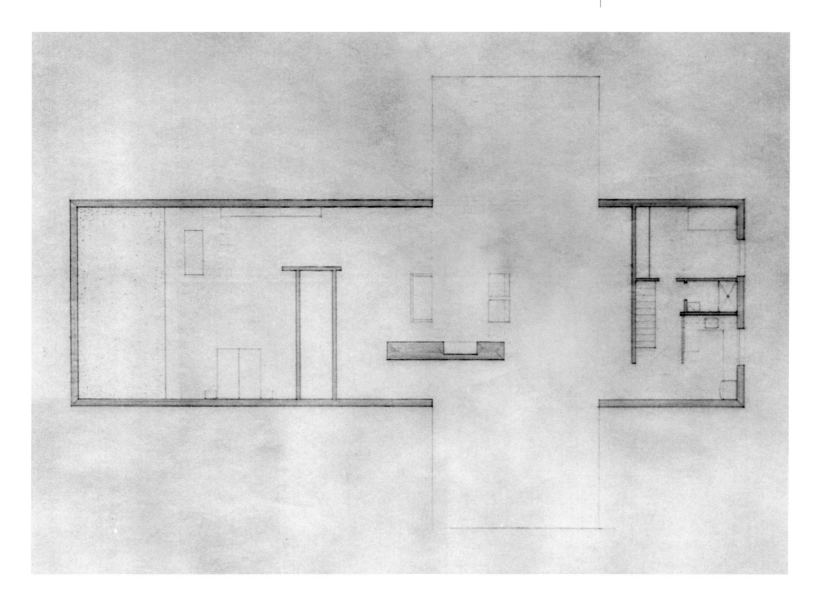

Schemes XVI and XVII

The studies that follow Scheme XV depart radically in overall planning strategies and representation. Scheme XVI depicts two pavilions, one glass and one brick, separate from each other but linked by a small paved terrace (fig. 96). The glass pavilion is sited at the edge of the promontory and contains the public spaces in this scheme: living, dining, and food preparation. The other pavilion contains two bedrooms and two bathrooms; the master bedroom opens onto an enclosed court. The fireplace has been removed from the interior and is expressed as a little masonry tower outside the glass walls, similar to the Townsend Farm barn of 1944 (fig. 31).

Glass House
Scheme XVI
96 Plan

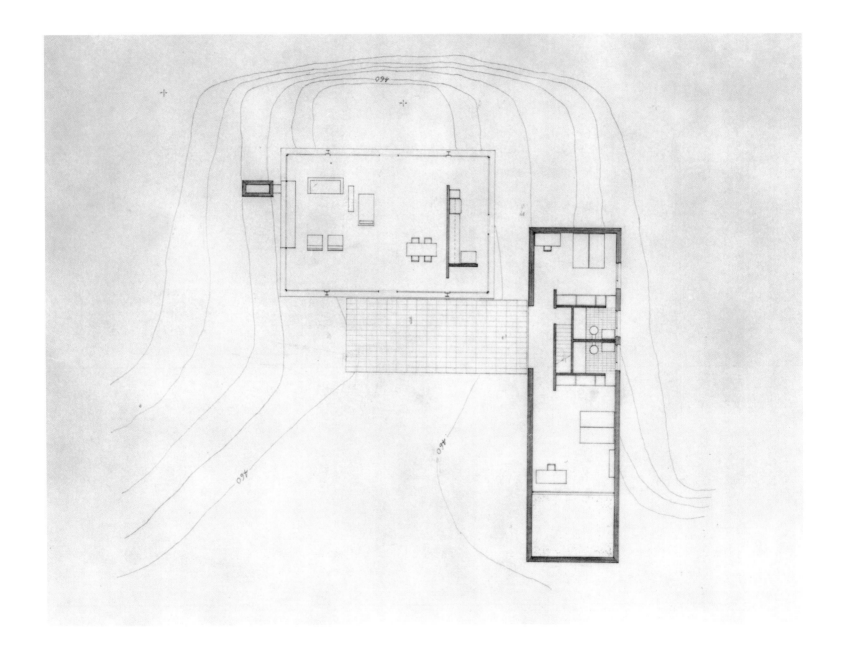

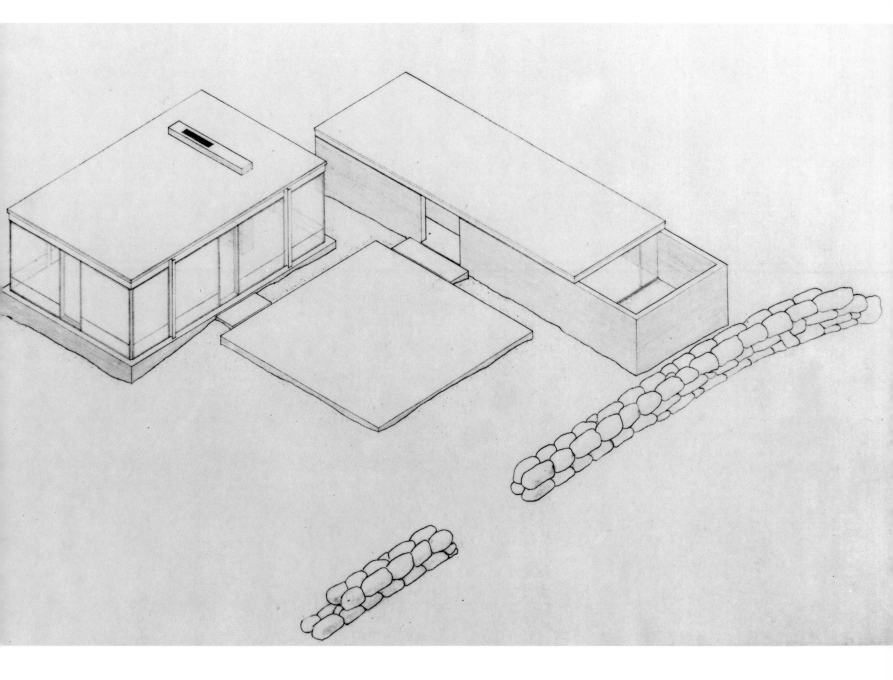

Scheme XVII is very closely related to the preceding one, with adjustments only in the size of the terrace and the reintroduction of the stone wall—with an opening in it—as a means of creating a forecourt for the house (fig. 97). Johnson looked back to Breuer for inspiration for these designs, but one might also recall Wright's strategies for his Usonian houses and their differentiation between public and private areas. One crucial development in this sequence of designs is the distinction between a glass pavilion for public activities and a brick one for private and service functions.

Glass House
Scheme XVII
97 Axonometric plan ("June 47")

Schemes XIX, XX, and XXI

In the summer of 1947, Johnson developed a very different set of designs that share attributes with the final project but depart from it stylistically to a remarkable degree. The houses in Schemes XIX, XX, and XXI are masonry and rectangular in plan, with, respectively, sets of two, three, and five arches on the front and rear elevations (figs. 98, 99, and 102). Scheme XX has become known as the "Syrian Arch" design. It includes another single arch on one of the short elevations as a part of a balcony extending out over a steep drop (fig. 100). The plan for that scheme shows pivoting doors within arches, which open onto a central public space (fig. 101). At one end is a bedroom with the balcony, while a kitchen and pantry occupy the opposite end. A raised terrace extends from this end of the house, opposite the end with the balcony. Additionally, a brick wall extends from the front of the house to create a loosely defined forecourt as an approach. One of the unresolved questions raised by these three schemes is whether or not a separate guest house was intended as a part of the design. The final design for the Guest House was apparently finished in the summer of 1947 and put aside while the design of the main house was completed.

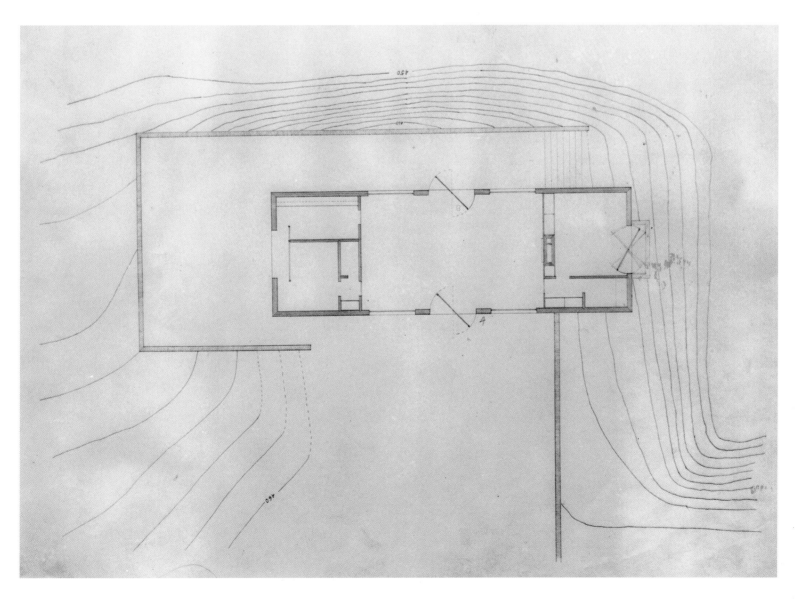

Scheme XXII

A sketch by Mies van der Rohe for a glass prism cantilevered off a slope (fig. 104) is almost certainly the inspiration for Scheme XXII, from the summer of 1947 (fig. 105). Johnson's major activity at this time would have been the Mies exhibition at The Museum of Modern Art. Although there is no correlation to the New Canaan site, one assumes that Mies had been working with a topography similar to that of Johnson's property. The Scheme XXII design, just a sketch, shows a single rectangular pavilion, mainly glass at one end and mostly enclosed at the other. The glass end cantilevers off a hillside, while the solid portion is attached to a foundation. As one would expect, the public areas are in the cantilevered end. Kitchen, bedroom, and bath make up the other end of the structure.

Ludwig Mies van der Rohe
Sketch for a house on a hillside, 1934
104 Elevation

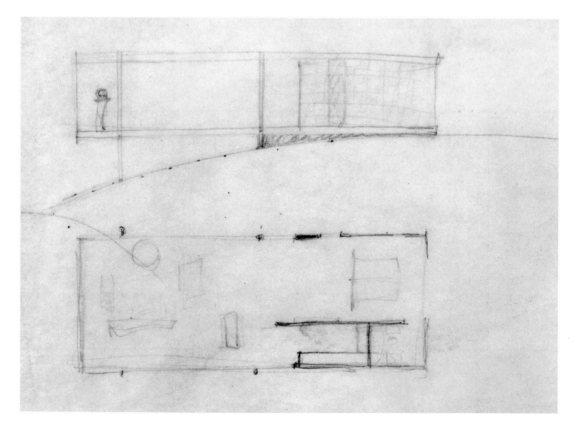

Glass House
Scheme XXII
105 Plan and elevation ("Aug 47(?)")

Schemes XXIII and XXIV

Scheme XXIII, from September 1947, is somewhat similar in organization to its predecessor: a single rectangular volume, with public and private functions at opposite ends (fig. 106). The difference is that Johnson added a second story underneath the private zone where the land falls away from the house. The use of glass is more limited than in the previous scheme, with large openings alternating with masonry walls primarily at the public end. A terrace created by a retaining wall affords access to the edge of the promontory at the public end of the

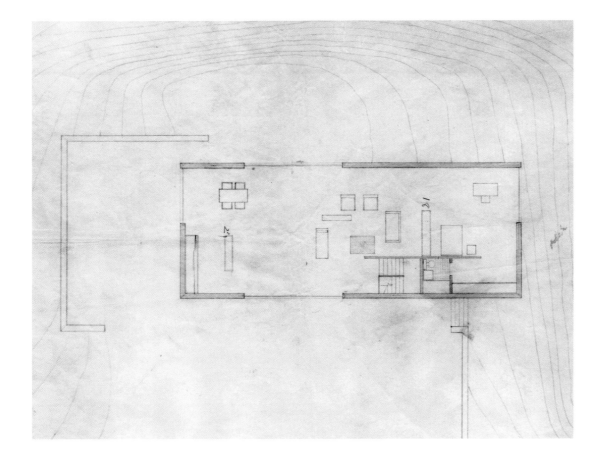

Glass House
Scheme XXIII
106 Plan

structure and ultimately flows back in the direction of the road to provide a level approach to the house. Elevations for this design show the fenestration in the two-story end of the house aligned, like the openings in the Abbott House project of approximately the same period. The fenestration is not symmetrical, however, and is clearly placed to favor the views down the slope. This project, the Abbott House project, and the Bramlette House project are Johnson's first two-story house designs; clearly the architect was exploring this theme in a number of different projects at the same time. Scheme XXIII was developed as far as some construction detail drawings. Its successor, Scheme XXIV (not illustrated) is really just a refinement of XXIII, with adjustments made in the extent of the retaining wall terrace and the relative location of the doorway on the southwestern elevation.

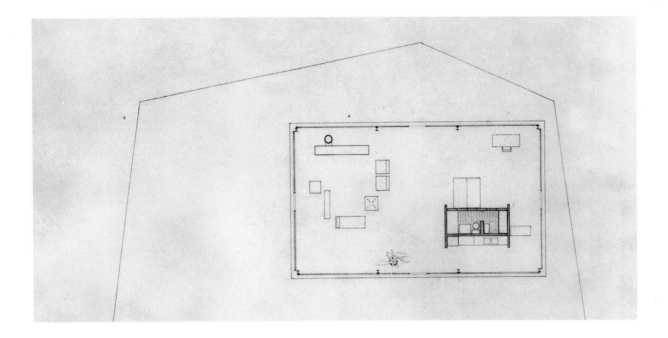

Schemes XXV and XXVI

At some point before autumn of 1947, Johnson returned to his podium and pavilion strategy from a year earlier; of all the schemes he had examined, he had developed this one the furthest. In Scheme XXV he revived the built-up profile for a promontory anchoring a rectangular pavilion, using virtually the same dimensions as for Scheme XI, almost a year earlier, and locating the pavilion in the same place—favoring the northern edge of the podium. There is a single rectangular core containing a bathroom, which also creates a separation for the kitchen, as well as a headboard for the bed (fig. 107). Living-area furniture is grouped in the southwest corner, and a small writing desk completes the internal arrangement of spaces and furnishings. In all likelihood, the inspiration for this design came from Mies's plans for the Farnsworth House, with its rectangular core enclosing bathrooms and tucking the kitchen area out of the sight of the main living spaces. In the next scheme, XXVI, he adjusted the shape and location of the rectangular core so that it occupies the central bay in the pavilion, with the living area directly in front of it (fig. 108). A bedroom alcove at one end and two small desks at the other complete the arrangement in this plan, which is a nearly literal adaptation of the Farnsworth House. The elevations are once again symmetrical, with a column grid set just inside the glazing and four doors centered on each elevation.

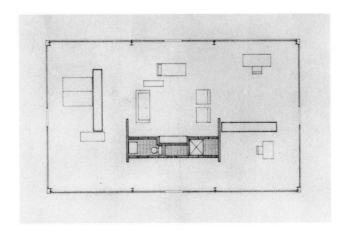

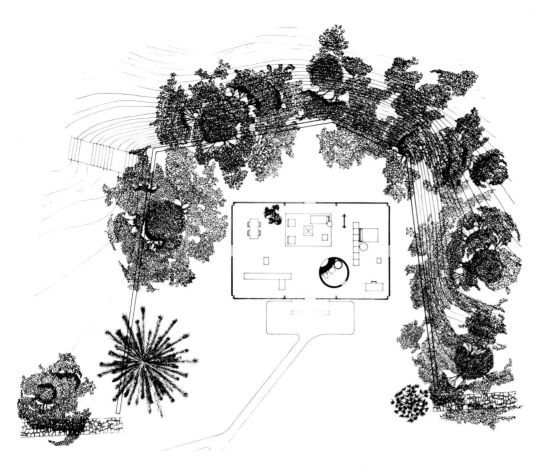

Scheme XXVII

In the final plan for the Glass House, Scheme XXVII of November 1947, Johnson retained the exterior of the pre-

vious design, but adjusted the interior arrangement significantly (fig. 109). Most notably, he returned to the use

of a cylindrical element, now a single brick core, off-center in the plan, incorporating a bathroom. A shallow arc

is carved out of the side facing the living space so that it reads as an immense fireplace. A six-foot-high free-

standing cabinet screens a space for a bed toward the north end of the plan. At the south end is a dining area

and a freestanding counter that accommodates the kitchen. The ele-

vations, all glass, remain much the same, save for the addition of a

chair rail along the glazing, broken only at the four doors; these, as

before, are centered on each elevation. The roof, as in all the pavil-

ion and podium schemes, aligns with the perimeter walls, with no

overhang. The structural columns are inside the glass, accentuating

the pavilion's transparency and the continuity of the surface.

Without a doubt, this final design is the most refined of all

the options Johnson considered for the Glass House. The elegance

and simplicity of its elements—plan, elevations, furnishings, and sit-

ing—belie its varied precursors. Even as the construction documents

were being prepared, Johnson was still willing to investigate, if only

Glass House
109 (above) Final plan, based on Scheme XXVII
Scheme XXVII
110 (below) Alternative court-house plan

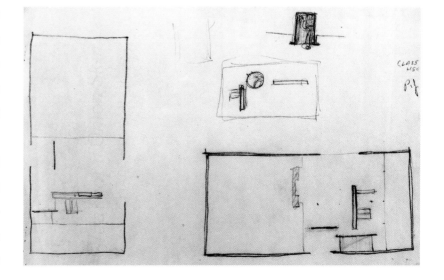

in sketches, other options. In December 1947 he returned to the idea of a court-house, specifically a double court-house (fig. 110). There is a strong resemblance in these studies to one of the Schlubach designs of a year or more earlier, but they seem to have never progressed beyond sketches nor derailed the progress on Scheme XXVII as the final design for the Glass House.

One change is evident between the drawings for Scheme XXVII and the built version, and that relates to the site conditions. The drawings show the return of the stone wall with a gap allowing for an entry to the promontory. As built, the wall breaks at each edge of the promontory, allowing the full width of the podium to be accessible. The choice of materials enhances the direct relationship of the Glass House to the surrounding landscape. The earth tones of the brick and steel sets these materials apart from the glass walls. The contrast between the transparent glazing—and the views through it to the landscape—and the more solid building materials is only one element of the Glass House's mysterious appeal.

The other very substantial issue in Johnson's design process is the relationship of the Glass House to the Guest House (fig. 111). The Guest House is not shown in the later phases of the design sequence. Its design was completed much earlier than that of the Glass House and then it was set aside and attention was devoted exclusively to the Glass House. Construction of both structures began together, with a groundbreaking in March 1948. The Guest House was actually completed before the Glass House (December 1948 and March 1949, respectively). Johnson lists the final Guest House design as Scheme XXVIIB, clearly tying it to the final version of the house. But its absence throughout the final phases of the design, at least in the representations, is puzzling. Its design serves as a powerful foil to the final version of the Glass House, as many critics have noted (fig. 112).

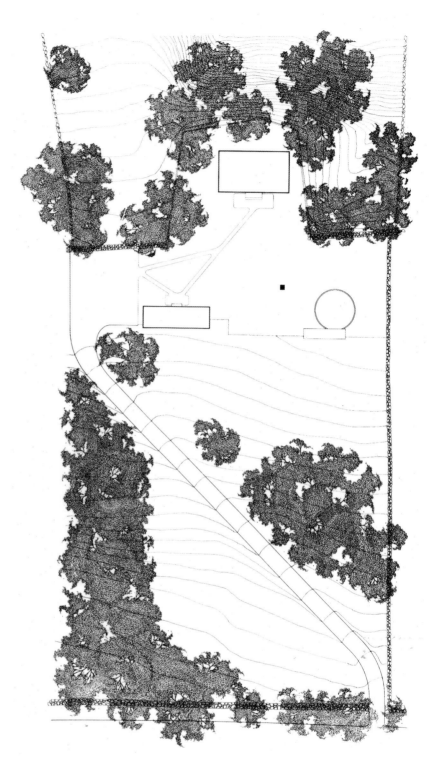

Glass House and Guest House
111 Site plan

Almost a completely closed brick box, the Guest House contains two bedrooms, a study, a bath, and utility functions for both structures (fig. 115). There are just three circular windows, for the bedrooms and the study, on the elevation facing away from the Glass House; a single door is centered on the façade facing the main house (fig. 113). The siting of the Guest House, well back from the edge of the slope where the promon-

tory begins, accentuates the perception of the Glass House as the dominant element of the design. In fact, by

virtue of both its closed surfaces and remote siting, the Guest House is so self-effacing it almost disappears.

Given Johnson's struggles, particularly early on in the design sequence, to elaborate a relationship between dif-

ferent pavilions—by court, loggia, or wall—the lack of a defined built relationship between the two elements

seems curious. However, whenever one examines that relationship spatially, it becomes quite profound. The

near-alignment of the southeastern wall of the Glass House with the northwestern wall of the Guest House, and

the relative siting of the two structures, creates a powerfully abstract space (fig. 112). The relationship is further

enhanced by the position of the stone wall, approximately halfway between the two structures, and the fact that

the wall is broken for the width of the podium. Moreover, the processional approach from the parking area

emphasizes the axis of the stone wall. Thus one is always turned toward the podium and the Glass House, while

Glass House and Guest House
112 View looking down the hill from the path in front of the Painting Gallery

Guest House
113 View of exterior

the façade of the Guest House operates as a receding plane that further delineates the forecourt of the main house. The Guest House is thus a foil for its crystalline counterpart.

The Glass House, then, seems to stand alone, a transparent pavilion on its own podium (fig. 115). Yet, for all its iconic architectural qualities, its greatest asset may be as a lens to focus a view of nature. The terrain falling away on its far side opens up views not only through the house but also through the trees on that slope to the sky above the valley beyond. The design is "worked out from the landscape point of view," according to Johnson, so that it will "take in nature from all sides."[43] The architect thus affirms the strong affinity with natural surroundings that has been a part of the American ideal since the first settlers. "The house was just a trick to make landscaping," Johnson remarked recently. "That house doesn't exist for me; it's where I stand, and the landscape goes on in all directions."[44]

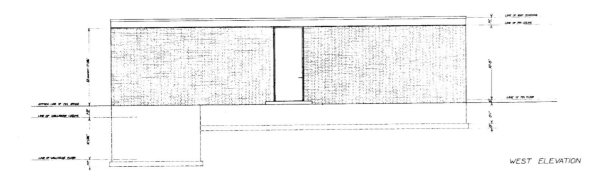

WEST ELEVATION

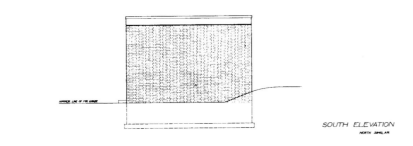

SOUTH ELEVATION
NORTH SIMILAR

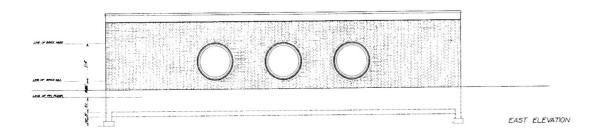

EAST ELEVATION

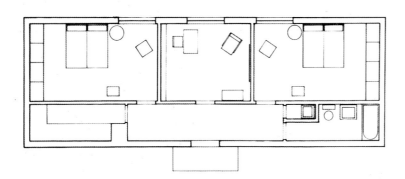

Guest House
114 (above) and 115 (left)
Final elevations and plan
Glass House
116 (pages 92–93) Interior

Progeny of the Glass House

4

Robert C. Wiley House
117 View of rear façade and living pavilion

The public and professional acclaim the Glass House received anchored it as one of the defining monuments in American architecture and bestowed on Johnson broad recognition in his profession. The process of designing the house also transformed him into a mature architect. In retrospect, that process was Johnson's second education, and it allowed him to develop his professional skills. In the 1950s he was able to demonstrate just how considerable those skills had become. Johnson's residential work of the early 1950s demonstrates that he had lost none of his willingness to explore new ideas about the nature of architecture. Just as importantly, however, he developed the discipline to see projects through to finished houses.

A close examination of the domestic projects of this period augments our understanding and appreciation of this period of Johnson's career. The house designs of the 1950s follow two related but parallel paths. The designs from the early years of the decade are, for the most part, dependent upon Johnson's Glass House and Guest House designs. Later in the decade, the architect made what he called a "conscious shift to break loose" from the earlier period, determined to try new ideas. This chapter deals with the earlier group of projects.

Far more sophisticated than his tentative residential designs of the mid-1940s, the houses that follow the Glass House show a more confident and refined practice. Johnson was fortunate that both his background at The Museum of Modern Art and the notoriety of the Glass House brought an increasing number of good clients to him. As Landis Gores remembers it, "The epiphany, not to say apocalypse, of the Glass House occasioned a rapid increase in the volume of work at 205 East Forty-second Street, first expansion to a second room for three summer volunteers and then a permanent increment of the same size."[45] In the mid-1940s his commissions were essentially favors from friends willing to help establish the career of a gifted young professional. The clients of the 1950s, however, were intent on establishing their own positions as exponents of modern art and architecture. His recollections of this period invariably turn to his relationships with these people. They not only brought a sympathy for both modern architecture and modern art; in the best cases they also came to Johnson with trust in his ability to create art and architecture that would suit their lives.

The broad themes Johnson explored in the design process for the Glass House—separation of private and public uses, open and closed volumes, the linkages between these oppositions, and the relation of the whole to the surrounding natural environment—are confidently carried forward in the houses of the first half of the 1950s. Many of these emphasize simple cubic shapes or primary forms. After absorbing the influences and lessons of the Glass House design process, Johnson used these forms as ideal types to be rearranged, reconfigured, and explored further. Reminiscent of J. N. L. Durand's codification of different ways of combining architectural elements, or of Le Corbusier's quest for ideal forms, these designs also reveal his desire to build upon Mies's Resor and Hubbe House projects (see figs. 8 and 6). Indeed, Johnson elaborated several of the formal arrangements that first appeared in early schemes for the Glass House: for example, there are projects that introduce a second story into the composition.

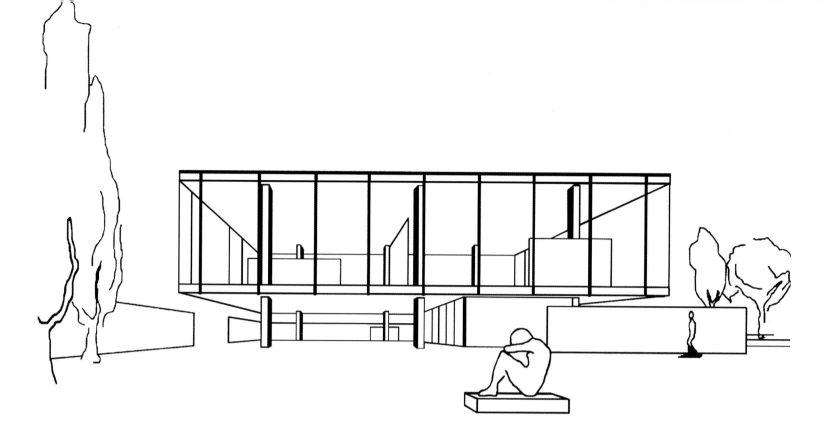

House of Glass, The Museum of Modern Art (project), 1948

Even before the Glass House was completed, Johnson had begun to expand on the possibilities inherent in its design. Three projects initiated in 1948 and 1949 illustrate this. The House of Glass for The Museum of Modern Art garden is interesting for Johnson's description of it, while two other art-related projects, both for Mrs. John D. Rockefeller III, demonstrate the intimate relationships in this period between Johnson's activities at the Museum and his private practice.

The House of Glass was intended as an exhibition gallery (fig. 118). The rendering of the project shows a glass-walled structure within the museum's sculpture garden, raised up on steel columns with individual works of sculpture surrounding it. Johnson described the project as a "prism," with walls of smooth plate glass, and floors and stairs of rough plate glass: "The building, as it is projected, will have the appearance of a huge crystal floating above the Museum's garden space in the center of Manhattan."[46]

The possibility of reaching a large new audience for modern architecture was not lost on Johnson. In his words, the pavilion was "intended to demonstrate in a dramatic and convincing manner to the Museum's annual one million visitors that glass is the lightest, most flexible, and most completely modern material available to architects today. The 'House of Glass' will have an impact on the public taste, and the resulting public acceptance of glass as an almost universal building material will advance immeasurably the cause of modern architecture."[47] Glass has almost romantic associations in the early designs of the modern movement as well as in such books as Paul Scheerbart's futuristic *Glasarchitektur* of 1914. Johnson was clearly drawn to such early modern projects as the House of Glass by Bruno Taut, also 1914, and Mies's skyscraper designs of 1919 and 1920.

House of Glass, Museum of Modern Art (project)
118 Perspective sketch

Mrs. John D. Rockefeller III Pool Pavilion and Art Gallery (project), 1948

Certainly the most prominent residential client for whom Philip Johnson worked during this period was Blanchette Rockefeller, wife of John D. Rockefeller III. Mrs. Rockefeller had recently begun collecting art, and she would eventually become president of The Museum of Modern Art. Friendly from their association at MoMA, Mrs. Rockefeller and Johnson engaged in two building projects together, one in the country and one in New York City. Both were Johnson at his most singular: pure settings for art. The first, in 1948, was a sculpture and pool pavilion, for the Rockefellers' Westchester County estate, where Mrs. Rockefeller could display art as well as entertain informally (figs. 119–20). Similar to a late study for the Glass House, Scheme XXVI from October 1947, the glass pavilion sits atop a terraced landscape, with cascading walkways and steps leading down from it. As in Scheme XXVI, there is a rectangular core, exactly centered in the space. It contains a massive fireplace with a private bathroom/changing room beyond it. The pavilion and surrounding terraces and walls are nestled into the slope of a hill and would have been concealed by mature trees. Glass partitions were intended as

Mrs. John D. Rockefeller III Pool Pavilion and Art Gallery (project)
119 Model photograph

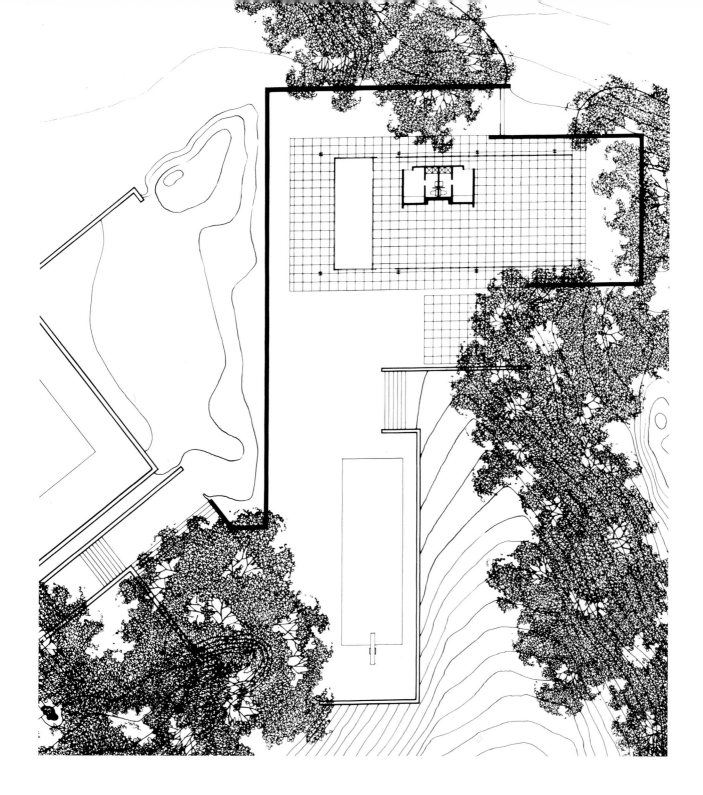

display screens for art, while terrace walls were to provide backdrops for sculpture. The pool would have been under a canopy of trees.

While the design greatly pleased Mrs. Rockefeller, her husband was not as enthusiastic, and the commission was not carried out.[48] Yet the project received attention in the professional press; an article about the pavilion in the January 1949 issue of Interiors was titled "New World Xanadu of Steel and Glass." The author noted, "There is one idea that most staunch advocates of modern architecture share with its staunch enemies, and that is that magnificence and luxury, like romance, are things of the past."[49]

Mrs. John D. Rockefeller III Pool Pavilion and Art Gallery (project)
120 Plan

Mrs. John D. Rockefeller III Guest House, 1949–50

Within a year Johnson had accepted a second commission from Mrs. Rockefeller, the design of a townhouse in Manhattan, on East Fifty-second Street (figs. 121–26). As much as this commission would mean to his career, coming as it did early in the establishment of his professional practice, it would be, ironically, his only built house for a client in New York City. Close to the Rockefeller apartment on Beekman Place, the townhouse would serve as an "adjunct space to her apartment. . . . She would show a portion of her sculpture collection there, serve tea and host receptions and parties, and even put up guests."[50]

Mrs. John D. Rockefeller III Guest House
121 (below, left) Street perspective
122 (below, right) Plan
123 (opposite) Street façade

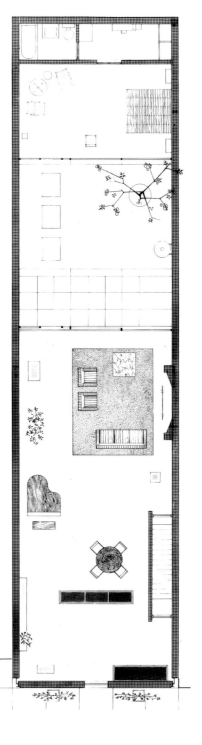

The Rockefeller Guest House design was as radical in its urban context as the Glass House was in rural Connecticut. The entire interior of the house is open, devoid of floor-to-ceiling partitions, creating a single space. A large living room extends from the front door to the middle of the site, with only a head-high freestanding cabinet to distinguish an entry foyer from the remainder of the space. Beyond the living room is an outdoor courtyard. There is a small covered terrace adjacent to the living room and a bedroom on the far side of the court. Both walls defining the court are made entirely of glass, and a pool of water stretches across almost the entire court, further separating the public and private functions of the house. Three stones, surrounded by water, permit access to the bedroom. Johnson remembers that an electric pump provided a cascading waterfall that "ran off the roof line into the pool like a liquid screen, a waterfall that you could turn on and off. Isn't that a marvelous idea?"[51]

The effect of the expansive interior volume flowing through an exterior court with a pool is striking. But unlike the Glass House, where the landscape moves through and is framed by the glass pavilion, the Rockefeller Guest House has a glass pavilion within it, which defines a moment of "nature" inserted into the urban fabric of the city. The effect of the courtyard is powerful despite its miniscule dimensions. The pool is the equivalent of a Roman compluvium: a room open to the sky into which rainwater can fall. In some respects, Johnson reassembled for the same client the programmatic and formal components of the Westchester pavilion in a site cleared out of the tight urban fabric of East Fifty-second Street. Nature, art, water, and even a massive hearth and fireplace come together again in a compressed but surprisingly serene space.

Of all his clients in this period of his work, Mrs. Rockefeller most closely shared Johnson's design sensibilities. The Guest House was "an ideal townhouse," he recalled later. "There I was in sync with the owner—a very close relationship." The pool of water created "a slight feeling of danger," making occupants of the house more aware of the architecture—and nature—around them. "Don't forget that Mrs. Rockefeller wasn't going to live there. She would visit, keep her art, and get away from her husband. She entertained her art-connected friends a little. When her husband didn't like [the guest house] she gave it to MoMA."[52] The museum kept the house from 1958, when Mrs. Rockefeller made the donation, until 1966. A subsequent owner was Mrs. Robert C. Leonhardt, co-owner with her husband of the cantilevered glass box Johnson designed in 1954–56. Johnson himself leased the Rockefeller Guest House from a later owner for a number of years in the 1970s.

Mrs. John D. Rockefeller III Guest House
125 (left) Interior view from living room to bedroom
126 (below) Interior view from bedroom to living room

Mr. and Mrs. Henry Ford II House (project), 1950–51

A project in Southampton, New York, for Ann and Henry Ford II, is the largest and most elaborate house project Johnson had attempted up to 1950 (figs. 127–29). It combines Johnson's earlier explorations of the Resor House type (see fig. 6) with new elements such as courtyards, verticality, and a complex entry and processional sequence. A largely open public area is centered between two closed ends of the house, which contain the private areas: bedrooms, kitchen, and storage. As with the Farney House in nearby Sagaponack, the main living floor is raised up to the second story of the house to align with the height of the adjacent dune and pro-

Mr. and Mrs. Henry Ford II House (project)
127 (left) Model photograph,
view of ocean side
128 (below) Model photograph,
view of entry side

vide views out to the ocean beyond. A large terrace off the central public space would have abutted the edge of the dune. The house itself would have been so large—the living space alone measures over fifty feet across—that he designed an interior glass courtyard in the middle of the public space, with shrubs and trees growing through the roof opening. At over eleven thousand square feet, the design clearly has ambitions beyond a typical domestic program.[53]

In many of the projects of this period, Johnson elaborated upon one of the most successful components of his earlier domestic architecture, an expansive private interior space. Yet he also brought a new idea to these compositions, a sense of monumentality. In many of the residential projects of the next two decades, Johnson moved back and forth from the modest yet refined scale of early modern architecture, evident in a project like his own Ash Street House, to a far more assertive and monumental modernism, represented by the Ford design. In many respects the Ford House is a modern version of a Roman seaside villa, a vast summer palace for the social set in Southampton. Henry Ford II was thirty years old in 1950, and the house was clearly intended to reinforce his emerging social standing and business prominence. The entry sequence expresses grand aspirations: the visitor would have entered through an arched opening, ceremonial in character, then climbed a wide stairway to the living areas on the upper floor. Arriving at the *piano nobile*, the visitor would have encountered a reception area defined by the glassed-in courtyard. This garden area, analogous to a compluvium in a Roman house, screens an immediate view of the ocean; one would have had to move through the large expanse of the house to find the views of the water. The master bedroom suite is generous, with a large dressing area. Both principal bedrooms face into an enclosed court. The wall along this edge of the house is entirely of glass, while the three surrounding walls of the court are of masonry, unbroken by openings. A similar arrangement of open glass and closed masonry takes place at the opposite end of the house, where the kitchen is located.

Johnson clearly had high hopes for this major project, but the house was never realized. His partner Landis Gores remembers that "by summer's end the Fords, back from Europe, vetoed the entire project, compensating Philip instead with an addition and alteration commission on their old shingled manse, which would bring down the curtain on the fantasized *pièce de théâtre*."[54] The addition was a stark modern contradiction to the existing Shingle Style house (fig. 130). A small two-story pavilion is separated from the main house by a glass passage. The exterior of the addition is essentially a curtain wall, with vertical fins for mullions. Louvers like those used in the Wolf House allow air to circulate. "I was out of sync with the period of the clientele," Johnson would recall later. "They [the Fords] loved the Glass House," but they had "no eyes, they never saw design. He had no idea what I was talking about. He ended up with a completely conventional house. But I saved a lot of time and trouble. I wasn't dumb enough to get into practical work. And I was kind of sick of working like [with] the de Menils, where I had to put the bathing suits right there and the silk stockings in that drawer."[55]

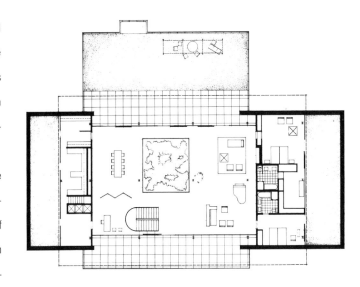

Mr. and Mrs. Henry Ford II House (project)
129 Plan of main floor

Mr. and Mrs. Henry Ford II House addition
130 View of façade

John L. Senior Jr. House (project), 1950–51

In 1950 and 1951 Johnson designed a project for a young businessman and art collector, John L. Senior Jr., on a thousand-acre site in New Canaan. Senior was thirty-four years old, son of a cement tycoon. He had graduated from Harvard and then received a degree in aeronautical engineering from MIT, but his interests were varied: he intended to create an organic farm and experimental dairy on the site. In addition, both he and his wife were devoted to music and art, and the program included two grand pianos and exhibition areas for the display of the thirteen Mondrian paintings the couple owned at the time.

The house was to be the centerpiece of their experimental farm. Johnson's design called for a double-height glass box atop a masonry base, cantilevering out on all sides (figs. 131–32). Entry would have been via the masonry box, which serves as a base for the living spaces above it. The ground floor contains the entrance stairhall, a guest room, and service areas.

A pair of chairs and panel behind them face the ground-floor entrance. However, aside from a guest/service bedroom, functions on the ground floor are only minimally indicated. The main space of the glass box is public, a modern *piano nobile* by virtue of its raised floor height and grand proportions. There are two groups of seating, a small dining area, the two grand pianos, and a kitchenette behind a partition. A raised platform over the kitchenette and one seating area provides for a sleeping loft, dressing cabinets, and bath. The effect would have been dramatic: the glass box contains two viewing areas, or belvederes. From the living

John L. Senior Jr. House (project)
131 Model photograph

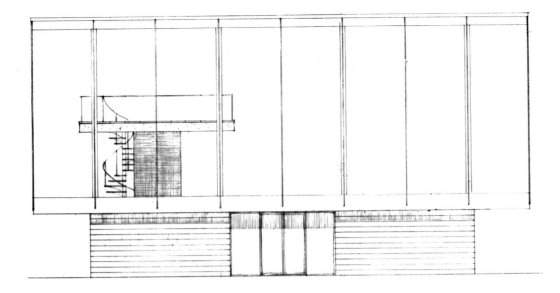

space, one would have looked out across the landscape of the farm, and from the sleeping loft, across the land-scape of the house to the farm beyond. Vertical circulation is by two sets of circular stairs: one larger set from the ground to the *piano nobile*, and a smaller set from the service quarters on the ground floor to the kitchen, and continuing on to the sleeping loft above. Freestanding columns in the glass box, in a grid aligned with the perimeter of the base, are held back from the glazed perimeter of the public spaces.

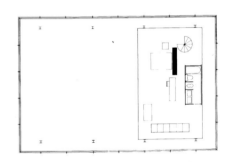

The overall effect of the Senior House would have been much more monumental than that of the Glass House, largely because of its height. In fact, it is a three-story structure, with the two-story glass volume lifted off the ground and thus made even more prominent in the composition. It would have had the appear-ance of the "huge crystal floating" in air that Johnson had contemplated two years earlier for The Museum of Modern Art Garden. Johnson has remarked on the effect of a second floor, "I mean, really, the one-story Mies house has no presence at all. The second floor adds about four times the height."[56] The grid of the structural system and platform support is reminiscent of Mies's Farnsworth House (fig. 75), while the cantilever at the perimeter is a device Johnson had used in the Wolf House three years before (figs. 57–58). Little attention was given to the site, although the model photographs show a freestanding wall that partially encloses a court adja-cent to the house. However, the idea of the belvedere overlooking the site was crucial to Johnson's conception. In utilizing it, he picked up a compositional element which had been important to a number of projects he par-ticularly admired: Schinkel's work in Potsdam, Le Corbusier's Villa Savoye, the Chamberlain Cottage of Breuer and Gropius, and Mies's Farnsworth House.

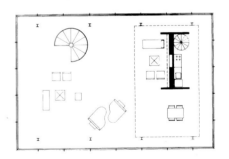

During the schematic design process, Johnson took the Seniors to see the small modern addition he had recently completed for Henry Ford II's traditional house in Southampton. Their reaction was not encourag-ing. "They were horrified! They said, 'Why do you show us this thing stuck on a very ugly house? It is very unsympathetic to the house, and the sea, and the neighborhood.' By seeing that project, they [the Seniors] could not imagine building their project."[57] The Seniors did move to the property, but into an existing colonial-style house.

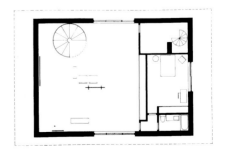

Kootz Gallery Exhibit House (project)
134 Model photograph

Kootz Gallery Exhibit House (project), 1950

In October 1950 a similar design was prepared for an exhibition, *The Muralist and the Modern Architect*, organized by the Kootz Gallery in New York. The exhibition, about the collaborations between modern architects and artists, presented drawings and models by five pairs of designers.[58] The dealer Samuel M. Kootz had a reputation as an activist and prophet on behalf of the "new American art," having been among the first to exhibit the work of the American Abstract Expressionist painters as a school.

Johnson collaborated with the painter William Baziotes. In a brief statement for the exhibition catalog, Johnson described the project as an actual commission for a family with three children, the client preferring "to remain anonymous." He went on to describe the design in basic functional terms: "Their requirements are separated into two distinct parts. 1) An area where they can all be together and where they will spend most of their time; an area elegant but washable. 2) Sleeping and general riot area."[59] Regrettably, only a photograph of the model exists (fig. 134). It recalls the Glass House, but it is raised up on a solid one-story podium—almost as if the Glass House had been stacked on top of the Guest House. Unlike the Senior House, the glass story is aligned with the masonry walls of the base. A steel structural system is clearly expressed, allowing for the walls to consist of glass and brick infill panels. That detailing and the fact that the second and ground floors align bring to mind the street façade of the Rockefeller Guest House completed the same year. Johnson noted in the catalog that the photograph did not accurately represent his design, in that the fenestration on the lower floor was not shown in the model. The Senior House project and the Kootz Gallery Exhibit House project continued the theme of the juxtaposition of a glass prism with a cube, reconfiguring it in vertical compositions. Entry, procession, and verticality link these projects. While neither of these projects was built, the willingness to explore different programmatic and compositional ideas would ultimately lead to the construction of one of Johnson's better known houses from this period, the Mr. and Mrs. Robert C. Wiley House of 1953 (see pages 132–35).

In two other projects of the early 1950s Johnson found clients willing to carry his ideas all the way to buildings. These houses, for the George J. Oneto and Richard Hodgson families, remain among Johnson's favorites. The clients were eager to work with him and gave him latitude to carry though his architectural ideas. The two houses resemble each other and make an interesting comparison. Each is composed of a simple one-story rectangular volume. The Oneto House follows the Glass House model through its use of a simple axial and symmetrical form, while the Hodgson House has more complex spatial interpenetrations. The results were widely published and admired by architects of the 1950s. The noted architect Richard Meier, for example, remembers seeing the Hodgson House as a student in 1956: "The courtyard house, the Hodgson House, was beautifully detailed and very serene."[60] These two houses served as precursors for several subsequent projects. Through the success of the Oneto House in particular, Johnson popularized the image of the Resor House as a model for contemporary domestic architecture, and it was much imitated.

Mr. and Mrs. George J. Oneto House, 1949–51

The Oneto House in Irvington-on-Hudson, New York, is in a subdivision that was originally part of a riverfront estate. The lot slopes to the Hudson and remains covered with mature trees. Mr. and Mrs. Oneto had no children, and the house is small at just under two thousand square feet. The plan is compact and compelling, with glass-walled public space, exactly centered, flanked by two equal brick-walled areas: bedrooms on the north; kitchen, dining, and storage on the south. Both ends of the house have large glazed openings looking out over the landscape, without any strongly defined exterior courts to limit interaction with the environment. The back of a large free-standing fireplace creates an entry area and ensures that the living areas remain screened from the arrival side of the house.

Johnson believes that the Oneto House is one of his best designs (figs. 135–37). In its simplicity, tight organization, and strong symmetry in plan and elevation, it recalls the most refined elements of Mies van der Rohe's architecture. Yet it also had qualities associated with classical architecture, as Colin Rowe noted when he used it to define the relationship between modern architecture and neoclassicism in a description of a "contemporary neo-Palladian building." Such a building, he wrote, "conceptually a pavilion and usually a single volume," would aspire "to a rigorous symmetry of exterior and (where possible) interior. If not Mies's Resor House, then Philip Johnson's Oneto House."[61] The orientation of the house to the site, with the open central section facilitating a view from the entry straight through to the Hudson River, is another classicizing element of the design. Johnson called it an "absolutely perfect house, pretty Miesian, about the most successful" of his career. Again,

Mr. and Mrs. George J. Oneto House
135 Entrance façade

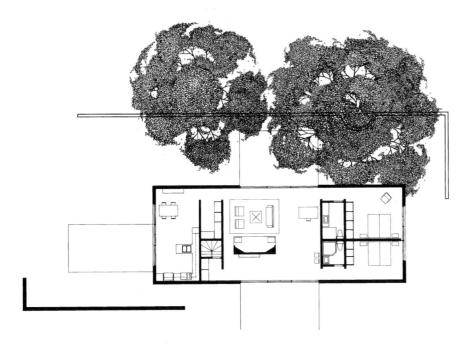

his relationship with the client was paramount. George Oneto "didn't have the foggiest notion of what he wanted. He just bought it—whatever I wanted. Isn't it funny how dependent all these houses are on the nature of the client?"[62] The house has recently been altered. A series of sculptural pavilions, designed by a former associate in Johnson's office, overlap and collide with the original house. They contrast sharply with the taut and refined horizontal lines of the initial design.

Mr. and Mrs. George J. Oneto House
136 (above) Plan
137 (below) View of interior, looking west toward the Hudson River, ca. 1951

Mr. and Mrs. Richard Hodgson House, 1950–51

The site for the Hodgson House is in New Canaan, directly across from the Glass House on Ponus Ridge Road (figs. 138–42). One afternoon Johnson saw a young couple inspecting the five-acre parcel, walked across the road to chat with them, and came back with the commission. Richard Hodgson was instrumental in developing the microprocessor industry, particularly several of the companies that came to define Silicon Valley in California. He and his wife, who raised four children in the house, remained neighbors of Johnson for nearly fifty years. While the house is outwardly quite distinct from the Glass House, it is similar in its sense of flowing space and in its compositional synthesis of several themes of modern architecture. In plan, it has elements of a Miesian court-house, particularly as that idea is expressed in Johnson's Row Houses project from his student days, as well as elements of Mies's Hubbe House (fig. 6).

A large exterior court is pulled into the center of a low, compact rectangular volume, with the living area moved to one side, and kitchen, bedroom, and study on the opposite side. Formal dining took place in the large entry vestibule, by moving a table out into the center of the room, inadvertently recalling the dining arrangements at the de Menil house. The court initially contained a fountain and a small covered terrace off the

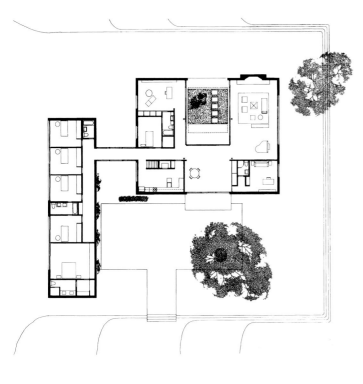

vestibule. While the fountain was later replaced with vegetation, the court still provides a dramatic backdrop to the vestibule and a visual separation between the two wings of the plan. The court also organizes the primary views of the house, which generally pass, from one space to another, through the court. While the plan of the house is simple, the spatial perceptions are complex. Much of this is due to the orientation of the public areas of the house around the court, and the possible views through the court. A large set of windows in the living room faces southwest, looking down a gentle slope to Johnson's property; this is the only major view that does not take in the court. In a sense, the house is organized about a partial glass cube, which is the court, almost as if the Glass House from across the road has been inserted, without its roof, into one end of the house, and the interior filled with nature. Thus the same spatial effects of standing outside the Glass House and simultaneously seeing space flow around and through it are a crucial experience of the Hodgson House.

Mr. and Mrs. Richard Hodgson House
139 (above left) Plan showing original house and 1955 bedroom addition
140 (below) View of arrival façade, from the north (before 1955 addition)

Hodgson built his house in stages, as a mortgage for a modern house in traditional Connecticut proved difficult to secure. Rather than alter the design, he and Johnson delayed the construction of the bedroom wing until his financial circumstances would allow it. But the major portion of the house, encompassing living and semi-private areas such as the study, were built as designed.[63] Thus for five years the Hodgsons used a study as a bedroom for their children, and the guest bedroom as their own. Finally, when they were ready for the second phase of construction, the bedroom wing was built. That element owed something to another student project developed under the guidance of Marcel Breuer at Harvard, Johnson's Freestanding House project (figs. 15–17). Expanding upon Breuer's idea of the binuclear house, Johnson attached a glass passage along the main circulation path, adjacent to the kitchen. Four bedrooms for children and guests and a master bedroom occupy this addition. The design and siting of the house are a significant achievement, especially given the fact that the Glass House is just across the road. The fact that Johnson utilized a different design idea from the glass prism he had chosen for himself not only expanded his architectural vocabulary but also augmented the visual separation between the two houses.

Mr. and Mrs. Richard Hodgson House
141 (above) View toward entrance, from living room (early 1950s)
142 (opposite) View of exterior court and living room (early 1950s)

Mr. and Mrs. Burton Tremaine Jr. Estate additions, 1951–55

Johnson's relationships with his clients ranged from the professional to the familial. Yet while he certainly culti-vated individuals whose prestige made it worthwhile, in some cases he maintained close and friendly contact with them for years. Emily and Burton Tremaine Jr. represented this kind of friendship. The Tremaines were prominent art collectors and patrons, with close ties to the Wadsworth Atheneum in Hartford. They were strong advocates for contemporary architecture; in a period of just two years, 1947 and 1948, they commissioned proj-ects from Buckminster Fuller for three identical houses, Richard Neutra for a beach house in Montecito, California, Frank Lloyd Wright for a visitor center at Meteor Crater in Arizona, and Johnson for a fluorescent light system which Tremaine's lighting company would market.

The Tremaines had a seventy-six-acre estate in Madison, on the Connecticut shore, which they used as a setting for their art collection. From 1951 to 1955, Johnson designed a series of improvements to the Tremaine estate. These included the renovation of an eighteenth-century barn; adding a glass pavilion to an existing colonial-style house; creating a sculpture court and pool adjacent to the glass pavilion addition; and

Mr. and Mrs. Burton Tremaine Jr. Estate additions
143 (below) Entry
144 (opposite, top left) Pool and courtyard
145 (opposite, top right) Plan of courtyard with pool
146 (opposite, bottom left) Glass barn exterior
147 (opposite, bottom right) Plan of glass barn and adjacent courtyard

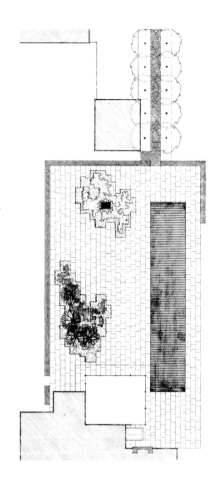

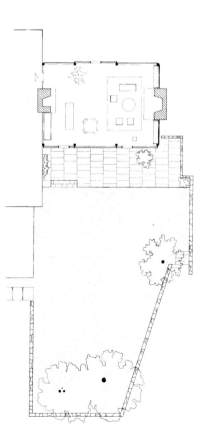

117 Mr. and Mrs. Burton Tremaine Jr. Estate additions

designing an entry pavilion, which also connected to the existing house (figs. 143–51). Johnson's additions are noteworthy for the unity he was able to establish between old and new construction and for how they enhanced the connections between buildings and site. The modern forms of Johnson's interventions contrast markedly with the traditional New England style, but the materials—rough-cut granite walls, bluestone paving—and landscape elements, such as the broad lawn and pool, contextualize the forms.

Mr. and Mrs. Burton Tremaine Jr.
Estate additions
148 (left) Entry pavilion
149 (opposite) Glass barn interior

Johnson's first designs for the Tremaines, from 1951, centered on the barn. He left its timber structure intact, but removed the siding on one face and opened up the opposite side, covering these openings with expanses of glass. A large stone fireplace occupies one short wall; the opposite wall is finished in plaster to allow for the display of art. A generous bluestone terrace was built running the full length of the barn, opening onto an irregularly shaped grass courtyard, which became a sculpture court. In 1955 he designed a pool house as a glass pavilion, attached to the existing house on one wall. The bluestone floor continues out from the pavilion to make the terrace of the pool, and an eight-foot-high wall serves as a backdrop for sculpture. Four delicate fountains, aligned in a row, shoot arcs of water into the fifty-by-fifteen-foot pool.

The Tremaines' relationship with Johnson had at its core a shared interest in modern art. Thus it led to one of the most rewarding, if informal, relationships between Johnson and a client: "I can't remember ever being hired as an architect [by the Tremaines]. All I remember is, we'd sit around of an evening and we'd say, Wouldn't it be nice if we had a swimming pool here or a place to put pictures over there? Or, This living room is really small, isn't it? So the pleasantest days an architect can spend are with friends, are with people that are sympathetic to your ideas. As far as I can remember we never had a disagreement."[64]

Mr. and Mrs. Burton Tremaine Jr.
Estate additions
150 (left) Glass barn interior at night
151 (below) Pool and pool pavilion at night

Mr. and Mrs. Burton Tremaine III House (project), 1952

In 1952 Johnson extended his services to Burton Tremaine III, for the design of a house for Farmington, Connecticut (fig. 152). Only a plan remains: it shows three pavilions linked together around a defined court. The largest pavilion houses four bedrooms (including the master suite, which forms an ell on the pavilion), a study, an informal sitting room, and a large kitchen. Opening off the kitchen is a dining pavilion and, beyond that, a generous living-room pavilion; these are mostly glazed. There is no indication of site or elevation.

The most interesting feature is the arrival and entry into the house. One would have entered in a lower level and ascended to the living floor, in a ceremonial manner. Due to cost, the house was not built. But Johnson must have liked several aspects of the design, particularly the arrival and the idea of wrapping the house around an elevated court, because ten years later he reworked the scheme, for another client, Wylie Tuttle, using a system of cylindrical perimeter columns and glass infill (see page 187).

Mr. and Mrs. Burton Tremaine III House (project)
152 Plan

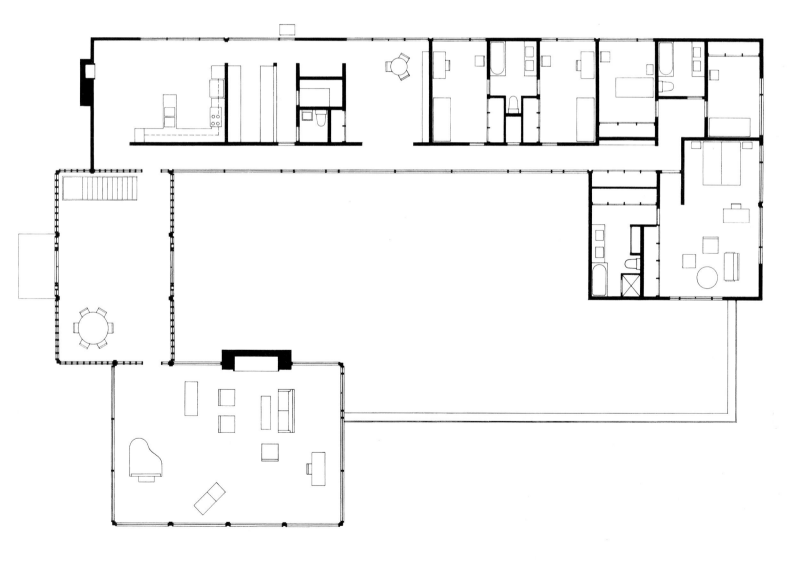

Walter P. Chrysler Jr. House (project), 1952

For the Walter P. Chrysler Jr. project in the Florida Keys, Johnson proposed a court-house of spectacular scale, defined by a perimeter of masonry walls and the edges of the low platform on which the house sits, at the edge of a mangrove swamp (figs. 153–55). Arrival would have been by water, so the house would have faced the estuary. The wall encloses about half of the compound. A large flat roof carried on a grid of columns covers two separate pavilions, mostly of glass. The walls are open to the outdoors, but within the space are two enclosed areas, the larger serving as a living and dining pavilion and the second as a bedroom, bathing, and dressing pavilion. The enormous roof contains four cut-outs, which were intended to bring light into various spaces below, including a separate outdoor court-within-a-court for sunning within the confines of the house; a planted area; and two miniature courts with translucent walls for outdoor showers.

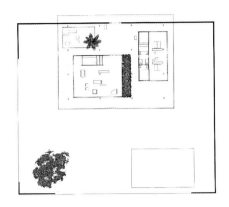

Walter P. Chrysler Jr. House (project)
153 (left) Model photograph
154 (above) Plan

Unfortunately, the only records of this design are two plans and photographs of a model; it is unclear if elevations or perspective drawings were ever made. Thus it is not certain whether the pavilions engaged the roof or had their own caps underneath that vast roof plan. Yet, even without an elevation rendering, the scale of the proposal is remarkable: the roof would have measured nearly 80 by 100 feet, and the compound wall facing the water, with the roof pavilion and entry centered on it, would have been approximately 190 feet in length, while the court would have been 165 feet deep. Approximately one quarter of the rectangular court is covered and the balance is open to the sky. Johnson had no particular use in mind for this uncovered area: "It was just space. In Florida you don't have to have lawn. It could have been swamp."[65] Within the court are three elements: the covered area, a pool, and one large oak or cypress tree. The living pavilion is centered in the court. One wall coincides with the perimeter wall and the three other sides are free. The house is almost an object in the space and is unlike anything in Mies's court-house projects.

The inspiration for such a monumental residence appears to be largely Johnson's. Yet elements of several of Mies van der Rohe's projects from the 1930s and 1940s are apparent in the Chrysler project, specifically Mies's project for a museum in a small city of 1942. In that project, Mies used a system loosely based on the regular column grid of the Barcelona Pavilion but put a series of compartmentalized spaces underneath the roof, rather than freestanding walls. For Johnson, the level of containment may have been a response to the natural wilderness of the site. In this setting, the need for contrast by territorial definition, through walls and compartments, seems apparent. The scale of the compound and the landscape would have matched. By pushing the extremes, as Johnson did in his own Glass House design, the artistic idea overcomes any practical considerations.

Ruth Young House (project), 1952

An unrealized project of 1952 for Ruth Young in Ridgefield, Connecticut, and a house built three years later for the Leonhardt family on Long Island (see pages 138–41) are directly indebted to a 1934 sketch by Mies van der Rohe for a glass house on a hillside (fig. 104). The drawing was shown but not discussed in Johnson's catalog of the 1947 Mies exhibition at The Museum of Modern Art. In the sketch, Mies proposed a glass pavilion with one end engaged in the ground and the other end cantilevered off a slope and supported by a set of piers. In the design for Young, Johnson replicated Mies's sketch almost exactly: a rectangular pavilion, mostly of glass, extends off a hillside (fig. 157). The point of contact with the hill is a terrace, and, in this respect, there are similarities with the Wiley pavilion cantilevering off its terrace (fig. 171). While the engaged end of the pavilion—containing kitchen, bath, and dressing area—is closed, the remainder, as it extends off into space, would have opened through its glazing to establish a dynamic relationship with the landscape around it. This end, of course, would have been the social space of the house, with seating grouped around a suspended fireplace (a precursor of the Wiley House fireplace), and with areas for dining and sleeping, the latter behind a set of freestanding cabinets, much as in the Glass House. The program and size of the house would have been virtually identical to the Glass House: about fifteen hundred square feet with living and dining area, one bedroom, a small kitchen, a study, and a bath. The portion of the Young design that rests on the base contains areas for private functions and would have been clad in cypress, while the public areas were located in the glass-walled bridge and cantilever.

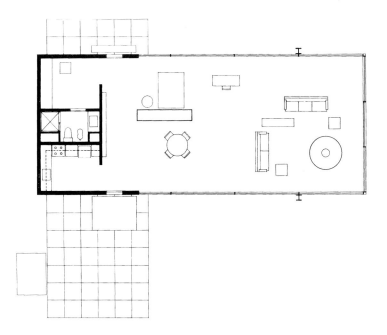

Ruth Young House (project)
156 (above) Plan
157 (below) Elevation

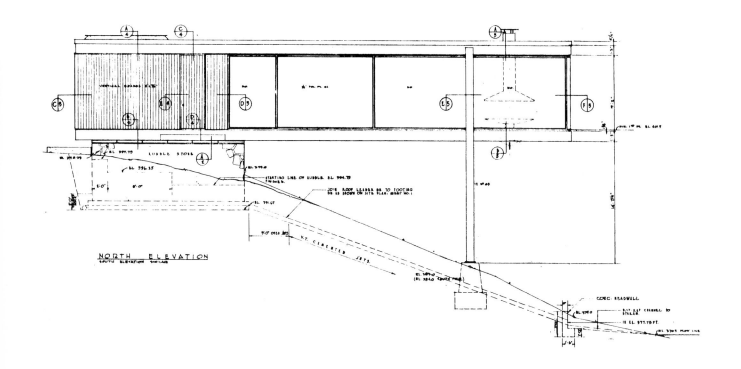

NORTH ELEVATION
SOUTH ELEVATION SIMILAR

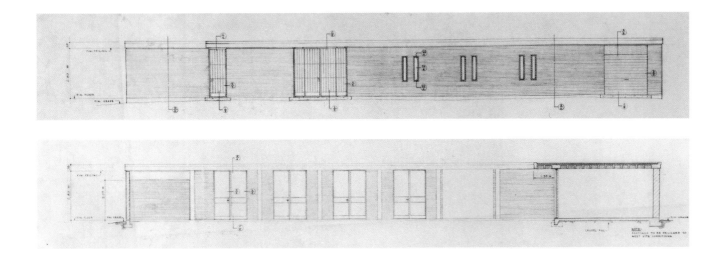

District Manager's House, Scheme 2 (project), 1952–53

In 1952 and 1953 Johnson designed two different schemes for a District Manager's Residence in Venezuela for the Schlumberger Company, which was owned by the de Menil family. The site was a corner lot in a residential neighborhood of Maracaibo, and Johnson utilized a court-house and perimeter walls for each project. However, there is a notable difference in the appearance of the two designs, indicating the two directions Johnson was simultaneously exploring in his residential architecture at that time. The first of these schemes is discussed in the following chapter, together with projects that explore architectural forms that depart from the Miesian vocabulary and articulation associated with the Glass House process.

District Manager's Residence (project)
Scheme 2
158 (above) Street and courtyard
elevations ("1953")
159 (below) Plan ("1952")

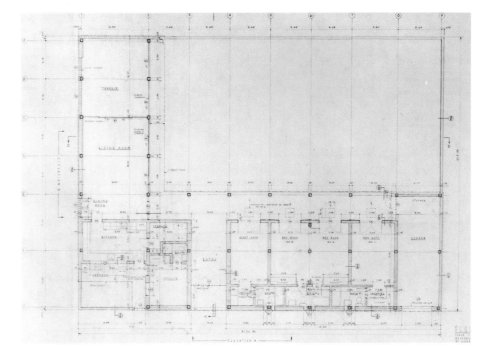

The second District Manager's House is sited on a corner, facing two streets (figs. 158–59). The design called for a one-story Miesian court-house, with a brick exterior. The rooms wrap against the street wall, leaving the balance of the site free for an open interior garden, like the one Johnson had included in his first *Ladies' Home Journal* design. The garden would have been visible from the street through the vertical slats of a metal entry gate, carefully detailed in a modern style. The entry divides the house into two separate areas, with the kitchen and combined living and dining area to the left as one would have entered, and bedrooms and a garage to the right. A covered loggia would have allowed direct access from the public portions of the house to the bedrooms. An enclosed terrace was provided off the living area, as Johnson anticipated that a tropical climate would make access to ventilation necessary.

Mr. and Mrs. Richard S. Davis House, 1953–54

With the 1952 Chrysler House in Florida, Johnson developed further the type of courtyard designed for the Hodgson family, one that is surrounded on three sides by the house itself and opens on the fourth side to the landscape. A design of 1953–54 built in Wayzata, Minnesota, for Richard Davis, a curator at the Minneapolis Institute of Arts and a leading art collector, adapts this type to a northern climate. In these two designs, and the earlier Ford House project, Johnson brought the court fully within the house, internalizing it as an atrium.

The orientation of the Davis House on a lakefront is similar to that of the Oneto House, as both are sited to take advantage of views toward the water. The plan arrangement resonates with the Hodgson House,

Mr. and Mrs. Richard S. Davis House
160 (below) Exterior view from lake side
161 (opposite, left) Exterior view from east with pool terrace. Main house is to the left and service wing is to the right
162 (opposite, right) Plan

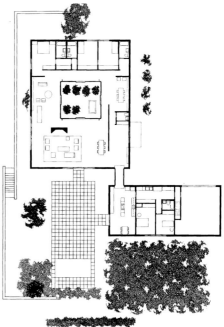

since there are two distinct wings of the house connected by a narrow glass bridge (fig. 162). In contrast to most of Johnson's domestic projects of this period, the perimeter walls of the house were largely solid, so that the client could display portions of his art collection.[66] The main pavilion of the house contains the living areas and master and children's bedrooms. The secondary pavilion incorporates service areas and a garage. A glass-walled, glass-ceilinged atrium, the house's major feature, is centered in the main pavilion. Glazed on all four sides, it was intended mainly to bring light into the center of the large plan. Like the winter garden in Mies's Tugendhat House, it was planted with shrubs and flowers and covered with a gridded translucent canopy.

In contrast to many of Johnson's houses in this period, the physical distinction between social and private spaces is not clearly articulated on the exterior of the Davis House, either by the overall spatial composition or through materials and fenestration. Instead, within the main pavilion of the house, there is a bedroom zone that incorporates three bedrooms, including the master suite. Two additional bedrooms, the garage, and the kitchen are located in the wing. This arrangement, recalling Marcel Breuer's binuclear plans, provides access to a raised terrace from each part of the house and also gives the terrace a sense of enclosure. The terrace serves as a podium for both pavilions, and a short set of steps parallel to the front wall leads down toward Lake Wayzata in the distance.

While a great deal has been made of Johnson's sources for his architecture (often by Johnson himself), far less attention has been paid to one important characteristic they invariably share: their proportions. From the Glass House on, the completed domestic projects demonstrate a high level of refinement in their dimensions, as well as in the relationship of materials to composition and in the overall sense of space resulting from these interactions. John Manley, architectural associate of over forty years, has noted, "It's not just that he's receptive [to ideas]. He looks for ideas. But most of his career has been a question of taking other people's ideas and usually doing them better."[67] This is certainly true of the Davis House: while the overall compositional strategy has clear debts to Mies, Breuer, and even Johnson's own Glass House, perhaps the most remarkable accomplishment in the house is its sense of space and scale. While the plan is unconventional—even for Johnson—it confidently and successfully embodies a modern way of life.

Mr. and Mrs. Richard S. Davis House
163 Exterior view from terrace

Mr. and Mrs. Richard S. Davis House
164 (left) Living room
165 (below) Interior court

Alice Ball House, 1953

Both the Hodgson and Oneto houses discussed above (pages 110–15) were important as precursors for sub-sequent projects. A house built in New Canaan in 1953 for Alice Ball displays much of the tautness of the Oneto House. The Ball house is smaller than the Oneto—indeed, even with two bedrooms, it is smaller than the Glass House—with only one end enclosed and apart from the social spaces (fig. 166). Unlike the Oneto House, which was symmetrical in both plan and elevation, the Ball House is asymmetrical, but balanced compositionally through its volume, chimney, garden wall, and glazing. This massing, along with its siting, gives the house the feeling of a romantic garden villa, as opposed to the more classical qualities of the Oneto House. Contrasting with its diminutive size, the public space opens out to the landscape on opposing sides, allowing a continuity of space through that portion of the house. Two simple bedrooms, a bath, and a kitchen are separated from the social space by a freestanding cabinet. Each bedroom looks out into its own private garden. The living area, surrounded by glass on three sides, is light and airy, giving one the impression of being in a little pavilion in the woods. As with the Oneto House, a garden wall makes a corner, suggesting some exterior enclosure. Despite its size, just fourteen hundred square feet, the structure was called the Pink Palace due to the finish on the masonry walls when it was complete (the color roughly matched the color of the Fortuny fabric Johnson used in the renovation of his own Guest House bedroom in the same year). The Ball House is now largely over-grown and difficult to study.

Alice Ball House
166 (below) Plan
167 (opposite) View of exterior

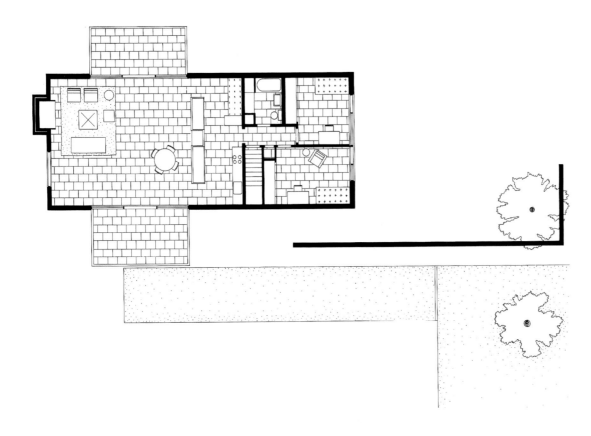

Mr. and Mrs. Robert C. Wiley House, 1952–53

Johnson returned to his idea of building an all-glass pavilion as a prism in three later designs from the first half of the 1950s. Unlike the earlier schemes for the "glass crystal," as he called it, two of these projects were built, and both received considerable attention at the time. The majority of these houses were built on semirural sites like that of his own house, but he also adapted this model to more suburban sites. Probably the best example is a design for Robert C. Wiley, a real-estate developer and speculator in New Canaan, from 1953 (figs. 168–72). The site was a wooded slope, adjacent to a barn and farmhouse, only a mile from John Senior Jr.'s experimental dairy. A double-height glass pavilion rests on a stone base, even cantilevering off the base on two opposite sides. The pavilion is the public portion of the house. It is comfortable in size without being generous; the area for seating is oriented around a suspended fireplace, and a low freestanding cabinet separates the living and kitchen areas. The stone base supports a large terrace, which is the primary approach to the house from the drive, at the side. Two short sets of steps, from drive to terrace and terrace to pavilion, define the approach to the house. The surface of the glass cube is heavily articulated, particularly with vertical structural fins or mullions separating the sections of glass, casting shadows and adding a three-dimensionality to the surface that is quite different from the Glass House.

Within the house, alongside the kitchen cabinet, is a stair down into the base, which contains four bedrooms and other services. In essence, Johnson has disguised the functional requirements for a typical family as a part of the base for the glass prism. As he described it in *Architectural Review*, this strategy was "one more attempt to reconcile the (perhaps) irreconcilable: Modern architectural purity and the requirements of living American families. . . . The Wiley house 'solution' of putting private functions below in a sort of podium to the 15 foot ceilinged public pavilion gives the architect great freedom. The client can design downstairs as he pleases. . . . The architect can design the pavilion above."[68] The house was sited on a gentle slope so that while the terrace is only three feet above grade at the entrance, on the far side it is a full story above the ground. This allowed for fenestrating the bedrooms and a study in the base, allowing views down the hill from the private rooms that do not conflict in any manner with the public views of, or from, the pavilion.

Mr. and Mrs. Robert C. Wiley House
168 (above) Approach
169 (below) Plans of main level
with terrace and lower level

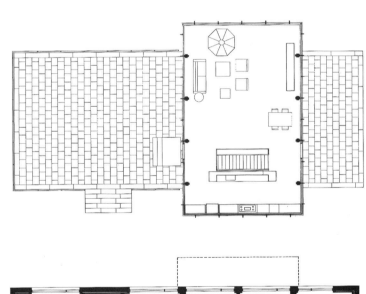

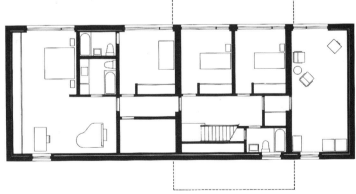

Mr. and Mrs. Robert C. Wiley House
170   Main level with terrace

Where Johnson prided himself on resolving the problem of designing around the living habits of the American family, others have seen a diagrammatic simplicity that enervated the overall architectural composition. Robert Venturi, in his seminal treatise *Complexity and Contradiction in Architecture*, singled out the Wiley House as an example of this kind of "oversimplification":

In the Wiley House, . . . in contrast to his glass house, . . . Philip Johnson attempted to go beyond the simplicities of THE elegant pavilion. He explicitly separated and articulated the enclosed "private functions" of living on a ground floor pedestal, thus separating them from the open social functions in the modular pavilion above. But even here the building becomes a diagram of an oversimplified program for living—an abstract theory of either-or. Where simplicity cannot work, simpleness results. Blatant simplification means bland architecture. Less is a bore.[69]

At least in his text, Venturi overlooked the debt that the rough masonry pedestal owed to the work of Le Corbusier, which Johnson had admired since his student days. The contrast of this rough stone with the glass prism above it may have less to do with the programmatic separation of functions than with a dialogue between history and the present, or traditional methods of building versus the articulation of modern space. The rustic, indigenous feel of the rubble-stone base, even if interpreted through projects by Marcel Breuer and Le Corbusier, heightens the sense of the glass pavilion as an expression of foreign, machined perfection in the wooded countryside of New England.

Mr. and Mrs. Robert C. Wiley House
171 (above) Exterior showing fenestration of lower level
172 (opposite) Interior of living pavilion

Wiley Development Company House, 1954–55
Mr. and Mrs. Joseph H. Hirshhorn Guest House, 1955

Johnson explored similar themes in two projects in 1954–55. One was a prototype for a modern house that could be reproduced widely, designed for Robert C. Wiley (figs. 173–74). The other was a guest house on the Canadian side of Lake Huron for the financier Joseph H. Hirshhorn (figs. 175–76). The two designs are almost identical; there are several minor variations and the plans are reversed, but in most respects they are quite similar. The design for the Wiley House is a single story in height. Based again on the Resor House, it consists of a main house in an L-shape, one wing housing public functions, the other private ones. A pergola over a stone terrace at the rear of the social pavilion provides a precarious link to the corresponding element at the other end of the design, the garage. But for whatever reason, at no point in the design does the house open to the landscape, either through an alignment of spaces or the establishment of a glass prism. Instead the house exhibits the tentative qualities evident in Johnson's earliest work. Just one house was built, and Wiley's development effort did not proceed.

How the design came to be used for the Hirshhorn Guest House, in Blind River, Ontario, is unclear. The two projects were designed at almost precisely the same time, in late 1954 and early 1955. Johnson carried out a number of other designs for Joseph Hirshhorn, and their relationship seems to have had thorny

Wiley Development Company House
173 (left) Exterior
174 (right) Plan

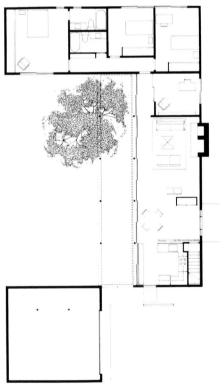

patches. Several of these projects were underway within weeks of the dates for the Blind River cottage. Johnson vaguely remembers some frustration in his dealings with the client; perhaps there were disappointments with the other projects, and he simply adapted an existing project to meet this client's intentions.

Mr. and Mrs. Joseph H. Hirshhorn Guest House
175 (below) Elevations
176 (bottom) Plan

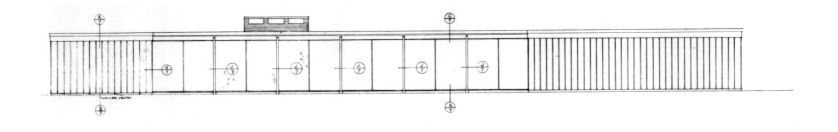

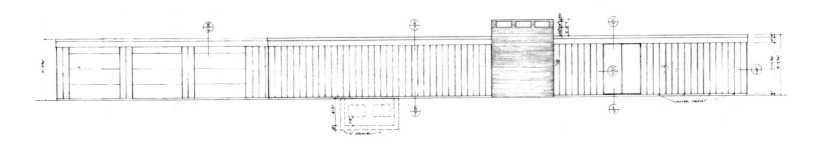

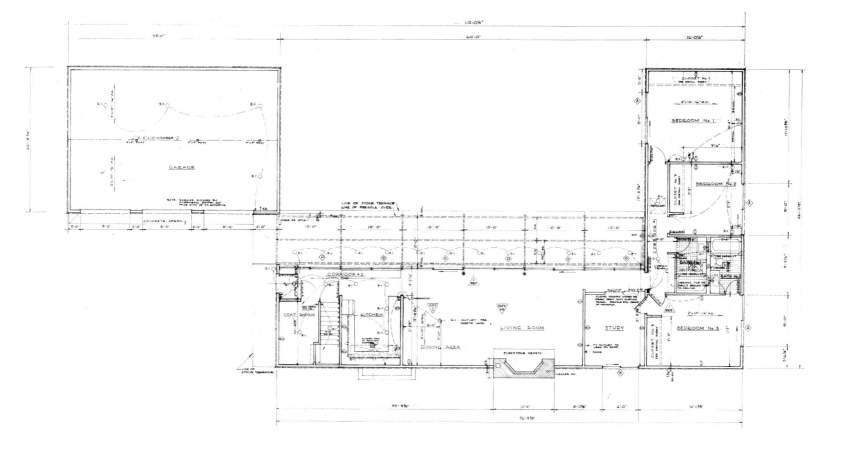

Mr. and Mrs. Robert C. Leonhardt House, 1954–56

For a house on Long Island commissioned by Mr. and Mrs. Robert Leonhardt, Johnson again cantilevered a glass pavilion, as in the Ruth Young House project (page 124), here realizing Mies's sketch even more literally (figs. 177–80). This is especially seen in such details as the steel tension rods running on the diagonal across the large windows. Yet in plan, at least, the Leonhardt House was an elaboration of other ideas Johnson had considered during these years. First of all, there were two pavilions, separated by an open terrace. Though set parallel to each other, they did not align, but were offset in a manner recalling his Freestanding House project done as a student under Marcel Breuer. Furthermore, the bedroom pavilion, anchored firmly on land, was a near-

Mr. and Mrs. Robert C. Leonhardt House
177 (below) Exterior showing cantilevered living room
178 (opposite) Final plans

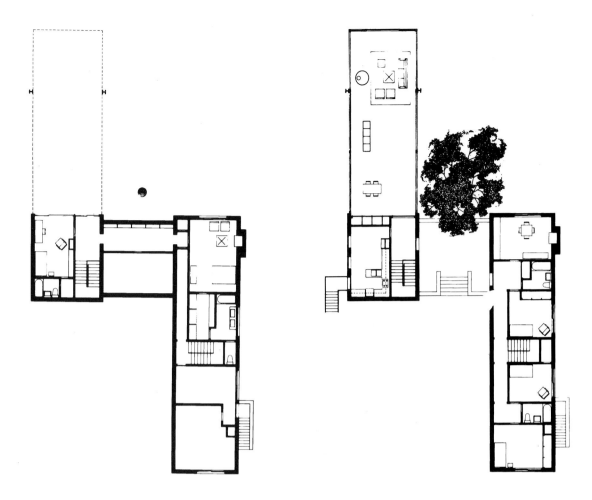

ly solid brick structure containing children's bedrooms on the main level and the parents' bedroom, a small kitchen, and the study on the lower level. However, there are important differences between Mies's sketch and the Leonhardt House. Most notable is the relationship of the solid pieces and the glass prism, and how they were expressed. The pavilion containing the living room and kitchen was no longer a single unified piece resting on a masonry base but a glass beam extending into space. There was a palpable sense of shear between the solid, load-bearing masonry of the grounded side and the cage-like steel and glass construction of the prism. The solid piece now served as an abutment, not a base, to the glass pavilion. The relationship between the private brick pavilion and public glass structure was a clear legacy of the final scheme for the Glass House. As the glass pavilion bridged and cantilevered out over the slope toward Long Island Sound, it afforded its occupants wonderful views of that landscape. Tragically, the house was altered beyond all recognition in the early 1990s.

The houses described in this chapter represent examples of the strategies Johnson derived from the process of designing the Glass House. They show fidelity to a fairly limited compositional vocabulary, yet they also reveal a willingness to experiment with that vocabulary. The results combine various design strategies, even as the basic ideas remain within a narrow range; one example of this is the linking of pavilions with differing programmatic elements—often by a court or on a podium. Another is the contrasting of solid and transparent surfaces. Johnson's inspiration can be seen in the work of Mies van der Rohe and Marcel Breuer, among

others. The glass pavilion juxtaposed with a solid pavilion, which reached its most refined form in his Glass

House and brick Guest House, is another model. Johnson later lamented, "I never had any good luck, as it were,

building in the design of the Glass House. Nobody ever wanted that done."[70] But in fact, to the degree that these

projects compromise with the idea of a pure glass prism-as-house, the results are far from vitiating. And

Johnson's willingness to redefine the glass prism has great value as well. It is impossible to study projects such

as the Hodgson House or the Davis House without concluding that the enclosed court, or atrium, serves as a

glass pavilion within the "landscape" of the surrounding house. Johnson in fact situated the glass pavilion as

the center of the composition for each project. Other elements that raise the glass pavilions in elevation, such

as the podium for the Davis House or the masonry base for the Senior House project, further enlarge the design

intentions of each project. The inversion of the glass pavilion in an urban context for the Rockefeller Guest

House—so that it defines the outside elements in the midst of an urban dwelling rather than interior spaces in

a natural environment—is evidence of his ability to creatively explore the limits of the architectural vocabulary

he had chosen for himself. Out of this limited vocabulary, inspired most clearly by his devotion and adherence

to the architecture of Mies, Johnson was able to compose a vibrant array of credible and poetic works of resi-

dential architecture. Yet by the middle of the decade, his design sensibilities had broadened, and his attention

turned in other directions. Ironically enough, this shift took place as he worked closely with Mies on the Seagram

Building commission. Even as the design process for that masterful expression of refined and spare modern

architecture was nearing completion, Johnson was investigating other ideals as inspiration for the creation of

new domestic forms.

A Conscious Shift

5

1953–1959

**Mr. and Mrs. Eric Boissonnas House,
New Canaan**
181   Night view of double-height living area

Each one of us says, I know I'm changing quite a lot. It gives us pause. But we do it, I notice. We're restless. We're striving for, I don't know what. Maybe this whole generation will be written off. I think we'll just have to wait for the history books. —Philip Johnson, 1955

In a 1951 article for *Interiors* magazine, Arthur Drexler—who would succeed Johnson as Director of the Department of Architecture and Design at The Museum of Modern Art—wrote, "It is hazardous to prophesy at this point what the next period in Mr. Johnson's development will be like, but that a new period is now beginning seems evident. One can be sure Mr. Johnson will continue to be insistent on fine workmanship and to maintain an almost ascetic devotion to simplicity; but, just as Mies himself several times in his career has experimented with richer and looser forms than those he favors at present, one may well believe that Mr. Johnson's next works will be less rectangular and less rigid. Certainly one can be sure he will build no more Glass Houses."[71]

Beginning in the early 1950s, Johnson had been introducing in his work a number of new forms and spatial ideas, along with the expressions and perceptions these implied. The forms are surprising for their non-Miesian, non-orthogonal geometries. He employs circles and ovals in plan and designs three-dimensional expressions of those forms such as vaults and domes. More orthogonal experiments used a highly ordered and centered spatial module, and he employed new structural expressions, particularly in adapting curved shapes to roofs. Most of the projects which feature these investigations were not built, not even fully developed. They were certainly not shown far outside his office. But the experiments were eventually reflected in a number of important built projects in the latter part of the decade, and in greater numbers thereafter.

Johnson's fervent advocacy of the architecture of Mies van der Rohe had endured for nearly three decades; his move away from such a strong engagement with Mies's architectural vocabulary could not have been easy. Johnson's relationship with Mies is important as much for its weaknesses as its strengths. Although their personalities were nearly polar opposites, for many years they found a means of working together in a manner benefiting both men. One example was the design of the Seagram Building. Johnson was instrumental in securing the commission for Mies, and he was from all accounts thrilled when he was asked—unexpectedly, and at the initial suggestion of the head of the building's construction company—to join Mies as a partner in the project. The client and contractor were concerned that Mies needed representation in New York, rather than be obliged to shuttle back and forth from his office in Chicago to the project site.[72] Johnson's office had undertaken several noteworthy projects by the time that he joined the Seagram effort, including an addition to The Museum of Modern Art and the museum's Abby Aldrich Rockefeller Sculpture Garden, completed in 1953. Even so, the Seagram Building surely polished his already substantial reputation.

If the working relationship between Johnson and Mies was, to all appearances, professional and productive, there was a restlessness in Johnson that caused him to turn away from Miesian forms even as he worked most closely with the master. John Manley, Johnson's associate since 1955, noted, "Once he worked with Mies and they didn't get along together at all, he didn't want to do Miesian architecture anymore."[73] Others have noted the stirrings of new inspiration for Johnson even earlier than his collaboration with Mies. Johnson's biographer Franz Schulze noted his "ravenous sensibility" for new forms in architecture, even if they conflicted with the precepts of modern architecture which were first defined in part by Johnson himself.[74] Or, as Manley put it, "He doesn't like rules, anybody's rules. Even including his own."[75]

The extent of Johnson's diverse engagements with the world of architecture has often deflected attention from his professional practice. He certainly has been aware of this, and he has tried to strike an effective balance between his practice and architecture as an avocation. He resigned from his position as director of the Department of Architecture and Design at The Museum of Modern Art in 1954, for example, soon after he joined Mies on the Seagram Building project. Yet his interests in all things architectural remained active. During the 1950s Johnson devoted time to the architectural programs at Cornell, Pratt Institute, and Yale University, held regular weekend salons for students and faculty at the Glass House, and supported important school journals, such as *Perspecta* at Yale.

His commitment to this work, and especially to the students, is well known, but there were benefits for Johnson as well, primarily in his contact with the architecture faculty at each institution. The chairman at Yale, George Howe, was an old acquaintance from the days of the International Style exhibition, and Howe deftly managed to arrange appearances in that department by many notable architects of this period, including Pietro Belluschi, Buckminster Fuller, Frederick Kiesler, Harwell Hamilton Harris, and Louis Kahn.[76] The opportunity to engage in discussions about the nature of architecture with such a distinguished group was no doubt just the kind of stimulus Johnson sought.

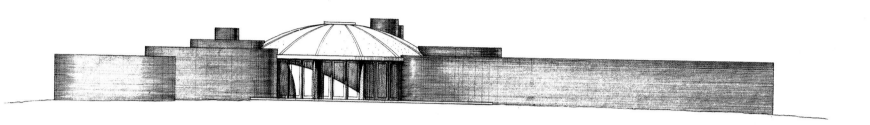

Mr. and Mrs. John Lucas House (project), 1953

Mr. and Mrs. John Lucas House (project)
182 Elevation

Johnson's willingness to investigate non-Miesian forms is evident in a project from early in this period, a vacation house on Nantucket for Mrs. John Lucas, who was his aunt (figs. 182–84). This scheme has little relationship to anything in his earlier work. Indeed, the clearest reference is a project by Frank Lloyd Wright from 1938, a house for Ralph Jester, which was based on a set of intersecting circles—unusual even for Wright.

Johnson's design set four circles on a nearly square podium, with another circle as a terrace extending to the south. On the north side is a rectangular bar—although a corner curves as it intersects with the living room circle—for bedrooms and for the kitchen and other service activities. Minor elements in the scheme, such as fireplaces and pools, are also circles in plan. The primary circle encloses the living room, with a piano and seating area adjacent to the fireplace. On opposite sides are circular pavilions for dining and informal seating or a study. The final circle, adjacent to the study and with glazed openings out to the terrace on the south, was a master bedroom suite. While the three minor pavilions were shown as cylindrical volumes of brick and glass, the living room walls were all glazed, and a wide dome carried over the entire space. The scale is quite large, even monumental: the diameter of the living room would have been over forty feet, and the height to the top of the domed ceiling would have been eighteen feet. (Johnson was already considered to be something of an expert on thin concrete shells, such as that planned for the dome of the Lucas House. In 1954 he was the featured speaker at a conference at MIT on this subject.)

Despite the obvious references to Wright's project, Johnson is unwilling to speak directly about his investigation of Wright. Their often thorny relationship dated to the International Style exhibition, when Wright felt snubbed by the organizers. Johnson has said that without a doubt, Wright is impossible to copy. He wrote openly of both Wright's genius and the wrenching difficulty—even impossibility—of working with him. Sometimes he did so even in the same presentation: he began an address to the Washington State A. I. A. Chapter in 1957, two years before Wright's death, with the words, "Mr. Wright has been annoying me for some time. (I didn't say he wasn't a great architect)." Yet he went on to state, "I wish to end with the same man I started with: a man that

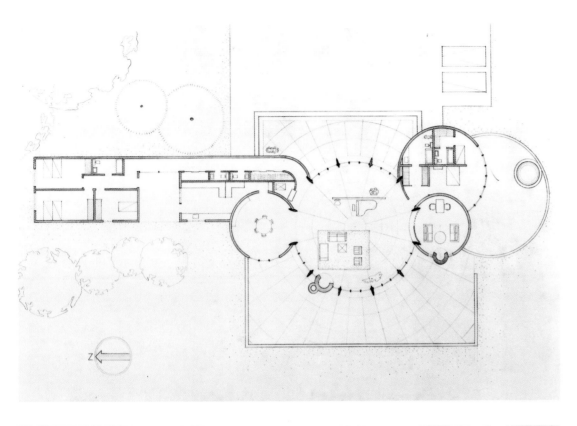

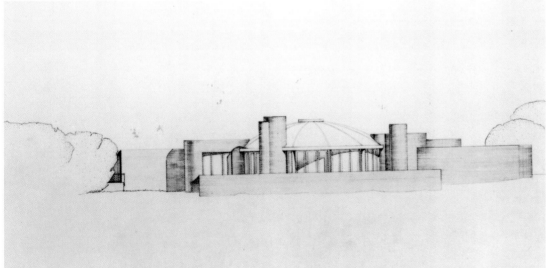

Mr. and Mrs. John Lucas House (project)
183 (above) Plan
184 (left) Ocean-side elevation

never gave up; the great American that perhaps we can admire at the same time we dislike him as much as I do—Frank Lloyd Wright. There is a man who creates space for its own sake and has never paid attention to any other things." And then Johnson went on to describe the arrival and procession through Taliesin West, Wright's compound in the Arizona desert, and in a grand finale to the essay, he concluded by describing that experience as "the essence of architecture."[77]

Mr. and Mrs. William A. M. Burden Apartment renovation, 1953

The Lucas House project was the first of five projects from the mid-1950s that showed the degree to which Johnson was experimenting with aspects of projects other than the plan. During the summer months of 1953, as Johnson was finishing the construction drawings for the Lucas project, he carried out the first of several renovations in the Fifth Avenue apartment of Mr. and Mrs. William A. M. Burden (fig. 185). Burden, a classmate of Johnson's at Harvard, served as a trustee for The Museum of Modern Art.

The project's scope was small: it encompassed special cabinetry and a new ceiling for the living room of the apartment. Johnson designed and had installed a shallow, rectangular-shaped dome in the room. Derived from the dome of the Lucas House project, it hung from above, floating completely free of the walls. It was illuminated from behind the shell of the vault, giving it a weightless quality, as if a giant section of an eggshell were hovering in the air. An elliptical light fixture was located in the center of the ceiling, acting as an oculus in the dome.

**Mr. and Mrs. William A. M. Burden
Apartment renovation**
185 Plans and elevations ("June 22, 1953")

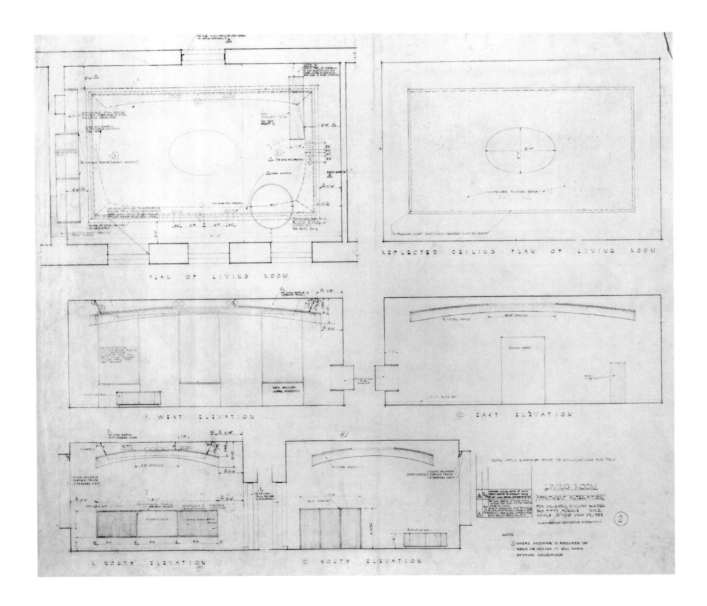

District Manager's House, Scheme 1 (project), 1953

At the same time, Johnson was experimenting with the idea of a series of connected flattened domes as a roof structure in the first design for the Schlumberger District Manager's House in Maracaibo, Venezuela (figs. 187–88). As noted in the previous chapter, the plan of the house was Miesian, as was the plan for the second design of the house (page 125). But the roof form for this first scheme has a different source, Le Corbusier's High Court at Chandigarh, India (fig. 186). Johnson had reviewed *Le Corbusier, oeuvre complète, 1946–1952* in the September 1953 *Art News*, and he paid particular attention to the roof of the High Court Building, referring to its "umbrella and parasol" forms. The most interesting feature of the District Manager's House is such a roof, supported by a Miesian structural system. The roof is made of spherical shells, joined together in squares, as if a number of round umbrellas had been cut into square shapes and glued together along their edges.

Le Corbusier
High Court, Chandigarh, India, 1956
186 View of façade

District Manager Residence, (project)
Scheme 1
187 Elevation
188 Plan

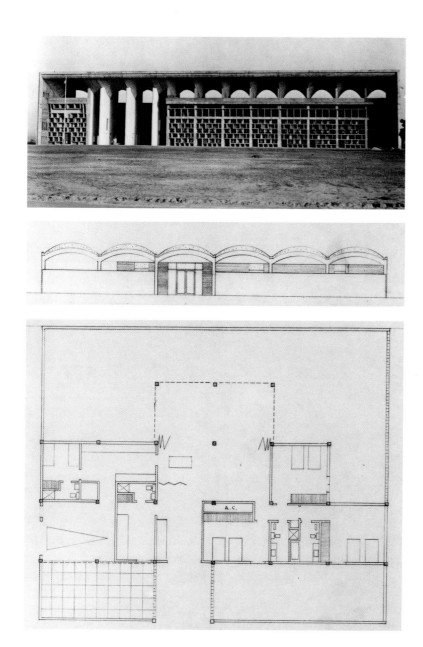

House for El Tigre (project), 1953

A much more utilitarian project, again in Venezuela for Schlumberger, provides further evidence of Johnson's interest in alternative roof forms. The House for El Tigre project (fig. 189) was intended as inexpensive, easily built housing for workers in the El Tigre oil fields and their families. Two housing units were efficiently combined in a single rectangular concrete bar with an arcade along the front elevation. The units were not minimal worker housing: with a screened-in porch, each pair of houses could have resulted in a single structure 120 feet long, with a colonnade along the entire front. Johnson designed a sloped roof, for the first time in his work since the John Wiley project of 1944, with a screened area underneath to allow air movement in the tropical climate. The plan is laid out with three of the six bays allocated to the public functions of living and kitchen areas and the remaining three for bedrooms and a bath. Circulation would have taken place through the screened-in porch, which provides a second family gathering area.

House for El Tigre (project)
189 Plan and elevations

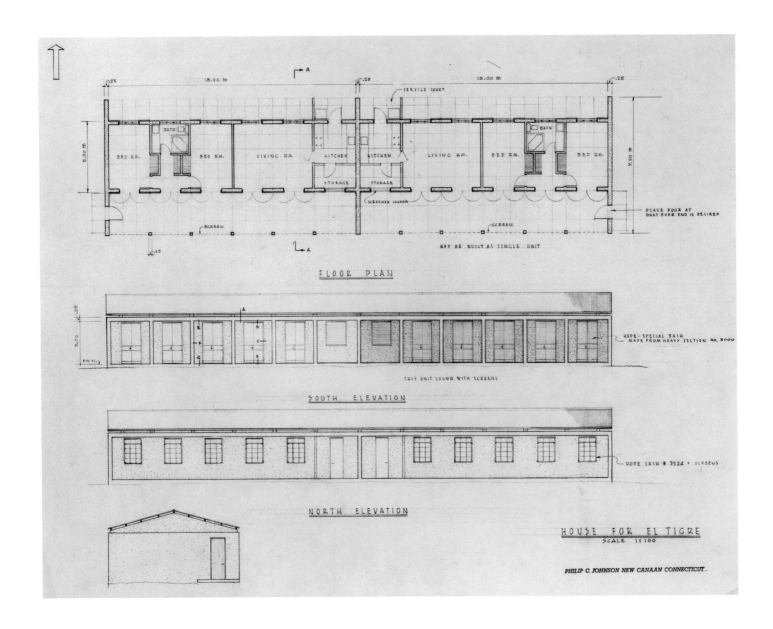

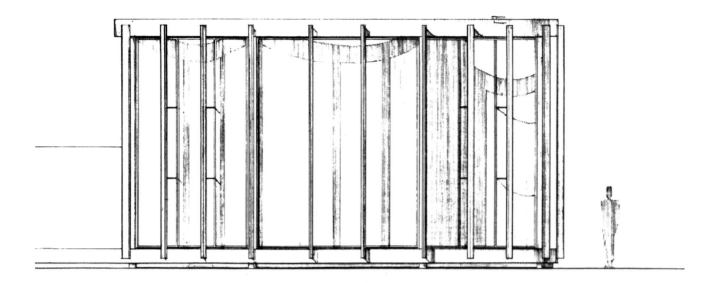

Thomas B. Hess Pavilion (project), 1953–54

A project in New York for *Art News* editor Thomas B. Hess was intended as a place to view and discuss the client's art collection (figs. 190-92). Located in the rear of Hess's Beekman Place townhouse lot, overlooking the East River, the design was an all-glass pavilion, either elliptical or circular in plan and with a domed roof. Its curvilinear form would have set it apart from its surroundings in a manner that brings to mind Frank Lloyd Wright's Guggenheim Museum, then being designed. One room, surrounded by planting, was to be linked to the townhouse by a narrow passage along the lot line. Although the elevations are Miesian in character, the plans and sections clearly are not. Fabric would have been draped along the windows and from the top of the dome, creating a tentlike canopy. The curved glass surfaces, which would not have been easy to construct, would have resulted in unusual reflections and shadows. The shapes of proposed furnishings are ovals and circles. Johnson and Hess were both intrigued with the idea of a salon, a gathering of people sharing an interest in a particular topic or issue. The Glass House served as a weekend salon for students and critics of architecture throughout the 1950s, and the Hess Pavilion would have facilitated this kind of activity for the art world.

Thomas B. Hess Pavilion (project)
190 (above) Elevation
191 and 192 (below) Plans

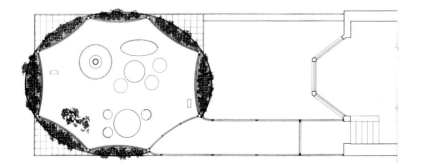

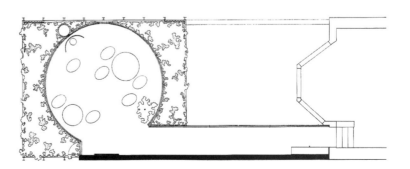

Mr. and Mrs. Eric Boissonnas House, New Canaan, 1954–56

One of the Glass House salons, held in late March, 1954, appears to mark a key moment in the development of Johnson's architectural thought. Invitations were sent to six leading practitioners: Gordon Bunshaft, I. M. Pei, Harry Weese, Paul Rudolph, John Johansen, and Eero Saarinen. He described the purpose of the weekend as follows: "Our purpose in these short meetings is for each of us to find out what the other six are thinking in terms of architectural design. It would be good if each of us could bring drawings or be prepared to sketch his ideas. We would like an exchange of ideas and not merely a mutual admiration meeting. There will be no minutes taken and will be no report to the press. I, for one, am preparing for March 20 more than I am for my clients. It seems so much more important."[78]

The weekend seems to have been cordial enough, ending on Sunday evening when the group relocated to the Rockefeller Guest House in Manhattan to celebrate the wedding of Eero and Aline Saarinen. Yet the dynamic of the meeting itself divided the group into opposing camps, and the repercussions were long-lasting. One participant, Harry Weese, later described the concept of the colloquium for *Inland Architect*: "Each [of us] was to sketch his latest project on blank tracing paper—no props allowed. Eero Saarinen drew his

Mr. and Mrs. Eric Boissonnas House, New Canaan
193 Night view of the "garden" facade

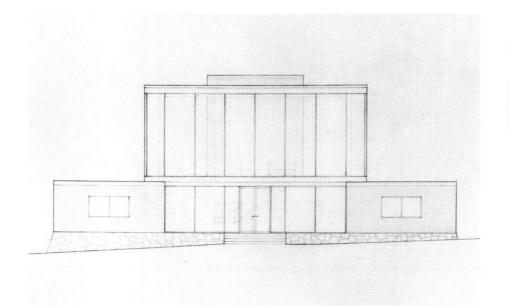

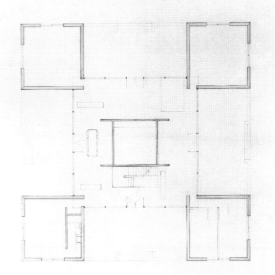

Lutheran Brotherhood Campus for Fort Wayne; I. M. Pei a ten-story building for Sun Oil in Atlanta; and so forth. As it became clear that Philip was plotting a funeral for functionalism and drafting us as pallbearers, the group polarized. The functionalist corner was held by Gordon Bunshaft, I. M. Pei, and myself; diagonally across the celebrated glass living room were Johnson, Paul Rudolph, and Jo Johansen. It was left to Eero to carry messages back and forth between the opposing camps."[79]

Johnson chose to present a design for a house at the salon. The program was loosely based on a commission he had recently accepted, from Sylvie Boissonnas, of the de Menil family, and her husband, Eric. The design he presented had overtly historical qualities which were uncharacteristic in this period of modern architecture. In many respects, the project was more closely related to the architecture of the late-eighteenth-century French architect Claude Nicholas Ledoux than to the final form the Boissonnas House would take (see below). Johnson had maintained an appreciation for the work of Ledoux from the time that Emil Kaufmann gave a presentation about him to the American Society of Architectural Historians at Johnson's Ash Street House in 1942. There is also a more than passing similarity between the elevations of Johnson's Square House and those of the sixteenth-century Villa Farnese in Caprarola, Italy, which must have seemed to be a jarringly different image to the architects gathered for the weekend salon (see fig. 225). Both have a clearly articulated geometric form resting perfectly on a broad geometric base. Johnson uses a glass cube on top of a smaller glass prism, anchored at the corners by masonry blocks (fig. 194), while the Villa Farnese has a five-sided prism over a wide, five-sided base, the entirety, of course, in masonry construction. But the composition is that of a classic fortress or castle, with a raised center block and a separate block or turret at each corner.

The plan shows five interlocking squares, the largest in the center of the composition and four smaller squares at each corner of the larger one (fig. 196). The perimeter squares are bedrooms, and on the lower level the center square would have provided

Mr. and Mrs. Eric Boissonnas House, New Canaan

First scheme ("Conference House")
194 (below) Axonometric plan
195 and 196 (above) Elevation and plan

informal seating and access to both the exterior—across four small courts between each pair of bedrooms—and to a primary social space on the second story of the central square. There, a large fireplace mass is set slightly to one side, which would have provided larger space for seating and a smaller area for food preparation. Both a piano and an organ are shown in the plan. The scale would have been large: the plan measures over fifty feet on each side, and the living space is double height. All of the walls are glass, of course. While that weekend colloquium has occasionally surfaced in Johnson's recollections, the Square House project itself has long been overlooked by Johnson and others. According to Johnson, the reaction at the time among the architects gathered in the Glass House was a stunned incredulity. Laughing, he recalled, "When I showed them, the silence was deafening."[80]

Around the design of the first Boissonnas House scheme pivot the three major themes that Johnson investigated in his house designs from the late 1940s to the late 1960s: the example of Mies, the role of history, and the opportunity for monumentalism. As a glass box on a solid base, the Square House continues the investigations begun by the Glass House design process and carried on through the mid-1950s. But this theme is overshadowed by the scale

Mr. and Mrs. Eric Boissonnas House, New Canaan
197 *(above)* Arrival elevation
198 *(below)* Final scheme (July), plan

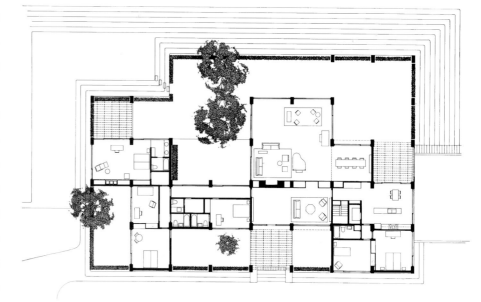

of the project and by the overt historical reference it makes to an architecture from a century and a half earlier. Increasingly, these last two themes predominate in the domestic commissions Johnson would undertake from this point on through the late 1960s.

The degree to which Johnson paid attention to the work of Louis Kahn, one of his most talented peers and a fellow instructor at Yale at the time, became evident with the final design for the Boissonnas House in New Canaan (figs. 181, 193–201). As an early design for it, the Square House project echoes Kahn's Adler House project of precisely the same time. The final design for the Boissonnas House combined some elements from Johnson's earlier vocabulary—the house was built on a podium adjacent to a court and included a large pavilion with extensive glazing for the public spaces—but there are considerable differences as well. Primary among these was the structural system for the house, which was an extensive column grid. Johnson had used the column grid in earlier projects, such as the Ford House, but that grid was clearly based on a Miesian vocabulary of refined steel construction. At the Boissonnas House, Johnson turned from column to pier, and the scale of the piers is quite large for the spaces they frame. Built of brick, the piers measure seventeen by thirty-four inch-

Mr. and Mrs. Eric Boissonnas House, New Canaan
199 Exterior of garden terrace

es each, on a spacing of approximately sixteen-foot centers. The depth of the piers provided an opportunity for Johnson to investigate one of Kahn's primary theses of this period, the differentiation of served versus servant spaces. Like Kahn, Johnson incorporated into the pier depth the servant, or secondary, elements of the house. This includes elements such as storage spaces, closets, the fireplace (no longer freestanding, but running from pier to pier), and, most importantly, the transitional areas, or thresholds, between primary public spaces.

The grid is extensive, running eight bays across the front of the house and extending back five bays. Not all of this area is enclosed by the house; several exterior terraces (which are on a podium and afford views down a slight hill) are defined by pergolas carried on the piers at the rear. All spaces except the living room are a single story. The main public space, however, is double height. In addition, the grid is broken at the living room, since one pier is omitted at the center of the space. "By doubling [the height at the living room], I made it into a house," Johnson said recently. "If I hadn't done that, it would have been a Miesian layout. The problem with Mies's houses, it occurred to me at the time, [is that] a one-story house [loses] its sense, if it gets over a certain size. The Glass House was easy. But to have anything that's large, a single story that shows walls, as in Mies's houses, they're boring, too thin. I had to put double height in somewhere. If I could get this room [the

Mr. and Mrs. Eric Boissonnas House, New Canaan
200 Master bedroom terrace detail
201 (pages 158–59) Interior view of living room

living room] big enough, then at last we had a house with a point. And I amazed myself that it was quite easy."[81]

The approach and entrance into the Boissonnas House also brought Johnson to a different perceptual experience of domestic architecture. Unlike the glass pavilion projects, where one enters a public space largely visible from the exterior, Johnson stretches out the entrance. One moves through the first bay of the grid, under a pergola, to arrive at the front door. After entering into the foyer, one turns right, setting up a view to a major painting on the wall at the end of the space. Moving toward that painting, however, the primary entrance into the living room appears at one's left. One turns, enters through the transitional space defined by the pier grid, and arrives at the refined and spacious living room, with views out to the landscape beyond through bays on the opposite wall. Johnson himself describes the procession from entry to foyer to living room as "one square–two squares–four squares, with double height."[82] Other major spaces circulate off the foyer: bedrooms to the left, and kitchen and staff to the right. Additional storage and a garage are situated in a lower story under the kitchen.

The sense of the Boissonnas House is that of a country villa, and certainly Mies's country house designs from the early 1930s partly inspired the composition. But while the design has the massing and material of a house such as the brick country house of 1922, the pier system and extensive use of brick announce Johnson's awareness of the work of Kahn. It is not a system of offset walls and the sliding spaces they make, but rather a grid of piers with cubic, defined spaces, and partitions locked into place by the piers. Johnson has grudgingly acknowledged the imprint of Kahn on this project, but only after he paid homage to Mies. The Boissonnas House, he explained, was "a Mies grid, but emphasizing the columns would not be Miesian, of course. Whether [the column] is round or square or rectangular became of great importance. It has none of the flow of Mies. There is no sense of in and out, of flowing. But there is the podium."[83] When pressed about Kahn, Johnson replied:

People said I was like Kahn, I forget why. I wasn't like Kahn, although it [the Boissonnas House] is different from Mies. God knows where . . . I probably got it from Kahn. You see, one gets things without admitting them. . . . The trouble with architects and any designer is that they're not to be trusted, because they always intend, they always use their own history. But now that you point it out, there's lots of this in my subconscious. This is still a Mies courthouse, and these are residuals of a Mies rhythm. But not used correctly. That's why, let's face it, Mies really hated it, because I wasn't being Miesian.[84]

The breakup and reassembly of the elements of the classical and formal in the composition of the Square House—the first design for the Boissonnas House—signals, metaphorically, a shake-up in Johnson's direction. By reassembling those blocks into the Schinkelesque composition of complex indoor and outdoor relationships, of shadow and sunlight, seen in the Boissonnas House, he replaced the sense of a commanding view from above with a design which, while still monumental, put the occupants of the house down on the land. In that relationship to their surroundings, they could sense fully their relationship with the natural surroundings as they moved through a series of different spaces and experiences.

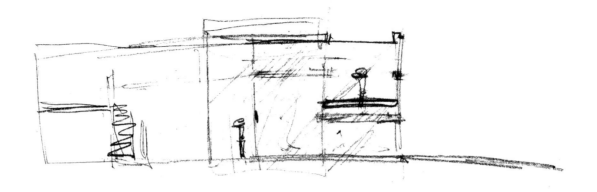

Mr. and Mrs. Joseph H. Hirshhorn House (project), 1955

Johnson carried out four projects within a year for uranium magnate and art collector Joseph H. Hirshhorn. One of these, a guest cottage, was discussed in chapter 4. For Hirshhorn's own house, designed initially for his lakefront property in Ontario and relocated to Campo Bello, Florida, Johnson returned to the Resor House model he had used in designing the Farney and Oneto Houses. The design progressed through several revisions, but the central features of the house, an innovative structural system and a large, two-story living space surrounded by walkways and balconies and containing a single massive fireplace, remained constant.

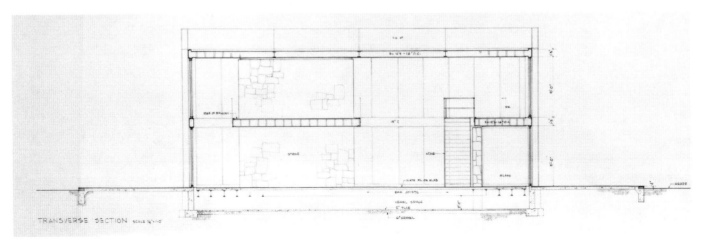

TRANSVERSE SECTION SCALE

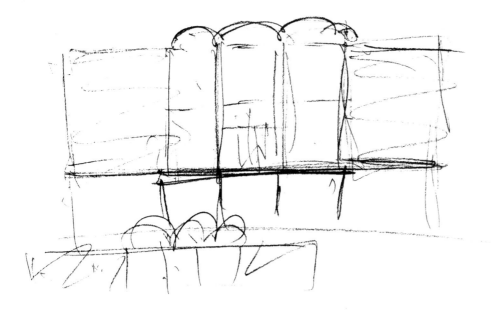

The central space is nearly twenty feet high, with the fireplace engaging a balcony off the master bed-room suite (figs. 202, 204, 206–8). This would have been a very large house, approximately fifty by one hundred feet in plan. The living space itself measures fifty feet on each side. Remarkably, there are no interior columns in this space. A system of steel H-columns and beams allows for a substantial roofspan; this is the same long-span raised truss system Mies used at Crown Hall in Chicago (fig. 203). Centered on the front (long) elevation is a glass wall, with a recessed opening providing an arrival vestibule, and a rubble-stone wall at the back of the recess. The opposite elevation is a two-story wall of glass facing Lake Huron to the south. On either side of the double-height living area are bedrooms and services that look out through large windows to both sides of the house. Just behind the stone wall at the entrance is a steel and wood stair with open risers; this rises to a balcony over the living area which connects both sides of the house, but is not directly linked to the balcony off the master bedroom.

Johnson also explored the use of different roof forms, including long-span shell vaults in the profile of flattened arches to span the double-height living space at the center of the house (fig. 205). These vaults would have extended out considerably beyond the perimeter walls of the house, providing covered areas both at the entrance and for a terrace facing Lake Huron.

Mr. and Mrs. Joseph H. Hirshhorn House (project)
205 (above) Elevation sketch showing shell barrel vaults
206 (below left) Longitudinal section of version with exterior steel beams (June/July 1955)
207 (bottom right) Plan of entry floor
208 (below right) Plan of second floor

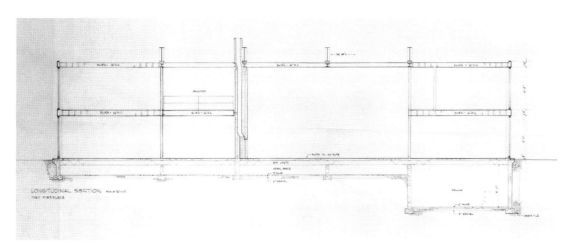

Mr. and Mrs. Joseph H. Hirshhorn Beach House (project), 1955

Besides the versions of his own house and the guest house, Hirshhorn commissioned Johnson to design a beach house and a town around a uranium mine he operated in Ontario. No site is given for the former, but one may assume the project was meant to replace the Florida house planned for the same site, a project cancelled in August 1955, just before the beach house was drawn (fig. 209). The beach house, also not built, would have been adjacent to some small mounds or dunes. The design clearly belongs to the Glass House progeny, though placing the glass box within an insect-screen box is novel. The living floor is raised, much as in the Farney and Ford Houses, to take advantage of the views, but it is supported by steel columns on the perimeter. A brick-enclosed ground floor contains two bedrooms, which look out on a small walled courtyard. The living floor was to have two entries, one from below and one from the dunes. The screened porch surrounding the glass box would have dulled the crystalline quality that defined so many of Johnson's pavilions in this period, but the climate necessitated it.

Mr. and Mrs. Joseph H. Hirshhorn Beach House (project)
209 Plans and elevation

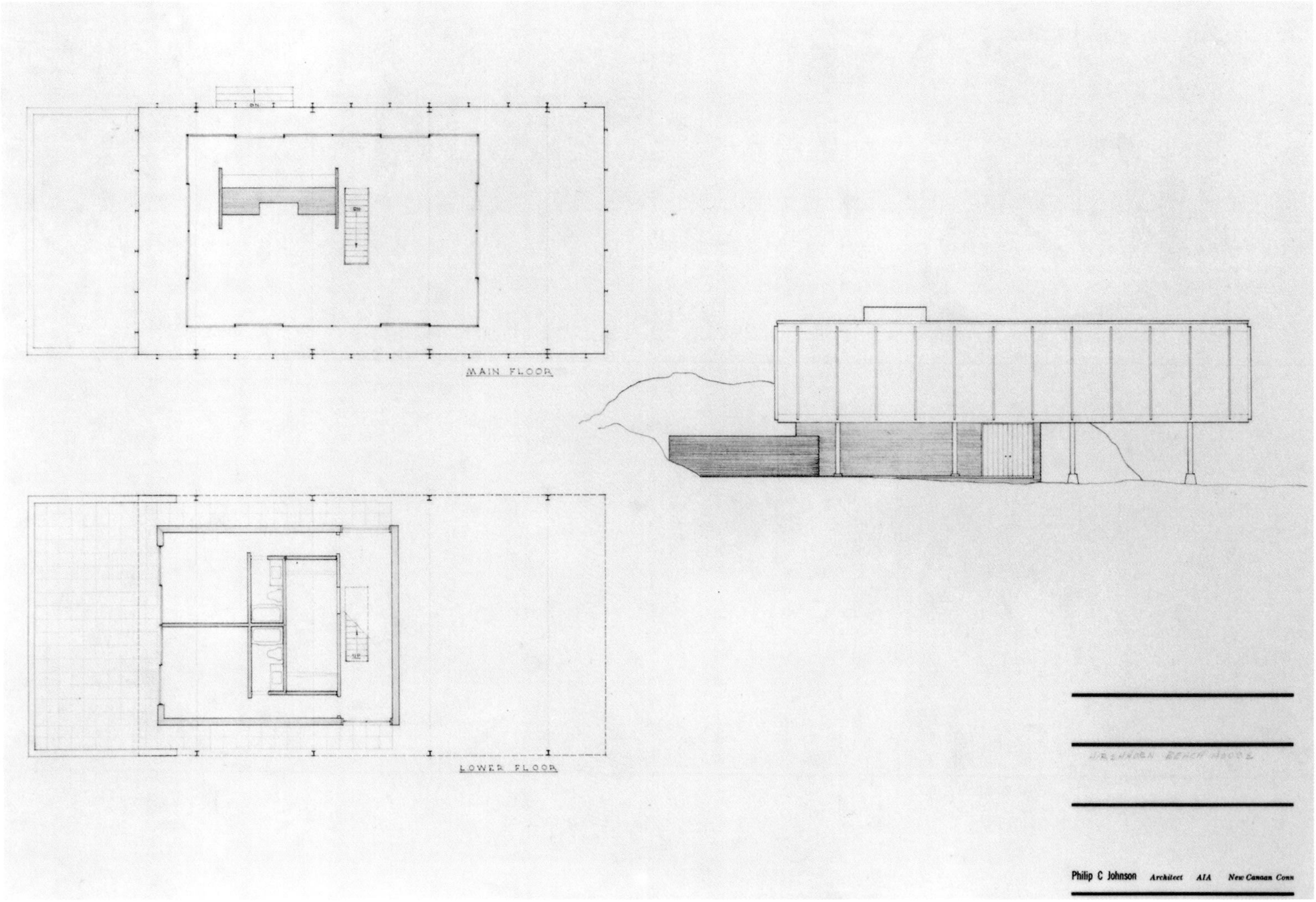

MAIN FLOOR

LOWER FLOOR

Philip C Johnson *Architect* *AIA* *New Canaan Conn*

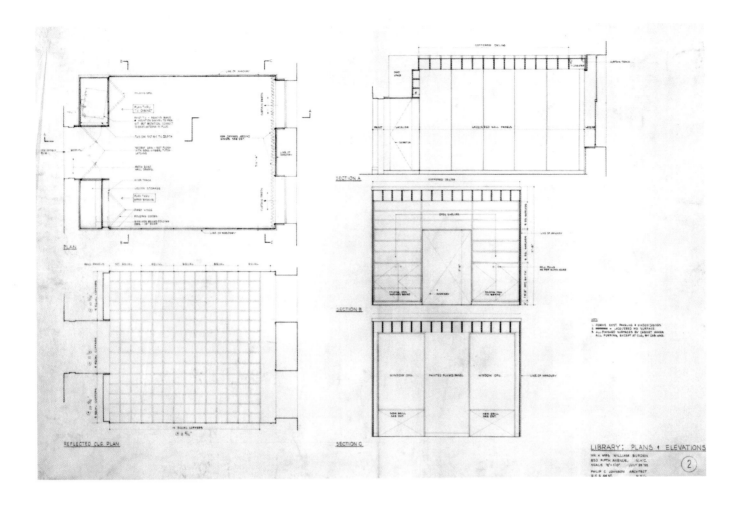

Mr. and Mrs. William A. M. Burden Apartment renovation, 1955
Mr. and Mrs. William A. M. Burden House (project), 1955–56

In 1955 Johnson carried out another small renovation of the Burden apartment in New York. Like the first effort, this project involved altering the ceiling of a single room, the library (fig. 210). He used an eggcrate design—in wood—recalling the ceiling Mies had designed for the Fifty-by-Fifty House of 1950–51 (fig. 214). That idea became part of a much more comprehensive, if unrealized, effort in a house that Johnson designed a year later for Mr. and Mrs. Burden in Mt. Kisco, New York. The scale, not to say the audacity, of this structure's design is extraordinary (figs. 211–13). Johnson suspends an enormous truss-roof system over a podium, with separate pavilions underneath the roof for the various activities of the house. The roof, 112 feet on each side, is raised nearly 40 feet above the podium.

There are initial similarities to another monumental residential design of the 1950s, the Chrysler House project, but also substantial differences. There is no column grid here as in the Chrysler House project; instead, the roof would have been carried by columns only at its perimeter and by deep three-way trusses spanning the interior space. Underneath there are three pavilions: a square social space near the center, a rectangular pavilion near the entrance for guests, and an L-shaped pavilion towards the rear for a master bedroom suite. In addition, there would have been five distinct landscaped areas on the podium, for vegetation and water.

Mr. and Mrs. William A. M. Burden
Apartment renovation
210 Plans and elevations

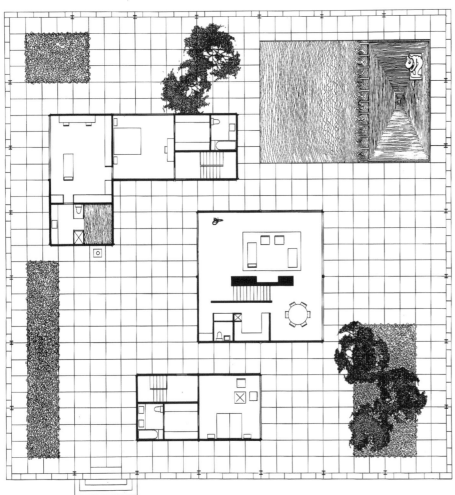

**Mr. and Mrs. William A. M. Burden
House (project)**
211 (above) Model photograph, arrival side
212 (left) Plan

Both the modestly scaled eggcrate ceiling of the Burden apartment and the steel roof for the Mount Kisco project offer modern versions of a classic coffered ceiling. Johnson had experimented with long-span truss construction in a design for an unbuilt office project for himself in New Canaan three years earlier. Franz Schulze describes the Burden House project as "a massive study of parts within parts within a whole."[85] The scale is monumental, dwarfing any earlier residential proposal the architect had made. Besides echoing Mies's Fifty-by-Fifty House project, the overall conception resonates with Mies's monumental institutional projects from the early 1950s, such as his 1953 Convention Hall project for Chicago and the Seagram Building in New York City, on which Johnson and Mies were working at the time.

Mr. and Mrs. William A. M. Burden House (project)
213 (above) Model photograph

Ludwig Mies van der Rohe
Fifty-by-Fifty House (project), 1950–51
214 (below) Model photograph

Mann House (project), 1956

A very different, but also monumental, residential project was designed just after the Burden House project, this time a townhouse on a downtown Philadelphia square. Only sketches and a perspective rendering of the façade remain (fig. 215). The house was designed as a single-family structure, but the character of the Mann House project is more institutional than residential. Masonry screen walls and a gate at the street level would have provided privacy, while the entire façade above is glazed and set back from the street. The façade is divided into three bays, each capped by an arched vault. At the top level of the house, balconies are suspended in each of the three bays, between the monumental piers that support the vaults.

Mann House (project)
215 Façade perspective

José M. Bosch House (project), 1957

Johnson's fascination with circular plans, undulating roof forms, and monumental volumes continued in a 1957 project for a beach house in Cuba for José M. Bosch (figs. 216–18). Mies had traveled to Cuba that year to work on the Bacardi Office Building; whether Johnson was involved with that project is unclear, but Mr. Bosch was president of Bacardi. The beach pavilion was not commissioned. Johnson prepared presentation drawings and a model, though he would claim later that the design never went any further than a sketch.[86]

  In plan, this huge circular beach pavilion is a polyhedron with twelve faces. (Drawings show that Johnson investigated an eight-sided plan as well.) The edge of the roof is defined by arches over each facet of the elevation. Vaults then taper in toward the center of the roof, so that the roof resembles a giant parasol. The main space is on the upper floor of the structure; it is not glazed, but screened, a response to the Caribbean climate. The structure can be understood as a concrete cage with infill panels that are Le Corbusier–style sunscreens, which were common in many designs of the period. Two distinct seating areas are seen in the plan, along with a freestanding oval cabinet containing a serving/pantry area. The diameter of the public space is nearly sixty feet, with a ceiling almost thirty feet high. The ground floor has three large bedrooms for the family and four smaller bedrooms for staff. A circular stair in the center of the plan would have connected the entry hall to the public spaces above. A smaller circular stair, intended for staff, connects to the serving/pantry area.

  Though the form of the pavilion is atypical in Johnson's work, the idea of a pavilion devoted to pleasurable activities was not. The billowing vaulted roof continued his interest in concrete-shell roof forms. Johnson would utilize several components of the Bosch pavilion in the design for his own water folly in New Canaan two years later. What is noteworthy is the degree to which he is willing to experiment in styles that depart so markedly from his past efforts.

José M. Bosch House (project)
216 (above) Model photograph
217 and 218 (below) Plan and section

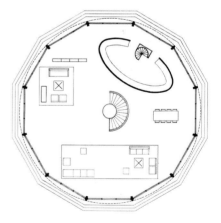

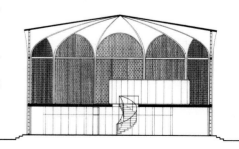

Mr. and Mrs. Robert Tourre House
219 (left) View of street façade
220 (below) View of entry gate

Mr. and Mrs. Robert Tourre House, 1957–59

In 1957 Johnson was asked to design a house in the Paris suburb of Vaucresson (figs. 219–23). Because of the distance, there were problems with monitoring the construction; Johnson felt that significant details in the house were not as refined as they might have been. Yet the house is interesting for its return to the Mies-inspired court-house strategy. It is also atypical of this period, since this is the only project from the mid-1950s through the 1960s to follow this course.

Returning to a theme of open and closed pavilions, Johnson fit them together in a T-shape. The closed, private wing extends back from the street and incorporates five bedrooms, a kitchen, and informal gathering areas. A glass pavilion, which contains the public areas of the house, attaches to the solid piece as the stem of the T. Johnson created an entry forecourt by running walls off the short side of each wing. As with his own Ash Street House, the perimeter walls are the same height as the house; and like the Boissonnas House in New Canaan, a grid of structural piers, regularly spaced, creates spaces based on squares. This plan includes the forecourt; the original design indicates a trellis, which would have covered the entire space. This was not carried out, but the central bay of the entry has a trellis-like metal construction that permits limited views into the forecourt and into the house. The entrance gate is centered on the wall facing the street. After passing through this entry, one moved along the wall of the

private wing to approach the glass public pavilion directly. The walls of the private wing are finished with large, rectangular French limestone panels, so the approach contrasts the stone lining the entry procession with the glazed public area.

Johnson's residential designs from the middle and later years of the 1950s are indicative of his insatiable appetite for architecture in all its forms. It is remarkable to see him working closely with Mies van der Rohe on the Seagram Building at the same time that he is experimenting with curving, vaulted, and radiating forms. At the same time, concern with issues of light, texture, and landscape are clearly evident in numerous projects to an extent that is not so evident in the work of Mies. Furthermore, the scale and size of his residential projects is increasing, making them seem more like small institutional buildings than large houses. This trend continues in the years to come.

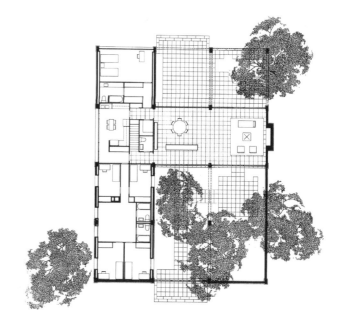

Mr. and Mrs. Robert Tourre House
221 (above) Plan
222 (below) View of rear court
223 (pages 170–71) View of pavilions and court

The Sixties:
Historicism and
Eclecticism

6

1958–1968

**Mr. and Mrs. Eric Boissonnas House,
Cap Bénat**
224 View from central court

There is only one absolute today and that is change.   —Philip Johnson, 1960

In the 1960s, Philip Johnson completed his transformation from following a strict modernist line to synthesizing an array of architectural traditions. In his work, he continued his effort of the late 1950s to integrate monumentalism into domestic architecture. And he retained the willingness to explore new ideas and forms that had increasingly characterized his work during this period. The number of residential projects dwindled through the decade as his institutional and commercial work expanded. By the late 1960s, he gave up on houses entirely, only returning to residential architecture a decade later when he investigated new living arrangements for himself.

The enormous cultural changes of the 1960s were reflected in architecture. Frank Lloyd Wright, Le Corbusier, Mies van der Rohe, and Walter Gropius all died between 1959 and 1969, and the dominance of the modern idiom practiced by these great masters came into question. Johnson described it in this manner: "The entire movement—modern movement—may be winding up its days. There is only one absolute today and that is change. There are no rules, no certainties in any of the arts. There is only the feeling of a wonderful freedom, of endless possibilities to investigate, endless past years of historically great buildings to enjoy."[87]

Antonio Sangallo the Younger and Baldassare Peruzzi
Villa Farnese, Caprarola, Italy
225 Plan

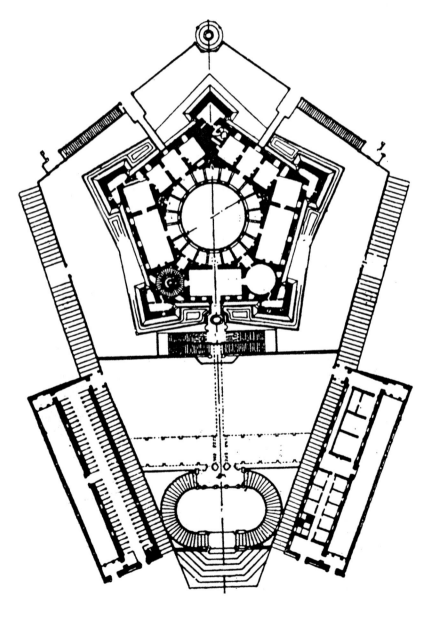

Mr. and Mrs. Eric Boissonnas House, Cap Bénat, 1958–64

In the late 1950s Sylvie and Eric Boissonnas returned to Johnson for a new project, a vacation house in France. The site was dramatic, on the point of the Cap Bénat peninsula thirty miles down the coast from Saint-Tropez. The site provided spectacular sweeping views of coastline stretching nearly 270 degrees around the head of the peninsula. The site was approximately one hundred feet above sea level, with groves of pine trees dotting the rocky landscape. Over the next five years, Johnson undertook two major designs for this house. Both are substantial efforts, although expressed in strikingly different fashions.

The first Boissonnas design (figs. 226–29) is, in effect, a modern interpretation of the sixteenth-century Villa Farnese at Caprarola, Italy, designed by Antonio Sangallo the Younger and Baldassare Peruzzi and begun in the 1520s (fig. 225). When asked by Neil Levine why he took the Caprarola plan as a model for the Boissonnas House, Johnson replied, "The only answer to that is, Why not?" That model had surfaced nearly a decade earlier in Johnson's work, in connection with the composition of the Square House (itself based on the program for the first Boissonnas House). Although it was a court-house, the first Cap Bénat scheme can only be described as a palazzo. The reference to the Villa Farnese is reinforced by the siting of the house on a slope, which accentuates its fortress-like quality. The plan assigns public and private areas to separate levels; an interior court opens through both stories. A large staircase, open to the court, provides vertical circulation. Massive concrete piers anchor the five vertices of the polygon and provide support for five-foot-wide balconies off most of the rooms, which would have afforded spectacular views of the Mediterranean coastline.

When the project was bid, the estimates were too high to proceed, and Johnson went back to the drawing board. Yet the direct confrontation between the narrow functional ideals of modernism and such an overtly historical precedent is noteworthy. It was not a matter of looking at—and sometimes borrowing—the best ideas of modern architects like Mies van der Rohe. By referencing one of the great Renaissance palazzos, Johnson called into question many of the basic assumptions about modernism's role in contemporary architecture.

Mr. and Mrs. Eric Boissonnas House, Cap Bénat
226 First scheme, site plan

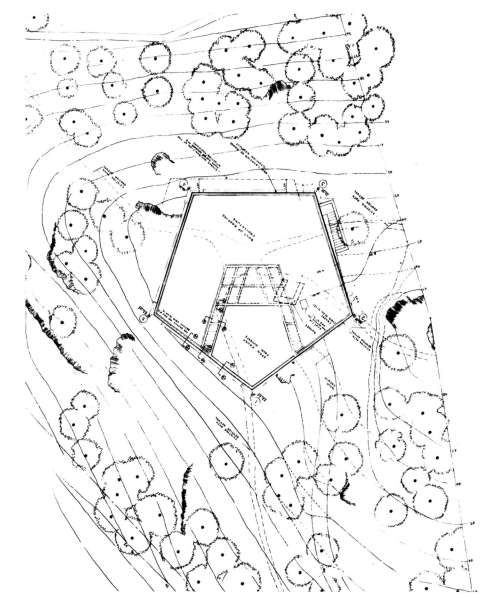

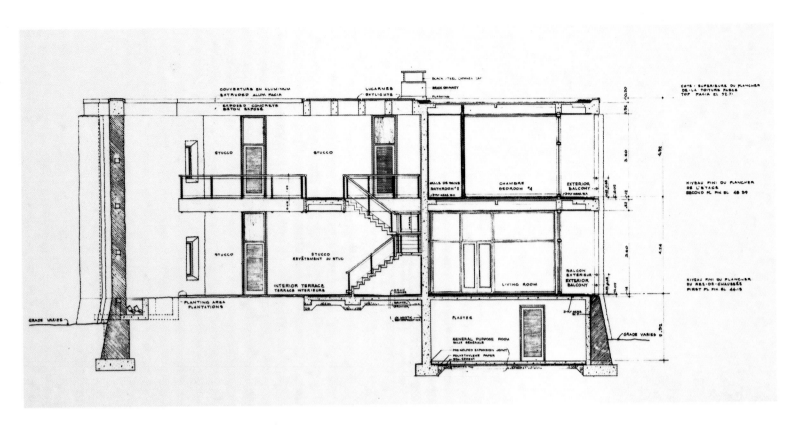

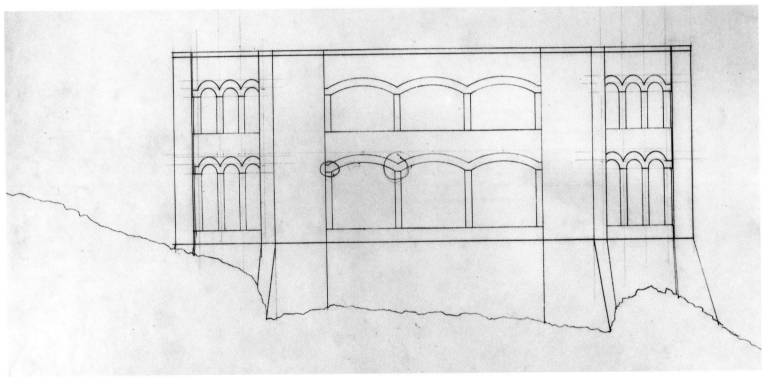

**Mr. and Mrs. Eric Boissonnas House,
Cap Bénat**

227 (top) First scheme, section through
entry court and living areas
228 (bottom) First scheme, preliminary
elevation

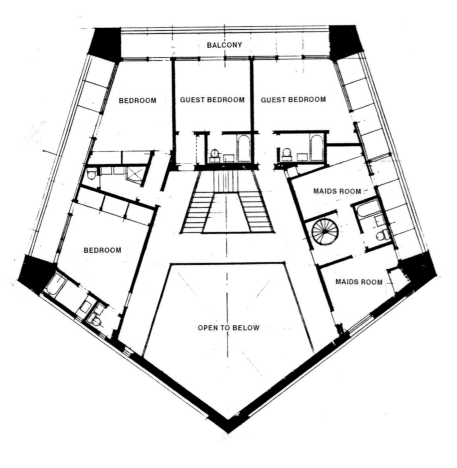

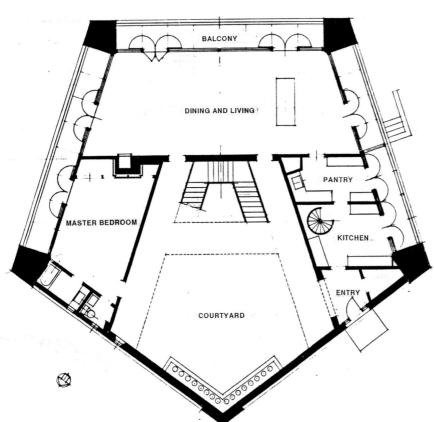

**Mr. and Mrs. Eric Boissonnas House,
Cap Bénat**
229 First scheme, plans of main floor (above)
and ground floor

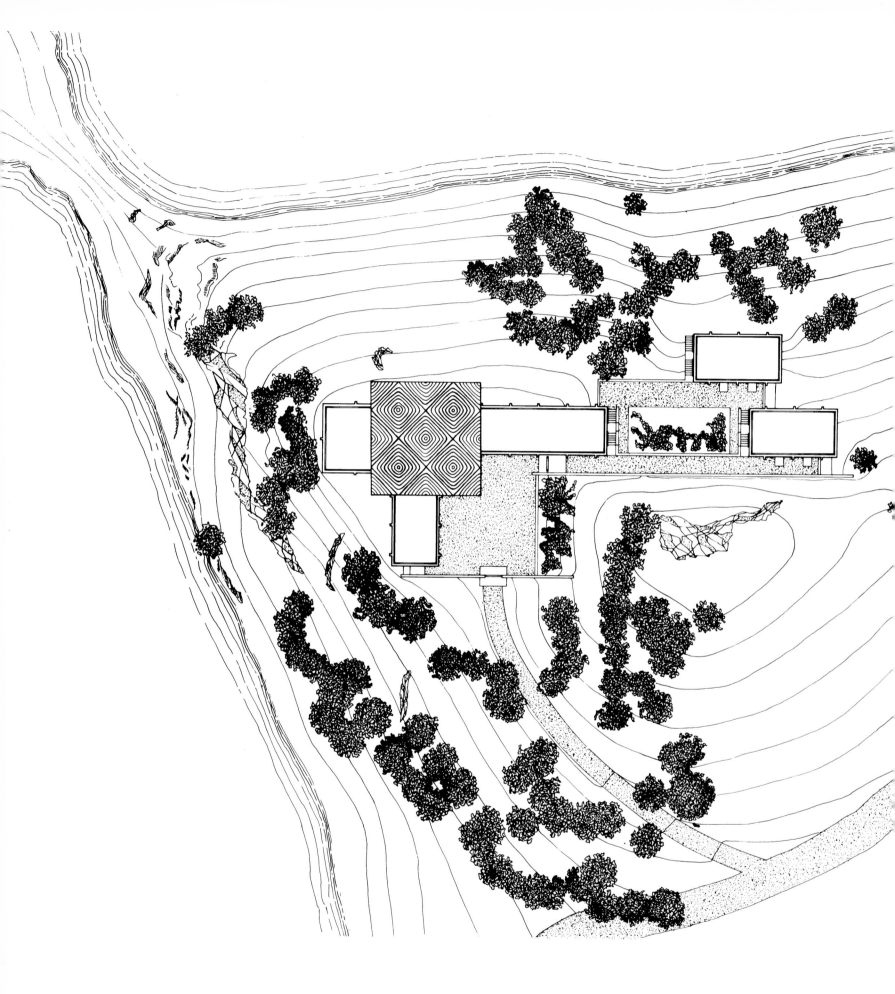

With the second Cap Bénat design, begun in 1960, Johnson demonstrated that he was no less interested in looking at history, although in this case he kept his gleanings to examples from his own century (figs. 230–38). After several years of design, construction began in 1963 and was completed a year later. Johnson revived the idea of the outdoor pavilion, open on all sides and covered by an evocative free-floating roof, with indoor spaces incorporated into separate pavilions around the court. It is an idea he had experimented with on a monumental scale in the Burden House project of 1955. For the Boissonnas House, he let the spectacular location direct the architectural composition, though in many respects, the siting of the buildings relates to a number of schemes for the Glass House.

One approaches the house up a short walk from the auto lane, and enters a gate in a freestanding wall. Inside the gate is an open court, with three separate pavilions visible, arranged around another court,

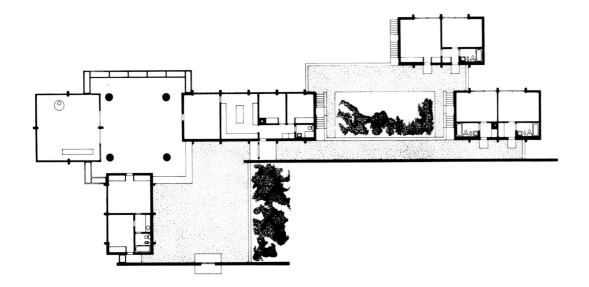

Mr. and Mrs. Eric Boissonnas House, Cap Bénat

230 (opposite) Final scheme, site plan
231 (left) Final scheme, plan
232 (middle) Final scheme, section through entry court and master bedroom with elevation of living pavilion (left) and service pavilion (right), looking south
233 (bottom) Final scheme, elevation/section, looking east

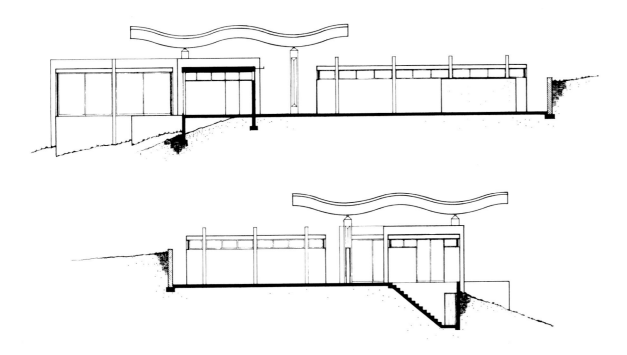

which is covered. In fact, there are five pavilions altogether, arranged across the hillside in a mostly linear manner; the remaining two are easily accessible along an open walkway behind a hedge at the far side of the entry court. Four of these pavilions are similar in their form and construction: piers are arranged in pairs to form simple rectangles; the walls align with the inside edges of the piers in the long dimension and extend beyond the piers on the short ends of these pavilions. The effect of this simple arrangement and construction recalls the work of Louis Kahn, for example, such as his trabeated pavilions at the Trenton Community Center Day Camp. Johnson intended the three smaller of these pavilions as private rooms, for either sleeping or study, and the larger one for kitchen, dining, and other service activities.

The fifth pavilion is the living area. While it has the same piers, they are arranged in a radically different manner from those of the other pavilions. Instead of aligned pairs defining a rectangle, the living pavilion has piers located at the midpoint of each of the four walls, which are of equal length. Thus the living room is square in plan, with its support placed not in the corners, as one might expect, but in the center of each wall. The reference is unmistakable: Johnson was looking toward Mies's Fifty-by-Fifty House of 1950–51 (fig. 214). As in Mies's project, expanses of glass open the pavilion up, in this case to views out over the ocean below.

Mr. and Mrs. Eric Boissonnas House, Cap Bénat
234 View toward entry court from covered courtyard
235 (opposite, above) View toward covered court from entry, looking south
236 (opposite, below) View toward bedroom pavilions

181 Mr. and Mrs. Eric Boissonnas House, Cap Bénat

The center of this house-as-village is the covered court, with pavilions arrayed around three of its four sides. Here Johnson drew upon one more reference—Le Corbusier. Four tapering columns carry an undulating concrete roof structure that cantilevers out beyond the court below to overlap the roofs of the three pavilions that surround the court. The effect is striking: the undulating roof set atop the piers seems to echo the mountains along the Côte d'Azur, turning the concrete construction into something that resembles the billowing of fabric in the sea breeze.

The use of the stylistic and tectonic qualities of these three major architects—workaday Kahn for the private rooms, taut Mies for the living area, and the exuberance of Le Corbusier for the canopy to tie everything together—served Johnson's design intention as well. The conjunction of these different styles enhances the sense that the house is a compound, more so than if it were designed in a single style. This approach also has the virtue of breaking down a program of substantial size, rendering it far less of a visual imposition than the fortress-like earlier design would have done. The Boissonnases were delighted with the house and have continued to use it for holidays since it was finished.

Mr. and Mrs. Eric Boissonnas House, Cap Bénat
237 (above) View of living room looking east to the Mediterranean
238 (opposite) Covered court at night looking toward the living pavilion

183 Mr. and Mrs. Eric Boissonnas House, Cap Bénat

Wylie Tuttle House (project)
239 First scheme, perspective (1961)

Wylie Tuttle House (project), 1961–62

Two other major house projects commissioned and worked on from the early to mid-1960s, one in Texas and the other in Connecticut, have similarities. Both began with an idea of a centralized four-sided villa which then metamorphosed—much as the Boissonnas design did—into largely asymmetrical projects. But what is most

remarkable about each design is how far their exteriors have come from the sleek, flush surfaces of the early International Style. Their skins are composed of repetitive modular colonnades forming the perimeter of the house. This system of columns and infill results in a highly articulated exterior. One, a Dallas residence for Henry C. Beck Jr., was built, while a design in Connecticut for Wylie Tuttle remained on paper (figs. 239–41).

The site for the Wylie Tuttle House was a fifty-acre plot near Stamford, Connecticut, where the client, a New York City developer, rode his horse. The house was to be on a bluff overlooking an open field, with a small lake in the distance. The first scheme for the Tuttle project dates from May 1961, and is in many ways a futuristic version of Le Corbusier's Villa Savoye. A square living platform, elevated completely off its rocky and wooded site, was to be suspended by a system of concrete Vierendeel cantilever trusses. The thin cubic shape seems to hover above the hillside, supported from below on four massive central piers. Within these piers, a stair rises up into the house, which is lit by skylights. Continuous strip windows wrap all four sides of the façade, and are broken only by the verticals of the trusses. Outdoor terraces are located at the perimeter of the structure, with living and bedroom spaces placed around the central stair and circulation hall.

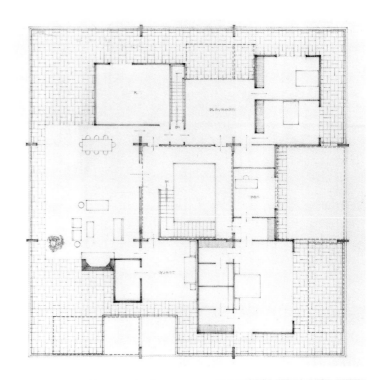

The overall effect of the first Tuttle House design would have been captured by the description of the Villa Savoye by Johnson and co-curator Henry-Russell Hitchcock in the publication accompanying the *Modern Architecture: International Exhibition* of 1932. The elevated living floor of the Villa Savoye appears "weightless," they said, and the "single square of the plan contains all the varied living needs of a country house."[88]

In the second and final scheme for the Tuttle House, dated September 1961 to March 1962, Johnson used wide, round brick columns spaced closely together to wrap a central courtyard (figs. 242–43). The diameter of each column was over two feet, and the spacing between each was only four feet, so the effect would have been one of dense, heavy structure. The plan was a variation on the Burton Tremaine III House project of a decade earlier, with rooms arranged around a loosely-defined courtyard. It shows living

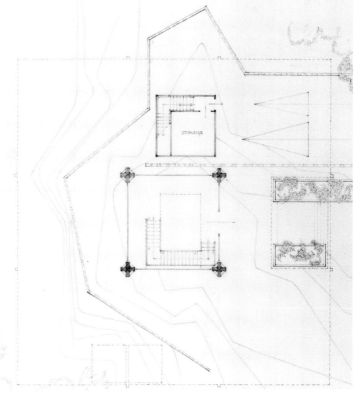

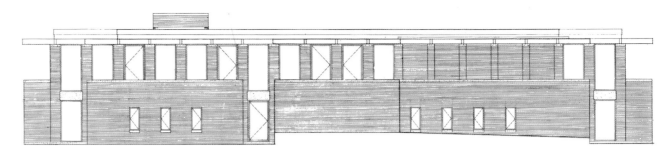

NORTH ELEVATION

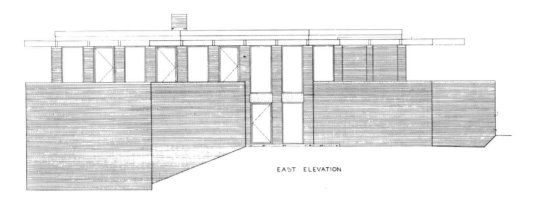

EAST ELEVATION

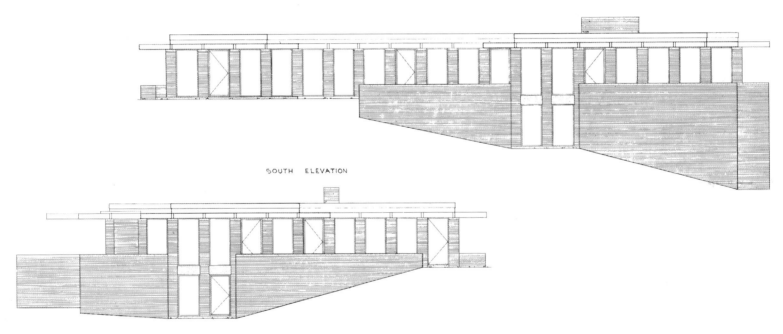

SOUTH ELEVATION

WEST ELEVATION

Wylie Tuttle House (project)
242 Final scheme, elevations

areas and the master bedroom at opposite ends of the courtyard, with children's rooms and the kitchen between them, stretching along one side of the courtyard. One side of the courtyard was left open and the ground sloped down into the landscape. Johnson worked with this level change to achieve what would have been one of his favorite types of processional: entering the house from below and rising into the light of an almost freestanding living pavilion above.

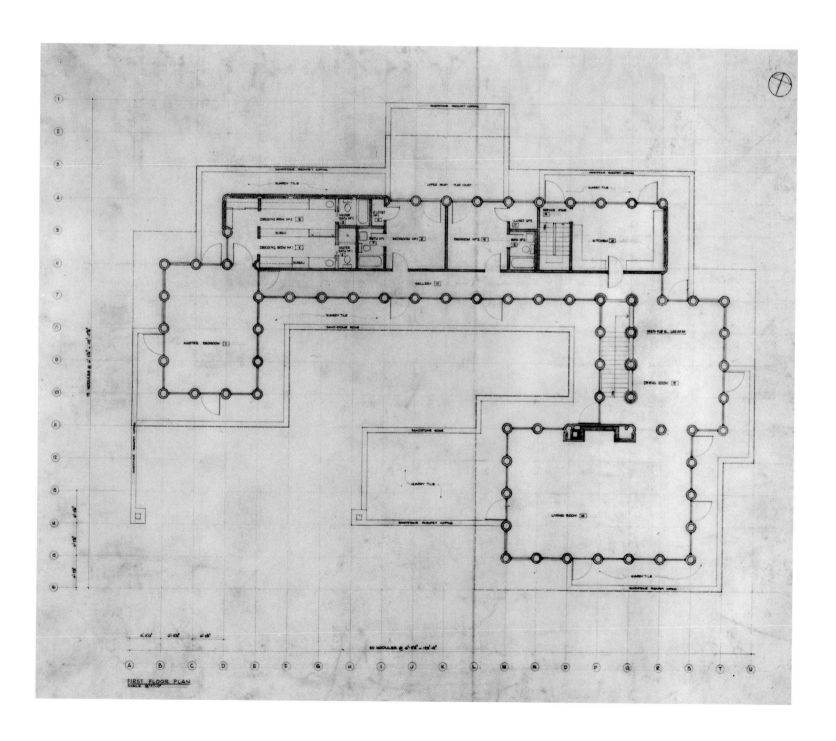

Mr. and Mrs. Henry C. Beck Jr. House, 1961–64

At the same time he was working on the Tuttle House project, Johnson built a house for Mr. and Mrs. Henry C. Beck Jr. of Dallas. The first design, from July or August 1961, shows a centralized Palladian villa plan. There is a central double-height space with balconies and a double ceremonial stair. That space is flanked on four sides by colonnades of circular columns. There are four blocks, each labeled with a function: foyer, living, dining and kitchen, and gym and study. A driveway passes through one colonnade, which also shelters the entry foyer. A service wing slides out from one of the sides. Though only a diagram, the plan contains many of the elements of the final design.

Schematically, the final plan was in place by September 1961. In it, a series of columns with arches in between carry around the entire perimeter of the house, and even are repeated in the second story of the building. Not as wide as the Tuttle House columns, the system of the Beck House emphasizes the arches (figs. 244–55). Johnson explored arches as a primary design element in several of the studies for his Glass House; at the same time he was designing the Beck House, he used arches in a pool pavilion on his New Canaan estate (see chapter 8). The columns underneath the arches are unusual in form: they splay out as they touch the floor. Johnson "derived the toe-ings of the columns from Delaunay's famous painting of the Gothic church of St. Severin."[89]

Mr. and Mrs. Henry C. Beck Jr. House
244 (below) Preliminary ground floor plan (July or August 1961)
245 (opposite, above) Final scheme, model photograph
246 (opposite, below) Final scheme, ground floor plan

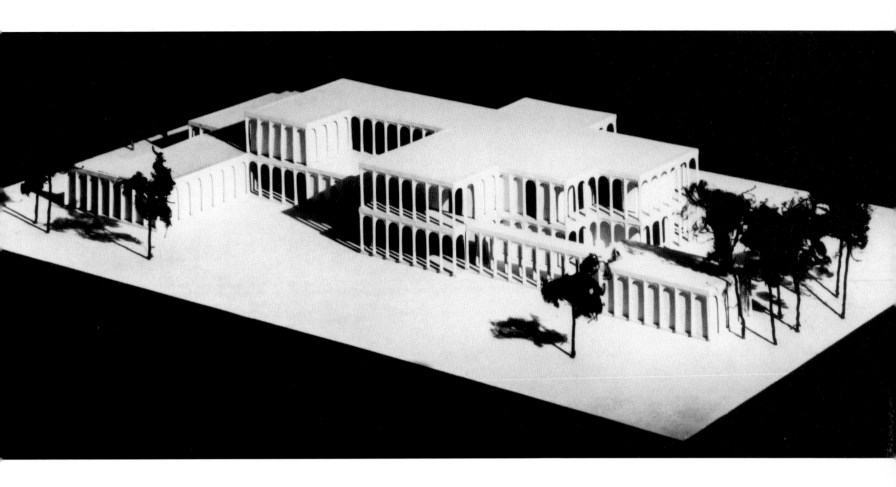

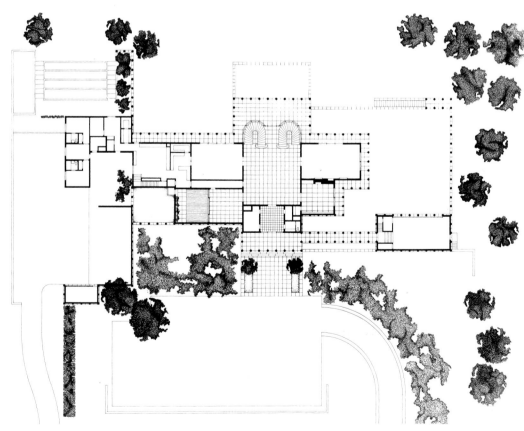

Mr. and Mrs. Henry C. Beck Jr. House
247 Corner detail showing elliptical arches and flaired column bases

Joseph Paxton
First sketch of the Crystal Palace,
June 11, 1850
248

The house is quite large, with the primary spaces arranged symmetrically. One enters through a vestibule into a double-height reception hall, with a pair of curving stairs at the far end leading up to a balcony. The arches create an arcade around most of the public spaces in the house, as well as along a large terrace at the rear of the hall; where they engage with the walls, the columns are treated as pilasters. The relentless quality of the arches around the entire perimeter, as well as the massive size of the house itself, give an institutional feel to the building. One of the most significant aspects of the design was the prefabrication, modular standardization, and site assembly of the building components. Playing against this standardization is an increasing concern with surface articulation, both in the surfaces of the house itself and in the loggias, which are created by extensions of the arches beyond the perimeter walls of the house.

Mr. and Mrs. Henry C. Beck Jr. House
249   View toward entrance façade

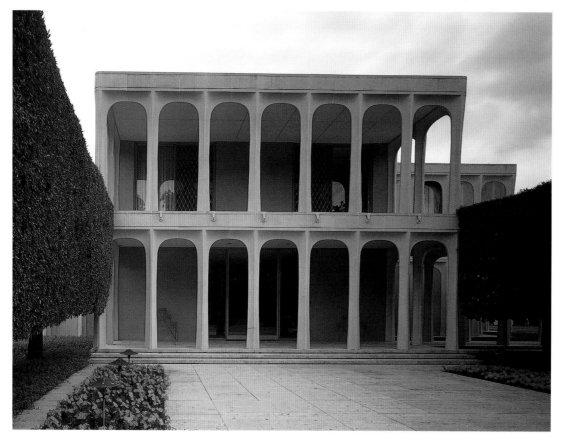

Mr. and Mrs. Henry C. Beck Jr. House
250 (top) View toward colonnaded court
251 (bottom) View of entry façade

Mr. and Mrs. Henry C. Beck Jr. House
253 (above) View of loggia and double stairs
254 (right) View of breakfast room and court
255 (far right) Living room, looking toward
double stairs

Mr. and Mrs. James A. D. Geier House, 1964–65

The Geier House, in Cincinnati, is unusual for a number of reasons (figs. 256–60). It is part of a group of three underground projects that Johnson worked on at roughly the same time, along with the Painting Gallery on his property in New Canaan and the Hendrix College Library in Arkansas. Rarely has a house been so completely subsumed by the landscape around it, albeit in a playful manner. The entire house is buried underground, by a highly stylized earth berm. The result echoes the ancient Indian burial mounds just north and east of Cincinnati, at Cillocothee, Ohio. The effect is further reinforced by the serpentine walk that leads down a gentle slope from the street to the house. Yet when one arrives at the front door—all glass, set in a sheer stone wall—

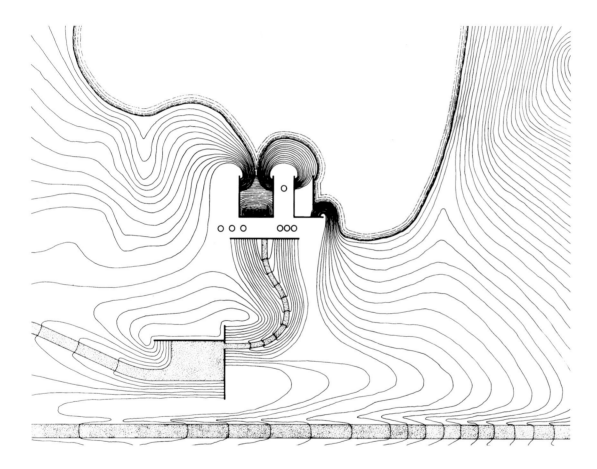

Mr. and Mrs. James A. D. Geier House
256 Site plan

one is greeted by a view of natural light and a vista. Part of this light comes through a series of cylindrical skylights which emerge out of the top of the berm like smokestacks from a buried ocean liner. But the primary means that Johnson used to create this effect is the sculpting of a pond on the far side of the house, so that a portion of the pond comes between the edges of the berms and into a central court of the house. The three wings of the house surround this court of water, ensuring a high level of natural light, even in this buried house.

The living room occupies one of these wings, and Johnson enhances the quality of light even further in it. Both the wall facing the water court and its opposite are glazed; the latter wall faces out to the pond. Thus from the bedroom wing, one can look out and across the internal water court, through the living room beyond, and ultimately to the pond in the distance. The overall effect of finding so much light and openness in a house that seems, on approach, to be buried, is profound and delightful.

Beyond the play of light and dark, both real and perceptual, Johnson may have had other reasons for designing a house which was entirely underground. First, the site was difficult. His longtime assistant, John Manley, remembers that the site had no inherent interest: it was "desolate."[90] There were only a couple of trees, and a single old barn, for context. More importantly, the site was completely flat. Johnson took the opportunity to sculpt the land and make it interesting. Additionally, Manley notes that the mid-1960s were a period in which Johnson had little confidence in his ability to design elevations. Putting the building underground seemed to solve that problem. Yet there may be still more to this. The Geier House came at a time of examination of large

Mr. and Mrs. James A. D. Geier House
257 View toward entry and lake beyond

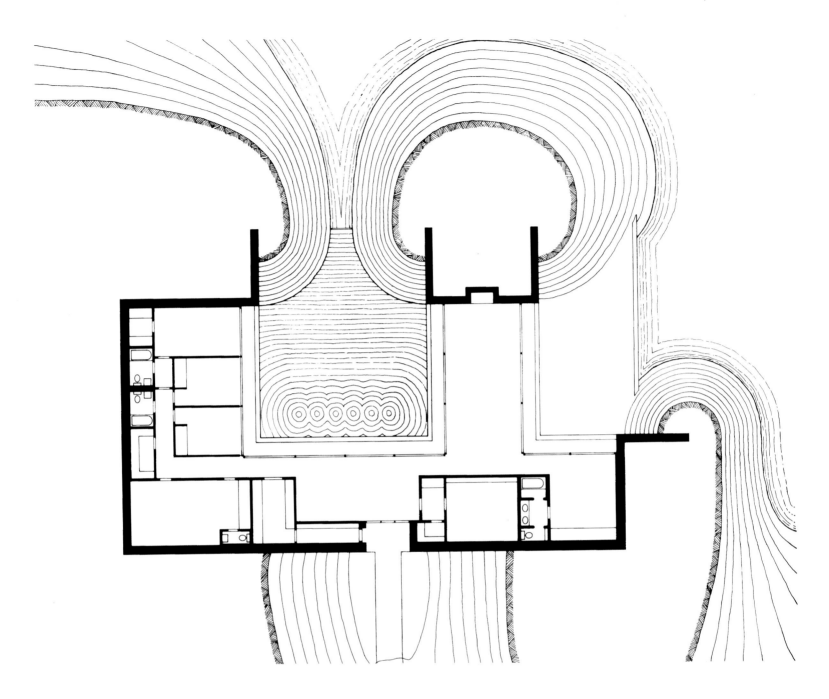

scale earth sculpture in the art world, a development of which Johnson would certainly have been aware. Also, a number of young architects were investigating different relationships between buildings and their environments, from large-scale constructions to individual structures. Whether he was confident in his elevation-making abilities or not, Johnson certainly delighted in the ironic juxtaposition of an underground house filled with light and water. It was yet another case, in Manley's words, of taking someone else's ideas and doing them better.

Mr. and Mrs. James A. D. Geier House
258 (above) Plan
259 (opposite, top) Water court looking toward living room
260 (opposite, bottom) View from lake

Mr. and Mrs. David Lloyd Kreeger House, 1964–68

Four years later, in 1968, Johnson designed a house in Washington, D.C., for David Lloyd Kreeger and his wife, that can be seen as either his most classically luxurious residence or his most institutional domestic work (figs. 261–66). The client was a wealthy art collector, attorney, and insurance magnate. The house is very large, roughly fourteen thousand square feet. It was designed to house Kreeger's art collection as well as to serve as his residence.

The overall organization of the house is based on two core areas. The first is a nine-square plan, which was a favorite organizing element for Johnson's institutional commissions, as it eliminates the need to double back for circulation. This gridded area houses most of the interior spaces and a large portion of the painting collection. In the center of this core is a landscaped courtyard or atrium, with views from all the surrounding rooms. It also contains the great hall.

The second core area is a giant outdoor room, a four-square covered porch for outdoor gatherings and sculpture display. In its location, orientation, and volume, this double-height space is an outdoor equivalent of the living room in the New Canaan Boissonnas House. The covered porch is on the garden side, overlooking both the surrounding landscape and a swimming court. Entry, dining, and service portions of the house are set adjacent to these areas.

Mr. and Mrs. David Lloyd Kreeger House
262 Ground floor plan

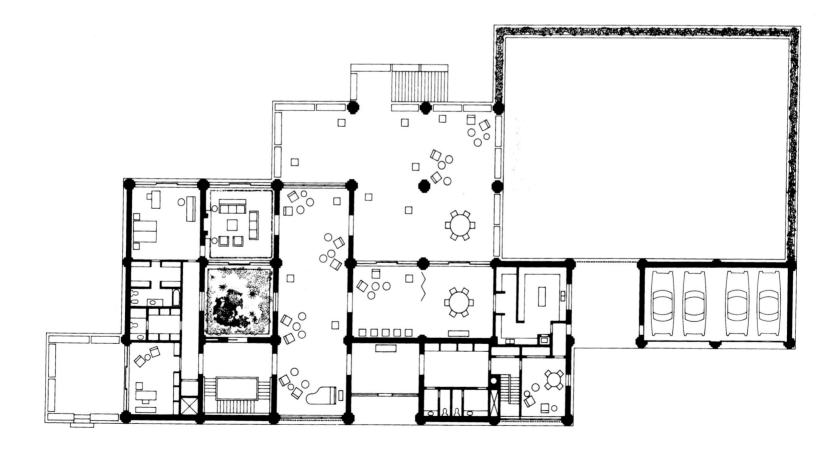

The architect used a system of heavy piers to organize a series of square bays, much as he had at the Boissonnas House in New Canaan. The piers themselves are cruciform in shape, and made of travertine. They are on a square module that measures twenty-two by twenty-two feet. Johnson even executed a variation on the Boissonnas entry sequence, moving from one bay at the entry to a vestibule of two bays, and then into a three-bay living room. Opening off the living room is a covered terrace of four bays, with a single uncovered bay attached to it. Additionally, other references to earlier Johnson projects abound: in the middle of one long wall in the living room, and taking up one full bay, is an enclosed atrium, much as in the Davis House in Minnesota.

The roof system is a series of repeating shallow domes, one for each bay. The use of the arch, even when segmented to flatten it, is noteworthy, and gives the composition a flavor of Islamic architecture. The overall size is enormous for a residence: over two hundred feet from one end to the other, and nearly one hundred feet wide. The effect, especially in Washington, seems institutional, more like a consulate than a residence. Appropriately, the house is now used as a museum.

Mr. and Mrs. David Lloyd Kreeger House
263 (opposite) Covered terrace
264 (above) View of covered terrace
from below

Mr. and Mrs. David Lloyd Kreeger House
265 (above) Pool court
266 (opposite) Living room

By the mid-1960s, Johnson's practice had grown significantly. He had either completed or was in the middle of major institutional projects for museums in New York, Texas, and Nebraska, and university projects for Yale, Brown, and others. Additionally, he was engaged with two major projects in New York, including the creation of Lincoln Center and the New York World's Fair. By any measure, his practice was among the most noteworthy ones in the country. Thus it is understandable that the domestic commissions he undertook were decreasing in number, and that those he did take on were significant in size and budget, to the point that they were, in fact, institutional buildings in the guise of houses, like the Kreeger House in Washingon, D.C. As the 1960s came to an end, Johnson turned away from domestic work completely and did not consider new residential commissions for nearly a decade.

Occasional Houses

7

1979–2001

Jerry I. Speyer House (project)
Scheme 4, ca. January 1994
267 Street elevations

For much of his professional career, Philip Johnson has worked with partners, for several reasons. One was his desire for intellectual stimulation; his partnership with Harvard schoolmate Landis Gores when he set up his practice in the mid-1940s, for example, was driven by recognition of Gores's intellectual abilities and education. Johnson had little interest in the administrative activity required to maintain a smoothly functioning professional office, so he sought partners with ability in that area. From the mid-1950s until 1964, Richard Foster served Johnson capably through several major projects, including the Seagram Building. In 1967, when John Burgee left Chicago to join Johnson's office in New York, Johnson began what would develop into his longest-lasting partnership.

Over the next twenty-four years, Johnson/Burgee Architects pursued Johnson's interest in major institutional and corporate buildings, but added another component: large commercial developments. The output of the office during this time was substantial, with major buildings in most large American cities. The list includes the Transco Tower and the Post Oak Development and Republic Bank Building (now NCNB Center) in Houston; the Boston Public Library addition; the IDS Center in Minneapolis; the PPG Building in Pittsburgh; and, among many projects in New York, the AT&T headquarters. The size of the office grew accordingly, and Johnson became an example of the globetrotting architect, jetting between major commercial projects in many cities.

One consequence of this changing nature of his professional practice was the de-emphasis of residential commissions. After he finished the Kreeger House in 1968, Johnson's house commissions were sporadic. Indeed, for nearly a decade after 1968, Johnson accepted almost no domestic commissions at all. When he did finally undertake new residential projects, they were for himself—a vacation house in the Big Sur region of California, and a pied-à-terre in a portion of a townhouse in the Soho neighborhood of New York City—and for his companion David Whitney, for whom he designed a house for the New Canaan compound. He also redesigned and moved into an apartment in Museum Tower, built as part of The Museum of Modern Art expansion of the early 1980s. Other commissions were taken on more as favors for clients who engaged Johnson/Burgee for large institutional or commercial projects. But far from being a substantial portion of the firm's work, the houses in this period of Johnson's career are at best tangential to the core of his practice.

One consequence of Johnson's commitment to his professional work was an increasing distance from contemporary developments in thinking about architecture, particularly in its relationship to the changing nature of the city. Orthodox modern architecture in America was under siege from the late 1960s through the 1970s. Increasing attention paid to the existing context of buildings and their historical linkages tended to undercut the autonomous culture of modernism. Johnson had been perceived to be a leader, even the ringleader, of the cause of modern architecture in America. As a younger generation of practitioners and critics challenged modernism, Johnson was suddenly in the uncomfortable position of not being in the vanguard of architecture in America, but rather watching and listening, and occasionally reacting to the criticisms of a younger generation. As his biographer, Franz Schulze, noted, Johnson "found himself for the first time in his adult life positioned off the pace."[91]

His response, as it developed over time, was to engage segments of this younger generation on its own terms. Paramount to that generation was defining a new relationship to history, particularly architectural history. Robert Venturi, in his seminal *Complexity and Contradiction in Architecture* (1966), chastised modernism for simplistic goals: "Architects can no longer afford to be intimidated by the puritanically moral language of orthodox Modern architecture. . . . I am for messy vitality over obvious unity."[92] Venturi's book was published by The Museum of Modern Art, with Johnson's knowledge and support, yet also with mixed feelings about its message. A decade later, the museum—or, more precisely, Johnson's successor Arthur Drexler—weighed in definitively on the relationship between history and the practice of contemporary architecture, in a 1975 exhibition of the architectural drawings of the Ecole des Beaux-Arts. The exhibition, with its accompanying publication, was a defining moment in the creation of postmodernism, where overt historical reference became a defining element of contemporary architecture. Johnson not only wholeheartedly embraced this movement in his own work, with projects such as the AT&T Building in New York City, he also promoted for major commissions other architects who shared these sensibilities, for example, Michael Graves for the Portland Public Service Building (1979–82), Graves's first major commission.

Just as important an influence on architectural practice at this time was an increased focus on vernacular architecture. Vincent Scully's *The Shingle Style Today: Or, The Historian's Revenge* appeared in 1974, and its commentary on the influence of American domestic architecture of the 1880s encouraged a new appreciation for the picturesque in architecture among younger practitioners and academics. It also served as a rallying point for opponents to modernism, implicitly rejecting that movement's own rejection of any historical references in the development of contemporary architecture. A renewed willingness to study the entire range of architectural history, and apply its lessons, took hold in architectural discourse.

As he nears the midpoint of his tenth decade, Johnson continues to practice architecture. Since 1993, he has worked in partnership with Alan Ritchie. Unlike much of his time in partnerships, however, his attention has moved away from commercial work and returned again to residential designs. Several new house projects are underway in the office, for locations as far afield as the Israel desert and the Turks and Caicos Islands in the Caribbean, as well as Teaneck, New Jersey, and Telluride, Colorado.

These new designs share a similar organizing concept that draws upon selected earlier domestic projects by Johnson. Various activities are dispersed into a number of discrete pavilions linked by a public space, which may not be as well defined as the pavilions yet has its own particular character. These recent houses are substantial in size, yet move away from the institutional quality that his big, expensive house projects of the late 1960s shared. And despite their big budgets, these later projects resonate with the earliest house projects, which emphasized relationships between separate small-scale pavilions. Most of them are for use as retreats or private resorts; Johnson has called them "pleasure camps."

Philip Johnson House, Big Sur (project), 1979–80

This enthusiasm for history carried over into two domestic projects that Johnson undertook for himself between 1979 and 1980 (fig. 268). At first glance, the design is based on a Shingle Style cottage, such as one might find in an 1880s Newport project of McKim, Mead and White, or in the work of Bay Area architect Bernard Maybeck, from the period around the First World War. Johnson remembers that his source was a church in Monterey, California, designed by Ernest Coxhead. Yet a characterization of the project as wholly historical in its references is not completely accurate when one examines the design, especially its fenestration. Contrasting with an eyebrow dormer window and an arch over the front door are a circular window and a single rectangular casement window in a wing of the house that projects forward. Both in their form and location, these windows have a greater debt to modern composition than to a sense of historical accuracy.

The most remarkable feature of the cottage is the use of the shingles themselves. As represented in the rendering, the same system of shingles covers the exterior walls as the roof. They even extend around a low wall defining a front terrace, and up the entire height of the chimney. On the public façade, instead of breaking the surface with large voids of glass, the windows are tight to the surface and composed of small panes of glass, emphasizing the continuity of the shingle surface. This effect is oddly resonant with early modern houses, such as Le Corbusier's villas, where the extensive use of a single material such as concrete is an essential characteristic.

The interior of the cottage was to be a single large room rising to twenty-one feet at the roof ridge. It was to contain a living area, a slightly elevated sleeping area screened by a low parapet, and a kitchenette; closets and a bathroom were to be in the attached extension. The rear of the house included extensive glass; the views would have been not to the ocean but to the mountains east of the settlement. In that way, it is reminiscent of several early projects that emphasized privacy over public presence, such as the Row House project from his student days and the *Ladies' Home Journal* Houses. Johnson intended to share the house with others, in a time-sharing arrangement common at that time for vacation residences.

Philip Johnson House, Big Sur (project)
268 Sketch

211 Philip Johnson House, Big Sur

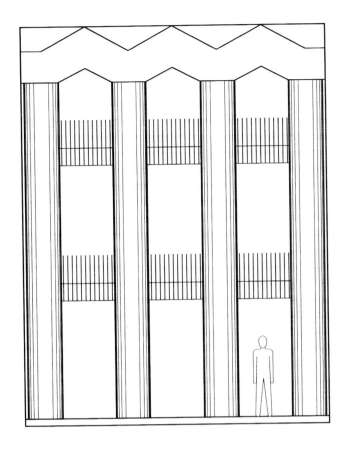

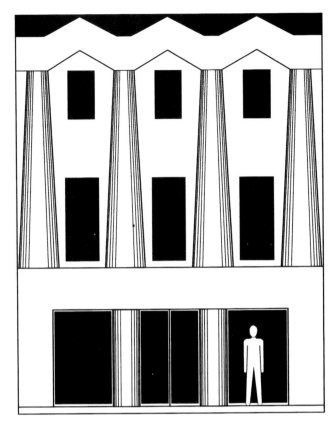

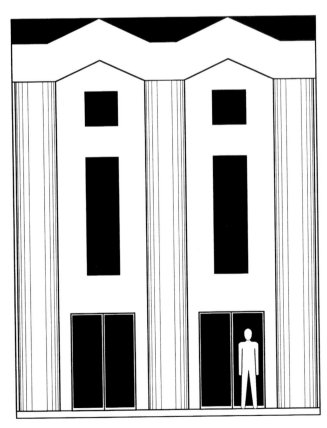

Philip Johnson Pied-à-terre (project), 1979

At about the same time, Johnson was investigating new living arrangements in New York. For a number of years in the 1970s, he had leased the Rockefeller Guest House (see pages 100–3) on East Fifty-second Street. (Mrs. Rockefeller had donated it to The Museum of Modern Art in 1958, and it was sold in 1964.) Although he ultimately leased an apartment in a new building for which he designed the façade—1001 Fifth Avenue— Johnson also considered renovating a portion of a small loft building in New York's Soho neighborhood. The design called for creating a new front elevation on the inside of the building (figs. 269–70). An internal wall would have divided the open space of the loft, and the side of this wall facing the open area went through several studies for possible elevations. Each of these involved the articulation of large abstracted classical columns. The loft was narrow, a bit less than twenty-three feet wide. But it was nearly thirty feet high and would have allowed for the display of significant pieces from Johnson's contemporary art collection. Behind this façade, on two floors, would have been the essential rooms for domestic life: kitchen, bedrooms, and other private areas. Johnson examined both two- and three-bay schemes, with engaged columns topped by variations of a classical pediment. When he could not reach agreement with the owner of the building, he decided to look elsewhere for his New York abode, settling eventually in the apartment on upper Fifth Avenue.

Philip Johnson Pied-à-terre (project)
269 (opposite) Elevation studies 1–4
270 (right) Elevation study 5, Johnson's preferred design

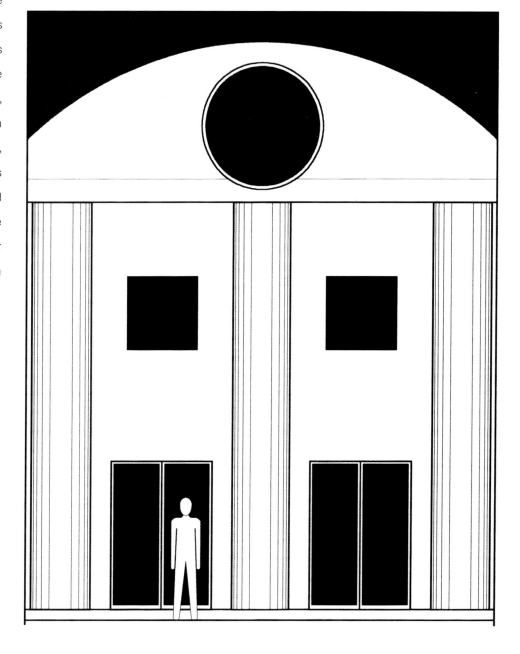

Philip Johnson Apartment, 1982–83

In 1985 Johnson moved to an apartment in the new Museum Tower, designed by Cesar Pelli, on West Fifty-third Street, at The Museum of Modern Art. The drawings shown here are dated March 1982 (fig. 271); final revisions are dated July 1983. His willingness to take up residence there was something of a surprise, since he had sought the commission for the tower but the museum's board did not select him. Johnson lived there quite comfortably until 1999, when he took up residence full-time in New Canaan, commuting three days a week to his office in New York.

Johnson's Museum Tower apartment is a product of its contradictory time. Located on an upper story of the tower, the apartment faced east, with a prominent view of Johnson and Burgee's AT&T Building. Like many other speculative apartment towers of this decade, the prominent views out were grander than the proportions within. Johnson detailed the interior with historical trim, and organized the spaces on historical models. A reference, if fleeting, is made to the work of John Soane, the early-nineteenth-century English architect whose own London house remains the paragon of eclectic historicism. The living room ceiling of Johnson's apartment is a flattened dome—the floor-to-floor dimensions of the tower's structure permitted little other vertical articulation—much as several of the most prominent spaces in Soane's house were domed. Yet little is known about the apartment; only limited construction documents are available. The apartment (and a contemporaneous house in the Caribbean for an artist) have never been photographed for publication. By all accounts, Johnson lived quietly and happily in this apartment until he relocated to the Glass House estate.

Philip Johnson Apartment

271 Construction drawings of living room elevations ("29 Mar '82")

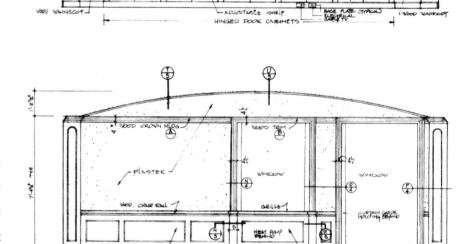

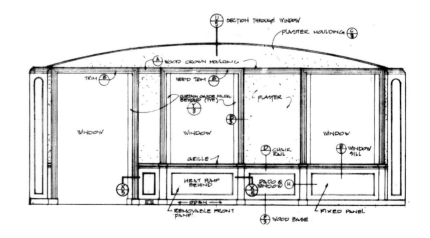

Ronald S. Lauder House/Study (project), 1986

Only in the mid-1980s, after nearly two decades, did Johnson begin to take on new residential commissions for clients. The first of these was for Ronald S. Lauder, a fellow trustee on The Museum of Modern Art board. Lauder owned property on Long Island, and asked Johnson to design a small studio for it, like the studio Johnson had recently added to his New Canaan compound. The design Johnson started indicates a single square room, approximately twenty feet across, with a small octagonal tower attached at one corner (figs. 272–74). Clad in shingles and intended as a combination library and cottage, its style was historical, a kind of Shingle Style cottage. The project seems to have lasted only a few weeks in the summer of 1986, and it did not even proceed as far as a presentation to the client; only a few sketches, a rendering, and a model were prepared. Still, the effort served as the foundation for a relationship with Lauder that extended for a significant period of time, leading to a new house project in the late 1990s.[93]

Ronald S. Lauder House/Study (project)
272 (above left) Drawing
273 and 274 (above) Elevation and plan sketches

Andy Williams House (project), 1990

Johnson's departure from historical models and his embrace of a much more abstract architectural vocabulary are not quite the sudden shift they seem. Postmodernism remained controversial in architectural circles throughout the 1980s, even crossing into public debate in a number of cultural venues. With considered opinion growing against it, Johnson once again moved into the position of a trendsetter when he co-organized the exhibition *Deconstructivist Architecture* at the Museum of Modern Art in 1988. The seven architects represented in the exhibition, along with others who shared certain formal qualities in their work or method, came to be known as the "Decons." They spurned any kind of historicism, preferring an abstract architectural language. Indeed, as Johnson noted in his preface to the exhibition catalog: "Deconstructivist architecture represents no movement; it is not a creed. It has no 'three rules' of compliance. It is not even 'seven architects.' It is a confluence of a few important architects' work of the years since 1980 that shows a similar approach with very similar forms as an outcome."[94]

As tempting as it must have been for Johnson to draw parallels with the *Modern Architecture: International Exhibition* of five decades earlier for the same museum, he refused to do so. That exhibition, he wrote, "prophesied an International Style in architecture to take the place of the romantic 'styles' of the previous

Andy Williams House (project)
275 Site model

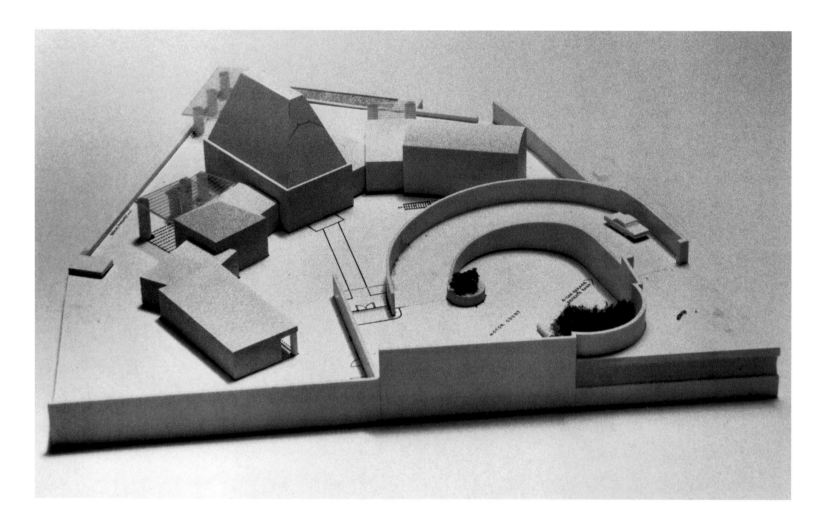

half century. With this exhibition, there are no such aims. Deconstructivist architecture is not a new style. We arrogate to its development none of the messianic fervor of the modern movement."[95]

While Johnson did not present any of his own work in the exhibition, his advocacy of this younger generation and their work thoroughly broke his ties to postmodernism. It also brought him into regular contact with a much younger generation of architects, facilitating the discussion of basic architectural values that had so captivated him throughout his adult life. Not surprisingly, it was to these architects that Johnson looked for professional inspiration as his work moved away from the historical tenets of postmodernism.

Johnson's first Deconstructivist project was a landscape folly, as usual an experiment for his own property in New Canaan (see chapter 8 for a discussion of all the building elements on the Glass House compound). Two additional house projects at the end of the 1980s include a design for the singer Andy Williams in Los Angeles, and a guest house in Cleveland for a major house project by Frank Gehry. Perhaps the most interesting feature of these houses is their marked departure from the culture of postmodernism and overt historical reference so evident in much of Johnson's work throughout the decade. Also, in a limited manner, these works indicate Johnson's return to strategies of domestic organization from his early career.

These characteristics are both present in the Andy Williams House project, from 1990 (fig. 276). Johnson used a series of separate pavilions to delineate different aspects of domestic life, much as he had done in a number of his projects from the 1940s. But unlike those earlier projects, in which rectangular building elements are carefully organized in orthogonal relationships to make regular external spaces, Johnson arranged the Williams pavilions in a segmental, arc-like system. One would have entered at the large central pavilion; to the left are a sequence of social spaces (study, dining room, and kitchen), followed by a pavilion for staff. To the right of the entrance are the private areas of the house: bedrooms, bathrooms, and dressing areas. The curving organization of the pavilions is reinforced by the semi-circular driveway. The arc of the road corresponds in size and orientation to the segmental connections between the pavilions. Contrasting with this arrangement, however, is the right-angle organization of the house's terrace.

The inspiration of Louis Kahn in the mid-century development of Johnson's architecture has already been noted, and there is more than a little of Kahn in the Williams House project. Kahn's Dominican Sisters' Convent project from the late 1960s arrays a series of rectangular building elements irregularly, so that they connect at their corners. Yet he also provides a larger rectangular frame for the three wings holding the nuns' residential quarters. The dominant aspect of the Williams composition is pavilions that appear to collide with each other, resulting in ambiguous relationships between them. The project illustrates how Johnson could take a theme he had developed decades earlier, and reconceive it as a novel composition consistent with contemporaneous directions in architectural thinking.

Andy Williams House (project)
276 Site plan

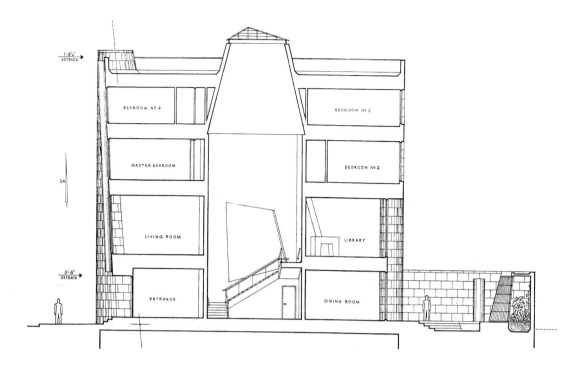

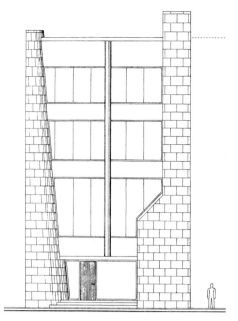

Jerry I. Speyer House (project), 1989–94

Working in the confines of a New York townhouse lot, Johnson prepared a series of designs from 1989 through 1994 for real estate developer Jerry Speyer (figs. 267 and 277–83). Although the designs are less radical than the Lewis Guest House proposals discussed below, the series shows a similar shift in Johnson's approach to design. The organization follows a pattern common to many townhouses on the Upper East Side: entry and dining room are on the ground floor, with access to a rear garden; living room and study are on the second floor, and two stories of bedrooms are above that. Johnson, however, enhanced that model substantially by the way that he articulated a major stair connecting the two lower floors. Set within its own pavilion and shifted at a slight angle off the orientation of the house, the stair hall is capped by a large skylight that would have provided natural light down through the center of the entire house, even the lower floors.

The stair itself would have served only the public portions of the house; to reach the bedroom floors access to an elevator or smaller set of stairs would have been required. Yet the most remarkable feature of this series of projects was the street elevation of the final design. Johnson warps the plane of the street wall so that it undulates in an organic and expressionistic manner, much like the early twentieth-century work in Barcelona of Spanish architect Antonio Gaudí, for example, the Casa Milà of 1906–11. The fenestration adapts to the undulations, and each element of the façade becomes an independent element in the composition. The effect would have been enhanced by the geometric rigidity of the adjacent façades, with their regularly gridded window patterns and stone coursings.

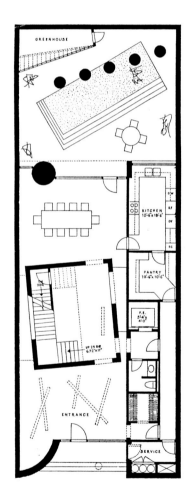

Jerry I. Speyer House (project)
277 (top, left) Section ("10/6/89")
278 (top, right) Street elevation ("10/6/89")
279 (above) Ground floor plan ("10/6/89")

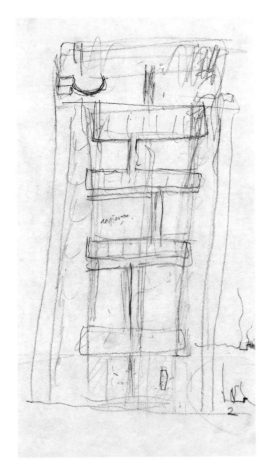

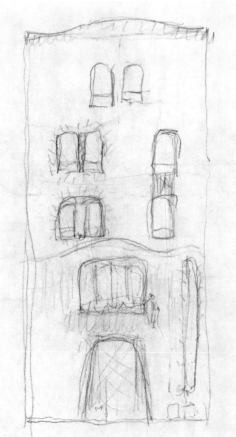

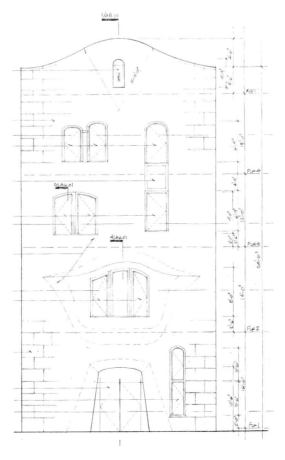

Jerry I. Speyer House (project)
280 (far left) Johnson sketch
of street elevation
281 (left) Street elevation ("12/21/93")
282 (below, left) Johnson sketch
of street elevation
283 (below, right) Street elevation
("Feb 94")

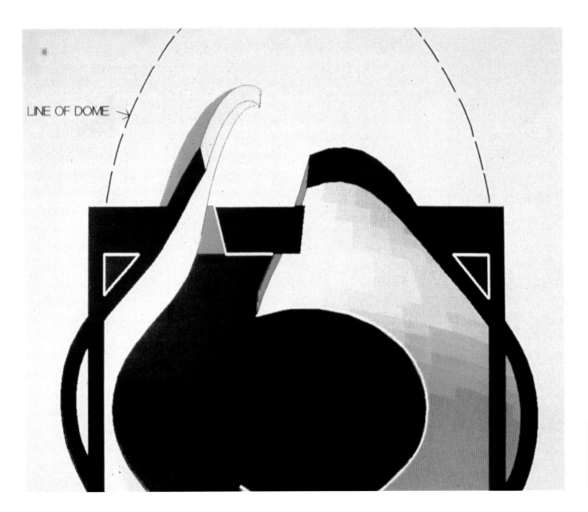

LINE OF DOME →

Peter B. Lewis Guest House (project), 1991–95

This series of designs for a guest house in Cleveland, for entrepreneur and philanthropist Peter B. Lewis, best illustrate the rapid shifting and explorations he was making following the break in his architecture after the Deconstructivist exhibition of 1988. Johnson's designs were part of a large house project on nine acres that Frank Gehry had been working on for six years by the time Johnson became involved; the project would continue for another five years before Lewis and Gehry abandoned it, construction having never begun. Johnson was brought in at Lewis's request.

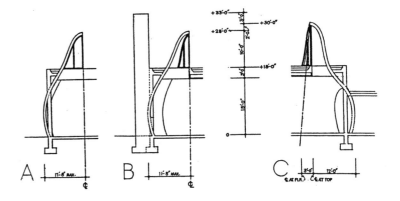

Johnson's contribution to the Lewis project would have included three separate components: a guest house within the main house compound, a gate house, and a totally separate structure called the Starfish House. The best record of the project is the guest house. From a series of interlocking cubes, it evolved into an irregular wedge shape, then to a pear-like form within a box (figs. 284–85), and ultimately mutated into an octopus shape (figs. 286–89). The progression of forms and ideas in the Lewis Guest House went from a Deconstructivist approach to a full-blown investigation of one facet of early modernism, Expressionism, with under-

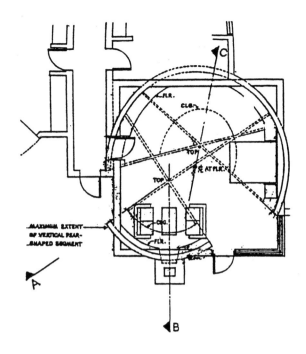

currents of a modernist primitivism, in which highly advanced ideas and experimental materials are mixed with natural forms. The futuristic ideas and forms of early modernism and the German Expressionists had fascinated Johnson for years. In the catalog of the Mies van der Rohe exhibition of 1947, describing the years 1919 to 1925, he wrote: "Never in its history had architecture been so influenced by painting. Beginning in 1919, the 'dislocated angles and distorted curves' of Expressionism became the basis of a procession of fantastic projects, very few of which were ever built."[96] Designs for the Peter Lewis Guest House show how Johnson had come full circle to a renewed interest in the fantastical undertones of early twentieth century Expressionism.

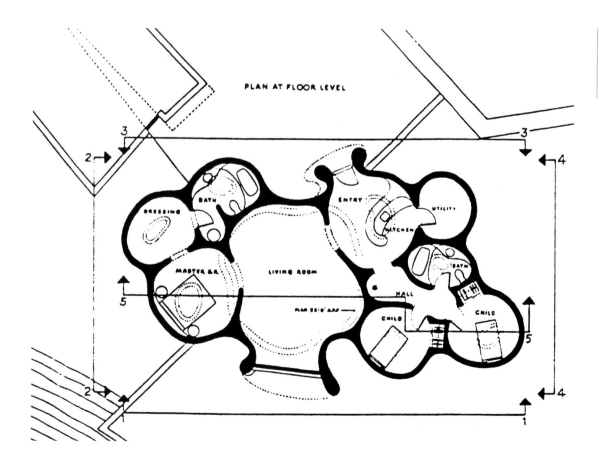

PLAN AT FLOOR LEVEL

Peter B. Lewis Guest House (project),
Preliminary scheme, "Octopus" (1995)
287 (left) Plan
288 (page 222, top) Section
289 (page 222, bottom) Model photograph

Peter B. Lewis Starfish House
290 (left) Model photograph
291 (below) Roof and floor plans ("24-1-95")

Peter B. Lewis Starfish House (project), 1995

Another structure intended for the Lewis property, the Starfish House dates from January 1995 (figs. 290–91). Unsolicited, it was designed by Johnson for a remote part of the site. It is a more animated version of the 1993 wedge design for the Lewis Guest House, and it demonstrates the same vocabulary Johnson was using for the Visitors Pavilion for his New Canaan compound (see chapter 8). The Starfish House plan describes a procession of expanding and contracting volumes, which provide for sleeping, bathing, and sitting areas, as well as a belvedere for views from the sloping site, which is adjacent to a pine forest and golf course. The warped wall planes were to be constructed of wire-reinforced foam panels with sprayed-on concrete. The floor, walls, and ceiling were to have as a surface small mosaic tiles, progressing from opaque ones on the floor to mirrored ones on the ceiling planes. "Theatrical lighting" was part of the scheme. The proposal was never presented to the client.

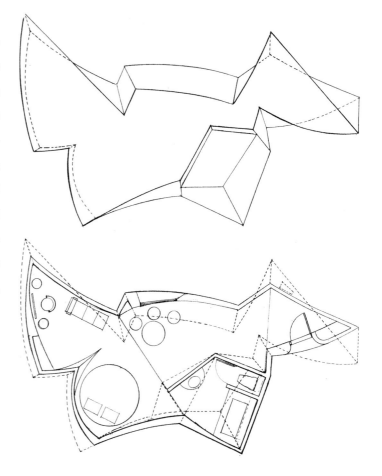

Thirteen Townhouses, Rotterdam (project)
292 (left) Model photograph, view of corner unit
293 (opposite, top) Plans: Ground, second
and third floors
294 (opposite, bottom) Model photograph,
street façades

Thirteen Townhouses, Rotterdam (project), 1996–97

This townhouse project, planned in the mid-1990s for Rotterdam, the Netherlands, called for thirteen town-houses arranged on the west side of a residential street (figs. 292–94). The three-story houses—identical except for the corner one, which adjusts to an oblique angle in the street grid—are designed to be small but efficient; there was to be a garage between each house. Public functions are assigned to the ground floor, with four bed-rooms and two baths on the floor above. The top floor could be a larger bedroom, or a bedroom/studio com-bination, with access to a roof terrace. The most interesting elements are the overall forms of each house and the fenestration: the side walls billow out slightly, in a manner derived from the Starfish House, and fold into a sail-like shape which is the street entrance. A vertical column of windows extends beyond the top of the house on the front façade, which angles back slightly from the street as it rises. The interplay between the functional normalcy of the plan and the gentle exuberance of the elevations is noteworthy.

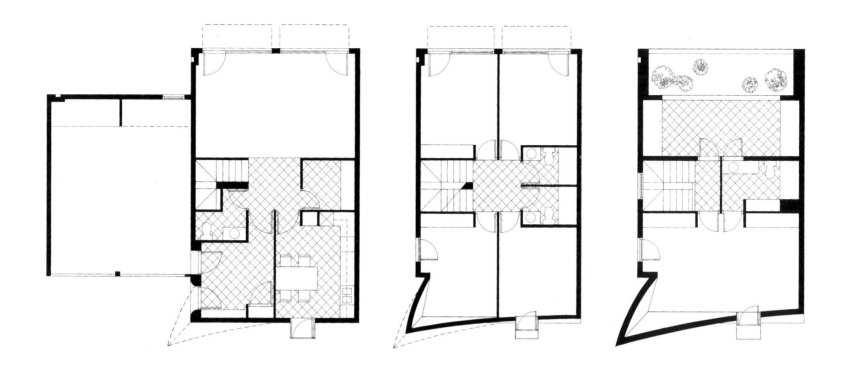

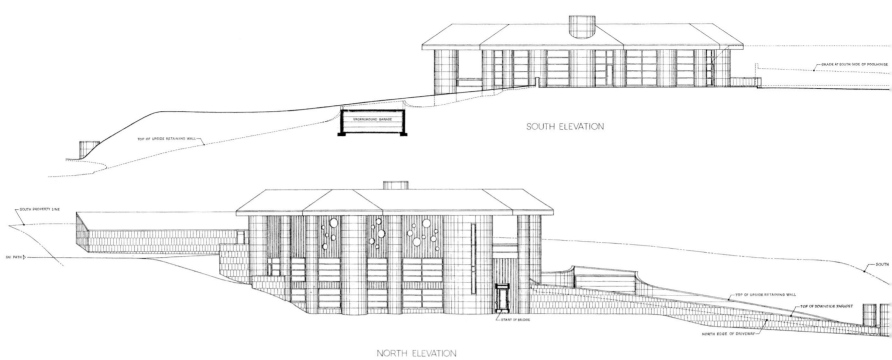

SOUTH ELEVATION

NORTH ELEVATION

John Buck House (project), 1999

The large cylindrical masses of the Buck House, planned for Telluride, Colorado, have diameters of varying sizes and seem to be randomly placed (figs. 295–99). According to Johnson's associate John Manley, the architect intended the cylinders to create the effect of large tree trunks in a forest. Panels of glass and wood set at different angles fit in between the cylinders and provide connections between them. The entry and the bedrooms are on the lower level, including a bridge connecting to a separate master suite. From the entry level, one comes up a stair into an open-plan living area, recalling 1950s schemes for the Wylie and Bosch Houses. This suite has two levels and is linear in nature, with a shed roof. Another structure contains a lap pool. A large gable roof covers the remaining interior spaces in the house, which one can imagine to be a clearing in the woods defined by the cylinders. After initially considering a flat roof, Johnson moved to a pitched roof to comply with local building codes. His preference was a single pitch, but due to the size of the house, that would have resulted in a vertical difference of nearly forty feet from one side of the roof to the other. Thus the gable roof was selected.

The cylinders are used for a variety of functions. In large ones, service functions take place: stairs, fireplace, closets, and storage. But they also define the perimeter of the house, as the cylindrical columns of the early 1960s Wylie Tuttle project would have done.

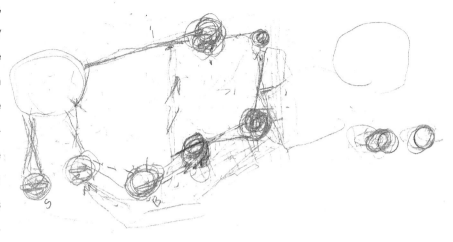

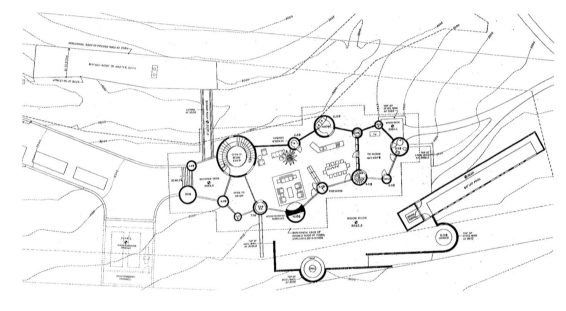

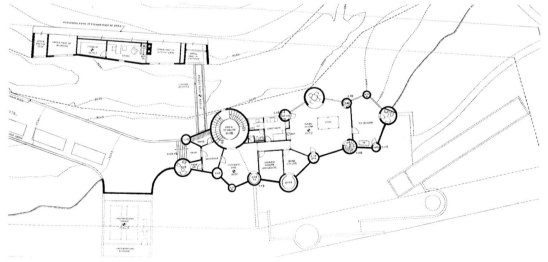

John Buck House (project)
295 (opposite, top) North and south elevations ("February 23, 1999")
296 (opposite, bottom) Model photograph
297 (top right) Johnson sketch of plan
298 and 299 (middle and bottom right)
Site plan, upper and lower levels ("February 23 and 5, 1999")

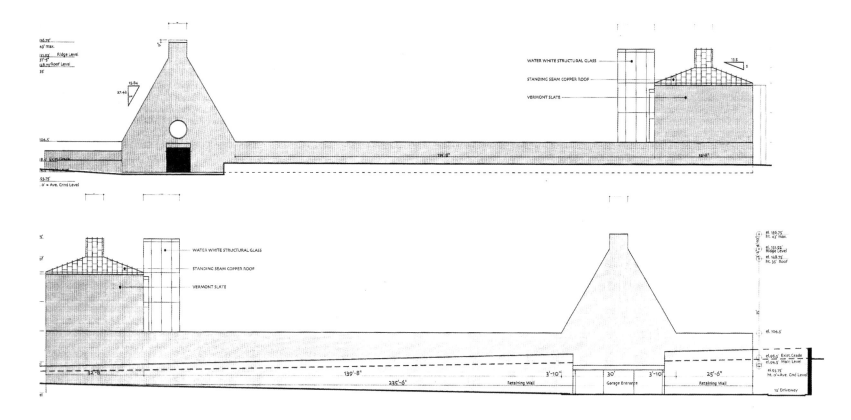

House in Teaneck (project), 1999–2001

A house in Teaneck, New Jersey, begun in 1999, is designed for a couple with four children and numerous grandchildren (figs. 300–2). The site is suburban, and the lot is 300 feet by 250 feet. The client came to Johnson for a glass house, but Johnson explained that while a glass house would work on a large, pastoral piece of property where neighboring houses are not close, it would not be appropriate in a relatively dense suburban neighborhood. So Johnson designed an inside-out glass house, in a reprise of the Miesian court-house. As opposed to the nearby houses, the scale is kept low by designing two separate structures at a distance from each other, grouped around a private courtyard. The perimeter wall of the court is solid stone. All exterior planes of the design are solid, while all the interior facing walls are glass.

The two pavilions are for different generations. The parents intend to live in the main house, while the second pavilion will be for the children and grandchildren. The two parts of the house are connected by two perimeter circulation walkways, which have glass walls on the side facing into the court. Unlike a typical Mies court-house, the pavilions are multi-storied. In the main house, the living spaces are thirty feet high. A master bedroom suite and study occupy the second floor, with large areas also open to the first floor below. The children's pavilion contains four identical pods, each three floors high, with common areas on the ground floor and two floors of bedrooms above. Each tower has a separate stair, a circular, glass-enclosed seating area, and a view towards a private garden opposite the courtyard. The courtyard width matches that of the Abby Aldrich Rockefeller Sculpture Garden that Johnson designed for The Museum of Modern Art, and it also is intended to provide for the display of sculpture.

House in Teaneck (project)
300 (top) South and north elevations ("05-03-00")
301 (opposite, top) Model photograph
302 (opposite, bottom) Plan ("05-03-00")

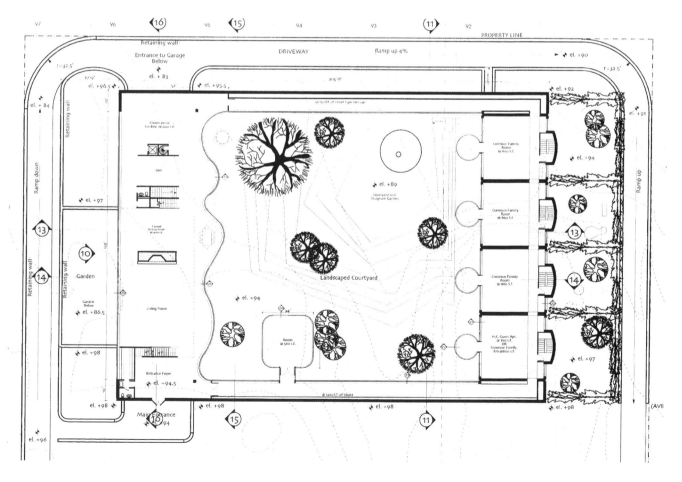

Ronald S. Lauder "Oasis House" (project), 1999–2001

As noted above, Ronald Lauder engaged Johnson to design a one-room Shingle Style study in the mid-1980s on Long Island. That design was not built, but in 1999, Lauder came back to Johnson with a considerably different program, this time for a retreat in the Israeli desert (figs. 303–7). The project has come to be called "Oasis House," and it is conceived as a literal desert oasis, though with no particular site determined. A small pool with palm trees is surrounded by roughly a dozen small pavilions, of varying sizes and shapes. Some are free-standing and several interlock. All are designed in the same architectural style as the Visitors Pavilion completed in 1995 for Johnson's New Canaan compound. Recreation areas for tennis and swimming are removed slightly from the oasis, as is a synagogue and staff parking areas.

Ronald S. Lauder "Oasis House" (project)
303 Model photograph

In the absence of an actual site, Johnson, working closely with John Manley, decided not to simply place the pavilions on the desert, but to submerge them in part, and berm up the land around them. As Manley described it recently, "You couldn't really see these outlying structures as anything but sand sculpture as you came to the house."[97] This was the strategy that Johnson had employed with the underground Geier House

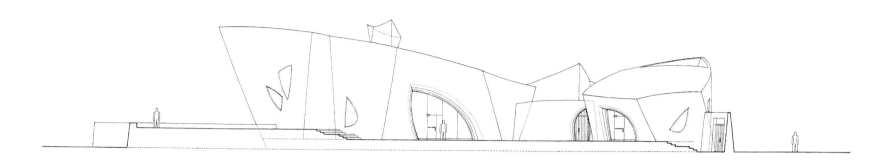

near Cincinnati when he believed that the relentless flatness of the site was a problem for a conventional building project. Originally, the central area was intended to be a covered court, like the exterior court of the second Boissonnas House in France, so that it would be protected from the desert sun. But that was abandoned as being too intrusive to the idea of adapting the architecture literally to the sand, so the concept of an oasis, with palm trees around a pool, replaced it.

Each structure has its own character, with one notable exception. The synagogue was modeled after a rock, about four inches across, which Johnson had picked up in Big Sur. After failing to model the structure through drawings based on the rock, his office calibrated the actual rock, and turned that into the architectural design for the synagogue. Within each pavilion, every important room would have an open garden within it. Only a few of these courts are designed with windows to the exterior, although each has a skylight.

Ronald S. Lauder "Oasis House" (project)
304 (top) Section through main compound looking toward living area ("1/3/00")
305 (above) Model photograph, view of main compound with swimming pool in foreground

Ronald S. Lauder "Oasis House" (project)
306 (below) Model photograph, view of
compound with service court (foreground) and
synagogue (upper right)
307 (opposite) Site plan ("6/5/00")

233 Ronald S. Lauder "Oasis House" (project)

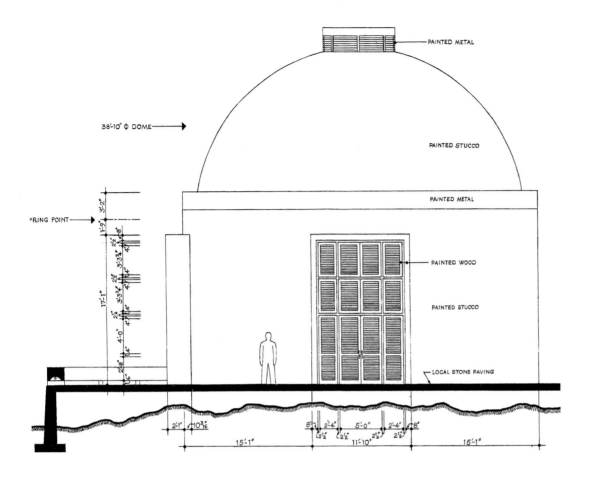

PAINTED METAL

38'-10" φ DOME

PAINTED STUCCO

PAINTED METAL

PRING POINT

PAINTED WOOD

PAINTED STUCCO

LOCAL STONE PAVING

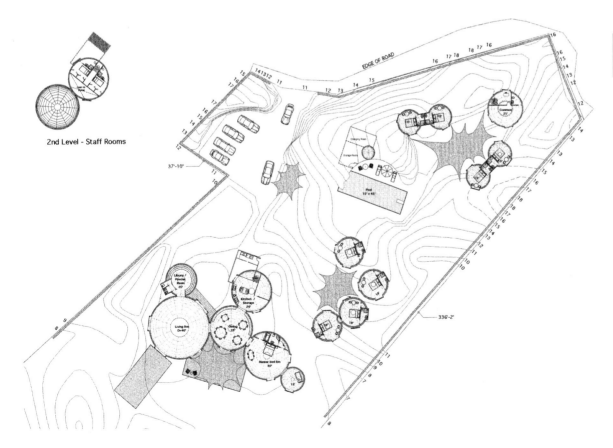

2nd Level - Staff Rooms

Mr. and Mrs. Alberto Fanni House
308 (above) Elevation of living room ("8/1/00")
309 (left) Ground level plan

Mr. and Mrs. Alberto Fanni House, 2000–1

A design for Alberto and Nicole Fanni, on the Turks and Caicos Islands, is quite similar in intent although not in style to the Lauder desert retreat. Groupings of cylinders are used to make the rooms of the residence (fig. 309). The cylinders vary considerably in size, although each has a half-spherical dome as a roof, with an oculus in the center (fig. 308). The cylinders seem to be scattered across the landscape, with little direct relationship to each other except for their programs. Tensile structures cover areas in between two of the groupings. As in the desert compound for Ronald Lauder, the pavilions are largely closed off from the exterior, with minimal fenestration. Instead, an oculus allows daylight into the pavilion as well as air circulation. The proportions of the domes recall the Pantheon, but the forms also evoke stellar observatories.

These recent projects emphasize Johnson's reawakened interest in residential architecture. He noted not long ago that he was old enough that no developer would hire him for a commercial project, but that was alright, since he realized that he could accomplish more in residential projects instead.[98] All on their own, these last two projects provide an appropriate summation of Johnson's domestic work. They affirm the primacy of the central issue he continually addressed from the time of the Glass House onward: the use of the pavilion in the context of residential life. One design uses abstract and contemporary building forms arranged in a pattern that goes back to the earliest human settlements; the other uses traditional form, materials, and construction, yet arranges the pieces abstractly across a site. If nothing else, they demonstrate Johnson's insatiable appetite for architecture: its entire history as well as its contemporary applications, juxtaposed in a manner that makes us consider our own age in the light of ages past.

Mr. and Mrs. Alberto Fanni House
310 (top) Southeast elevation
("June 7, 2000")

The Glass House Compound

8

1953–2001

Guest House Interior Revisions **1953**

Caretaker's House (project) **1954**

Swimming Pool **1955**

Dining House (project) **1956–57**

Entrance Gate **1957–77**

Water Pavilion, Pond, and Fountain **1959–62**

Footbridge **1962**

Painting Gallery **1965**

Sculpture Gallery **1968–70**

The Red House (project) **1977**

Studio/Library **1978–80**

Gehry Ghost House **1984**

Lincoln Kirstein Tower **1985**

Deconstructivist Folly (project) **1988**

Slat House (project) **1991**

Visitors Pavilion **1986–95**

Footbridge
The Sculpture Gallery is seen
at the end of the path

Over the last half-century, both the popular and architectural press have ascribed numerous iconic qualities to Philip Johnson's Glass House. Certainly the house itself has earned these accolades; it is one of the most recognized and recognizable dwellings in America. We have already discussed the dynamics of the relationship between the Glass House and its brick Guest House in chapter 3. Yet the process of designing and building the Glass House inaugurated an intermittent yet five-decade-long effort by Johnson to shape not only the structure in which he would live but the entire estate. Over that period of time, he purchased additional land, expanding the original five-acre parcel to forty. From the outset, he spent considerable time shaping the landscape to his liking: "I could see the potential of the five-acre slice. . . . I could see where I could sculpt it, after I'd cleared it, and gradually I found the knoll where the house was going to be, and now is. The knoll at that time was deep in the woods where nobody could see it. So I cleared the field from the road down to where I was going to build the house."[99] Those efforts have continued throughout Johnson's life on the estate: "I went ahead—cutting, cutting, cutting. I still cut down fifteen or twenty trees a year. I realize I shall be in trouble with the local nature lovers, but I have to free us from the terrible curse of New England, which is the tree. New England is a jungle, and it has to be beaten back."[100]

As Johnson has shaped his natural landscape, he also has shaped his built environment. Even from his first years in the Glass House, he planned for an eventual series of pavilions and other structures on the estate. These now serve a variety of functions, from service to personal to public. But the process of their creation and the ensemble they form is also a defining element of Johnson's engagement with the evolving dynamic of architectural form in the twentieth century.

Glass House
312 (right)   Site plan
313 (opposite)   View past the Glass House to the Water Pavilion and Kirstein Tower

Guest House Interior Revisions, 1953

His revisions to the estate began at its core: the Glass House and the Guest House. Although the exterior of the Glass House is unchanged, its use has been altered. In the years just after the Guest House was completed, the structure was used primarily for guests. Its original layout indicated this clearly: two bedrooms of equal size, flanking a study, with basic services off a shared hallway. In 1953, however, Johnson combined one bedroom and the study into a master suite, and this bedroom became an alternative to the sleeping area in the Glass House (fig. 314). A pair of flattened domes flowing continuously from paired triangular columns was incorporated into the design of the room, one dome over the bed, the other over a small sitting area (figs. 315–16). The style of the columns—almost freestanding pilasters, abstracted away from their surface—and their primarily decorative function conflicted with the modern ideal of clarity of form related to clarity of purpose. While Johnson had explored the use of arches in several of the later schemes for the Glass House, the primarily decorative use to which they are put in the Guest House renovation indicates how quickly he was willing to move in other stylistic directions and to explore historical sources.

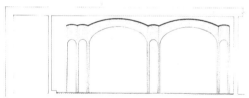

Guest House Interior Revisions
314 (left) Interior of bedroom (1950s)
315 and 316 (below) Section through bedroom and plan

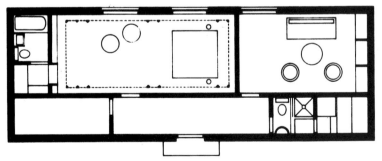

Caretaker's House (project), 1954

A year later, in 1954, Johnson contemplated an addition to the estate, a house for a caretaker. Intended for the site where the Painting Gallery would ultimately be built a decade later, the project went through several variations. A two-story rectangular bar was considered, as well as single-story schemes in both a bar and a U-shape. There are similarities to the Wiley Development House, which dates from the same period. The two designs shown here, however, present an octagonal pavilion attached to the house, on the downhill side of the site (figs. 317–18). While no function is given in the drawings, it is reasonable to surmise that the octagon was intended as some kind of dining pavilion or belvedere. The wall to the caretaker's structure behind it is solid in each scheme, so that the octagon would have read as a sculptural element against a brick wall.

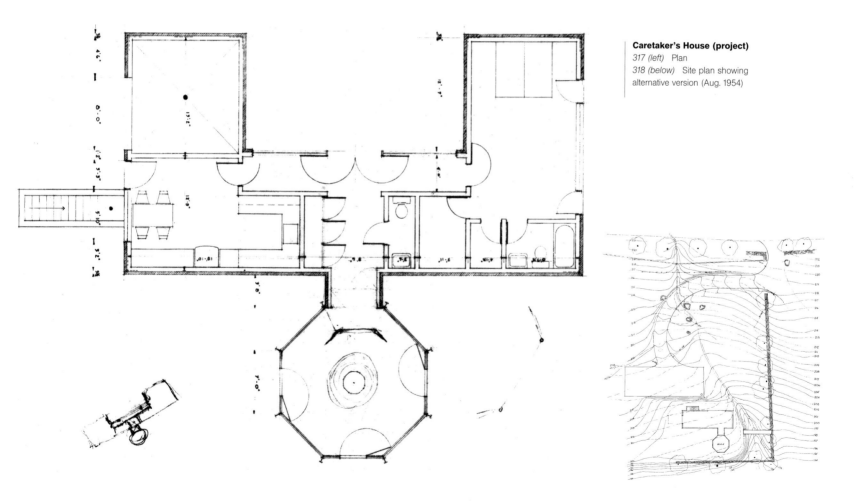

Caretaker's House (project)
317 (left) Plan
318 (below) Site plan showing alternative version (Aug. 1954)

Dining House (project), 1956–57
Swimming Pool, 1955

The notion that the octagon in the Caretaker's House might have been intended as a dining pavilion is supported by a subsequent project Johnson considered for the estate. Located on precisely the same site as that considered for the Caretaker's House, this new project was called the Dining House (fig. 319). In plan it appears as an arrangement of squares, the corner piers of each square being quite large: forty inches on a side. The design is sheared along one axis, so one square pulls free at each end. A barrel-vaulted roof system was planned (fig. 320). The function of each square is different; closest to the Glass House would have been an open-air terrace, connected to an enclosed terrace. That would have led to the kitchen and service area, from which one could have continued into the caretaker's apartment, open to the estate on just one side. The composition must be seen as a variation on two contemporaneous projects: the design of the first Boissonnas House, in New Canaan (fig. 152), which similarly utilizes a square grid and large piers as organizing elements, and the vaults of the Mann House project (fig. 215).

While neither the Caretaker's Pavilion nor the Dining Pavilion were built, Johnson did carry out at this time his first built addition to the New Canaan estate. It was a pool, for swimming in hot weather; for viewing at other times (fig. 320). Located just west of the front of the Glass House, it is a pure circle in plan, and bowl-shaped. Originally, Johnson had intended to place a sculpture by Mary Callery on that particular site.

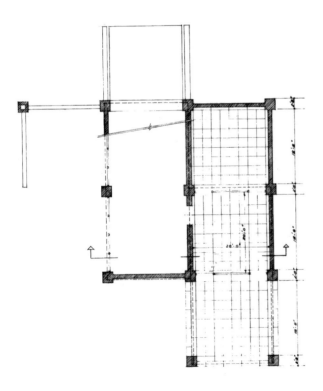

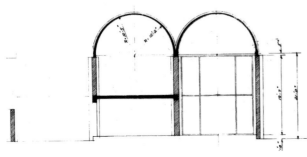

Dining House (project) and Swimming Pool
319 (left) Plan and section, showing barrel shell vaults
320 (opposite) Pool

Entrance Gate
321   View of gate from Ponus Ridge Road
322 *(below)*   Final scheme, elevation

Entrance Gate, 1957–77

Two years later, Johnson prepared a design for a gate to the driveway off Ponus Ridge Road, as he contemplated moving the entrance to the south. The effect of the driveway relocation would have been substantial, for it would have taken away the vista of the Glass House on its promontory as seen from the road. Instead of a visitor crossing in front of the Glass House, he or she would not really have had much of a view of the house before arriving at a small parking area adjacent to the Guest House, getting out of a vehicle, and looking over the stone wall framing the parking area. Thus the approach to the Glass House, solely from the oblique, was accentuated. A frontal view of the house would have been discovered as a part of a walk across the estate and up to the entry of the house.

The November 1957 design is for a courtyard, with a wide opening where a car would enter off Ponus Ridge Road (fig. 323). A motorist

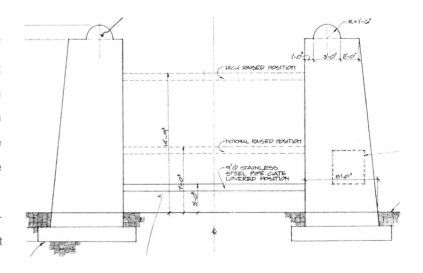

would have found himself in a court, sixty-six feet long by thirty-four feet wide, enclosed by eight-and-a-half-foot-high walls, facing a pair of swinging gates. These were to be simply two circles on hinged panels set in the long wall.[101] The driveway was to run diagonally through this court.

A second scheme was developed in about 1962, around the time the final design of the Water Pavilion was established. A pair of square pavilions, with arches like the Water Pavilion, would have flanked the driveway entrance (figs. 324 and 328). Lit from within at night, these would have looked like immense lanterns.

In 1964 the driveway was in fact relocated to its present position. In 1977, around the time the Studio/Library was created, Johnson designed and built the Entrance Gate that visitors to the compound now encounter (figs. 321–22). It consists of two pairs of thin, flat piers that enclose a mechanism, based on that of a vertical lift bridge, which raises and lowers a horizontal barrier across the driveway entrance. The design is substantial—perhaps overbearing—but it does serve to locate the entrance to the estate for new visitors and to intimidate uninvited guests.

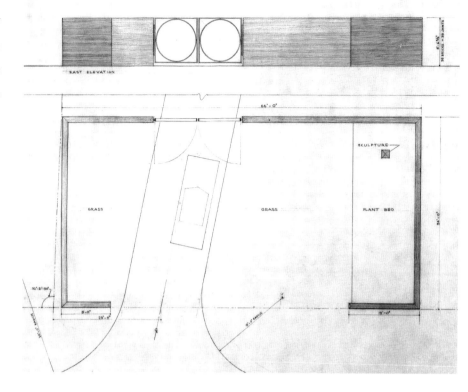

Entrance Gate

323 (above) First scheme. Elevation and plan (1957)
324 (below) Second scheme. Pavilion elevations and site plan (ca. 1962)

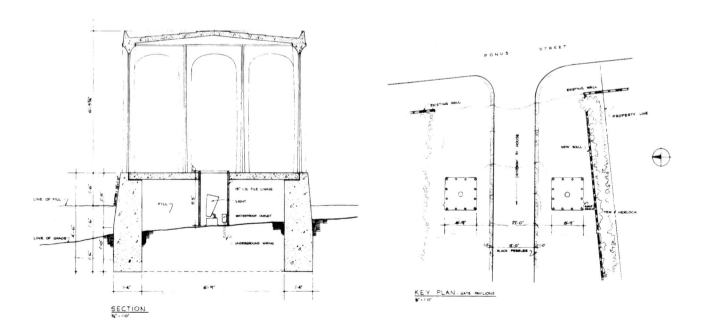

Water Pavilion, Pond, and Fountain, 1959–62

The first major addition to the New Canaan estate was built in 1962, with the creation of a pond with a pavilion in it, along with a jet in the middle of the pond. Three years earlier, Johnson had explored a ten-sided polygonal temple form for the pavilion, topped by a pointed roof with a crescent moon at its peak (figs. 326–27). Each side has a pointed elliptical opening, a design Johnson was experimenting with for his New York State Theater project at the same time. In its form and its detail, the pavilion was intended as a garden folly.

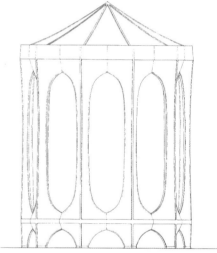

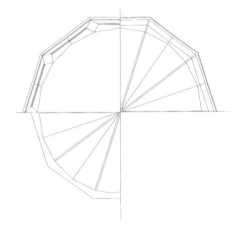

Water Pavilion

325 (left) View of Water Pavilion and water jet (1960s)
326 and 327 (below) First scheme, elevation ("Nov. 1959") and plan
328 and 329 (opposite, above and below) View of Water Pavilion and plan

By 1962, however, Johnson moved to a more abstracted idea of a folly-as-pavilion. The Water Pavilion (also called the Lake Pavilion in writings on the Glass House compound) consists of four orthogonal arched structures, two square and two double-square, with an open square at the center of a loose pinwheel arrangement (figs. 328–29). Three other uncovered areas, as well as a part of the platform for the pavilion, are attached. Several of the squares are covered, their undersides treated with gold leaf. At the center is yet another square area, uncovered, for a pool with small fountains. The arches are linked seamlessly to columns with a kind of cornice running across them. The columns, four-sided and tapering, are turned diagonally, like the cruciform columns of the Barcelona Pavilion. Johnson described their form later: "I derived the 'toe-ings' of the columns from Delaunay's famous painting of the Gothic church of St. Séverin."[102] The most remarkable feature of the Water Pavilion, however, is not so much its form as its scale: it has been miniaturized to the point that one must duck one's head

to move through the arches, or risk a lump at best and a soaking at worst. There is no bridge or catwalk to the pavilion; one must jump from the shore of the lake to its edge. A fountain, removed in 1977, further exaggerated the diminutive scale. This vertical water jet, intended to send a column of water nearly one hundred feet into the air, was at the center of the pond (fig. 325).

Reaction to the Water Pavilion was, at best, dismay. Kenneth Frampton wrote in *Architectural Design*, "One step further along the road to complete architectural decadence has now been taken by Philip Johnson, with yet another addition to his idyllic estate in New Canaan. Although it is passed off by the architect as a 'folly,' by virtue of its entirely false scale, it is, nonetheless, in its trivial historicism, quite typical of Johnson's recent work. It is indeed hard to believe that this is the same man who once designed and built the thirteen-year-old famous Glass House in which he still lives, or that a former admirer and collaborator of Mies can, in a few years, come to conceive such feeble forms as these."[103]

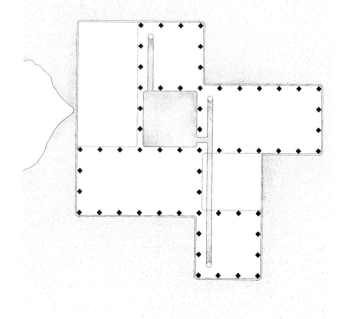

Footbridge, 1962
Painting Gallery, 1965

Johnson's response to this criticism, printed the same year in *Show Magazine*, was cheerfully sardonic: "The overtones of Puritan disapproval deriving from years of indoctrination in the 'only-useful-can-be-beautiful' philosophy show that some of the British have forgotten their glorious eighteenth-century heritage. We need more of this pointed, beautifully written criticism in this country!"[104] Yet his domestic architecture in the years following did not offer such an easy target. In 1965, at the same time he designed the Geier House outside Cincinnati to be largely underground, he undertook the next major pavilion on the Glass House estate: a pavilion devoted to contemporary painting (figs. 330–33), approached from the Glass House by way of a footbridge, which crosses a small stream bed (see fig. 311).

In the early 1960s, Johnson, with the assistance of his companion, David Whitney, had amassed a significant collection of contemporary art works. In order to exhibit them regularly, he devised a system of movable partitions on a circular system. The gallery is composed of three such circles, which allow partitions to

Painting Gallery
330 (top) View of entrance
331 (above) Site plan
332 (opposite, above) Gallery interior, view from entry
333 (opposite, below) Plan

rotate around a center column support. Thus six panels are visible at any one point from a central viewing area, yet they can be quickly reconfigured by hand to reveal another set of paintings. The site is the same location at one time considered for the Caretaker's Pavilion and the Dining Pavilion. The entrance faces down the hill, with a view of the Glass House. A ramp cut through the berms around two of the gallery cylinders provides entry, and is built of steel panels. Like the Geier House, the Painting Gallery is underground. While this certainly solved the problems that three large circles in plan would create in designing an elevation, it also precluded the issue of designing the elevation as well.

Sculpture Gallery, 1968–70

Five years later, Johnson completed the next major structure on the estate, this time a pavilion for sculpture. The design process involved at least two very different schemes, over nearly three years of work. The site is northwest of the Painting Gallery. In the first design, Johnson organized four distinct, rectangular gallery spaces along a linear circulation spine that descends with the slope of the hill (figs. 334–35). Each gallery would have been three feet lower than the previous one; a small storage/work area is separate from the gallery itself and provides a terminus to the approach leading to the gallery entrance. The sloped roofs are glass.

The version of the Sculpture Gallery that was built compresses the four separate galleries into one structure. Its spiraling circulation system descends as one moves through the space (figs. 336–39). The galleries alternate between purely rectangular spaces and rectangles with one wall turned on a forty-five-degree angle. Thus the perimeter of the structure is irregular, and a rich and varied spatial interior results. The exterior wall is brick painted white, and the entire roof is a gable of glazed panels in a brick-row pattern. Given the changing orientation of the galleries along the circulation spiral, one's perception of the light coming into the space from above is constantly changing. Johnson is able to use the differing orientations of the perimeter walls to shape the sense of light in each space and, ultimately, on each sculpture.

The response to the Sculpture Gallery was immediately positive. In *Time* Robert Hughes wrote, "Johnson's new sculpture gallery is a brilliant attack on the problem of how to avoid a long, boring, enfiladed room of sculpture without chopping the space up into unrelated cubicles. . . . The ambiguity of space, and its constant surprises, allows each sculpture to make its own zone of authority."[105]

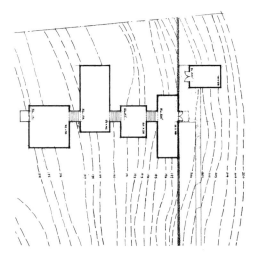

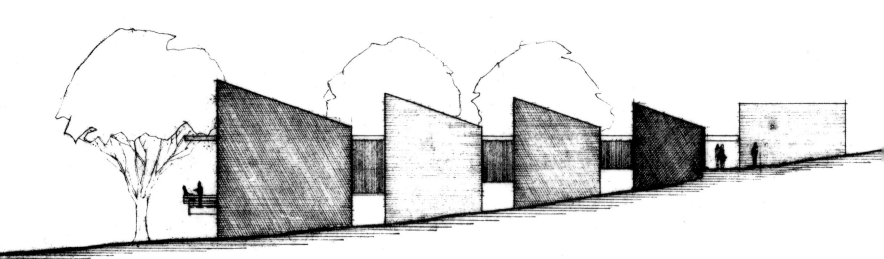

SOUTH ELEVATION

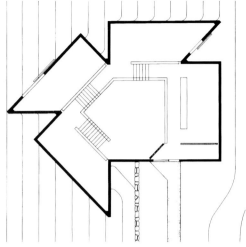

The Red House (project), 1977

By the late 1970s, new issues were emerging in Johnson's thoughts about the estate. Certainly he was examining other avenues for his living arrangements; this is the period when he considered both a vacation house in Big Sur and a pied-à-terre in Manhattan (see chapter 7). Additionally, he seems to have become more aware of energy efficiency in the wake of the mid-decade energy crisis. Two projects from this period reflect these concerns, drawing the architecture in closely around his private world and its workings. The first, from 1977, is a design for a house for his companion, David Whitney (figs. 340–42). The house was to be built at some distance south and east from the Glass House. Both its architecture and its appearance would have been striking: it was intended to be painted a "rich red—grenadine—which reads like one of the houses of the 1700s which was built nearby,"[106] thus earning the name "Red House." The plan is shaped like a horseshoe, and it is quite small: the living room is just twenty feet in length, which is its largest dimension. Yet it is a three-story house, with a living space that is nearly thirty feet high, which would have provided a sense of space more in keeping with a loft than a house. The curve of the horseshoe has three separate levels: a kitchen on the ground floor, bedroom on the second, and library at the top. Each of these spaces opens onto the three-story main space. Four square arches, successively narrowing, would have framed a view of the landscape to the south. Finally, three cylinders of varying heights, attached to the curve of the horseshoe, would have provided spaces for a bathroom, entry, and a circular stair. The only major fenestration for the Red House project are windows facing south; from all other points of view, the house would have been closed, a private place. As Jeffrey Kipnis has written, "Johnson presented the project as an ecological-mythological nest, discussing it as an odd mixture of mandalas, mysticism, and energy efficiency."[107]

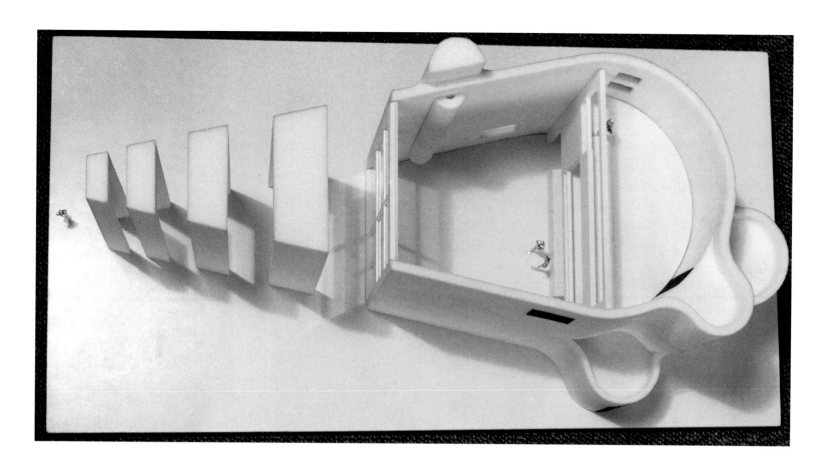

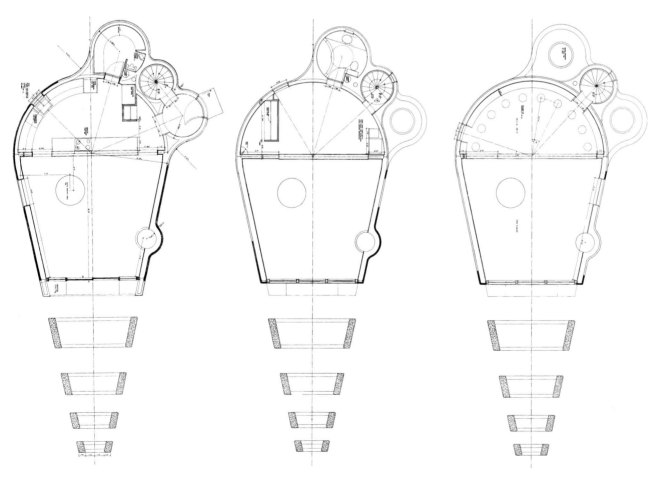

Studio/Library, 1978–80

Only a few years later, in 1980, Johnson built a different structure just up the hill from the intended site of the Red House. This time the program was even simpler: a studio for himself, a place to work alone without distraction (figs. 343–46). The most notable features are the volume of the studio and its scale. The interior is a single space; the exterior is dominated by two strong vertical elements: a rectangular chimney stack and a conical shape above a curved wall that protrudes from the main body of the studio. Both of these elements denote major features on the interior, even though they are integrated into the overall spatial conception. The fireplace under the chimney is a major feature along the west wall, while Johnson's work desk is located under the skylight at the top of the cone. Most of the walls are lined with bookshelves for his architecture library, and several of Frank Gehry's bentwood chairs surround the work desk. No other amenities are provided: no telephone, bathroom, kitchenette; the studio is only for work, a monastic retreat where Johnson can pursue architecture in isolation and without interruptions.

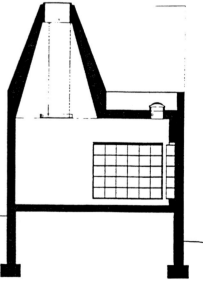

Studio/Library
343 (below left) View of Studio/Library, looking south from Glass House
344 (below right) Section

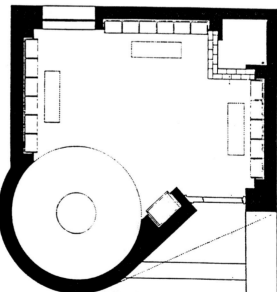

Studio/Library

345 (above) Interior of Studio/Library, view from Johnson's desk

346 (left) Plan

Gehry Ghost House, 1984

In 1984 Johnson designed and built a small enclosure of chain-link fence, down the hill from the Studio, and named it the Gehry Ghost House (fig. 347). It was built in honor of his friendship with Frank Gehry, who has used chain-link fencing to great effect in a number of his projects.[108] The "ghost house" is built on the foundation of an old farm building. The fifteen-foot square enclosure is used to protect young plants from the burgeoning deer population in the area. The form of the Gehry Ghost House is reminiscent of traditional New England architecture, and certainly Johnson was delighted to poke ironic fun at architecture of the past through the structure's name and use.

Gehry Ghost House
347

Lincoln Kirstein Tower, 1985

A year later, Johnson honored another close friend, Lincoln Kirstein. Kirstein had served as director of the New York City Ballet for many years and shared Johnson's strong appreciation for the arts and New York City. The construction is located across the pond from the Glass House, at the edge of a grove of trees (fig. 348). It is an abstract assemblage of cubic concrete blocks, eight inches on a side, which step up in an irregular path that one can climb to the top of the tower. But there is no handrail, and the path is only two bricks wide, so as one climbs higher, the ground seems dangerously far away. One is reminded of Johnson's assertion, at the time he was designing the Rockefeller Guest House, that a bit of danger can make one appreciate architecture to a much greater degree. Those with the fortitude to make it to the tower's top can read an inscription honoring Lincoln Kirstein on a small plaque embedded in the highest block.

Lincoln Kirstein Tower
348

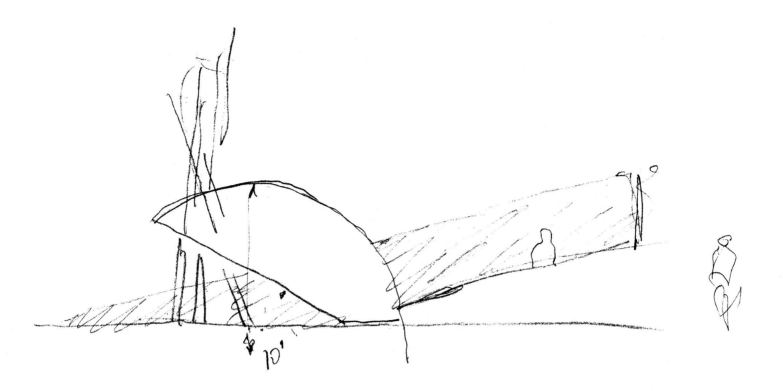

Deconstructivist Folly (project), 1988
Slat House (project), 1991

Deconstructivist Folly (project)
349 (above) Johnson sketch of elevation
350 (below) Plan and elevations ("9/14/1988")

Slat House (project)
351 (opposite) Model photograph

Two other small-scale projects for the estate, designed in 1988 and 1991, were not completed. They are,

respectively, the Deconstructivist Folly and the Slat House. The Folly, designed at the same time as the *Deconstructivist Architecture* exhibition at The Museum of Modern Art, marks Johnson's transition from historicism and postmodernism to an abstracted version of Russian Constructivism (figs. 349–50). A large fragment of a sphere, a rectangular length of brick wall, and a single pole are arranged in a composition that emphasizes the unstable way they intersect. Both the sphere and the wall cantilever out of a circular plinth raised slightly above grade. The Slat House combines a right-angle wall system with a curving wall that turns over the right angles to make a roof construction (fig. 351). Wood lath runs vertically on the walls, horizontally on the curved section of wall.

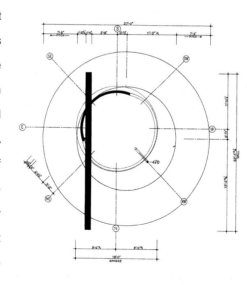

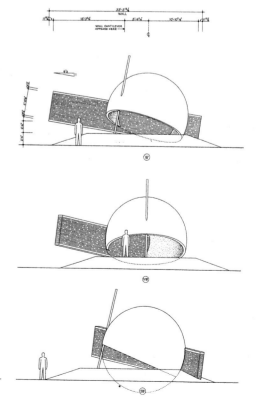

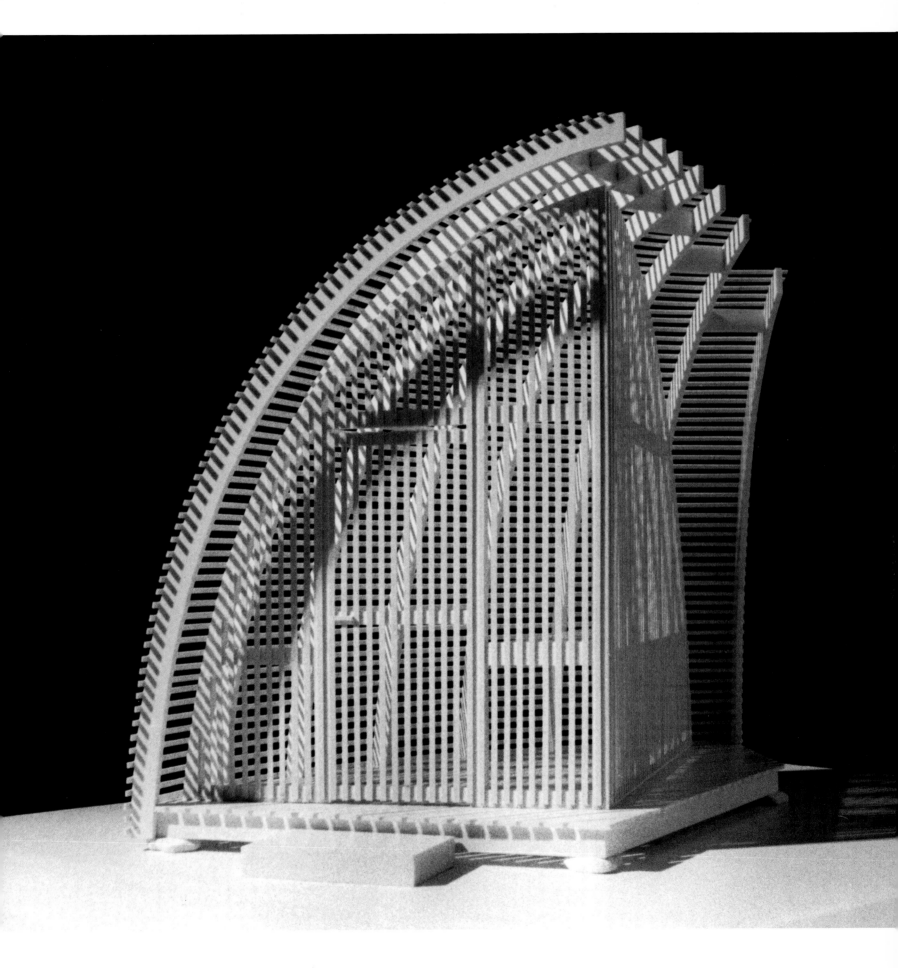

Visitors Pavilion, 1986–95

The most recent major addition to the estate is the Visitors Pavilion. Johnson has deeded the Glass House to the National Trust for Historic Preservation, and upon his death, the trust will administer the estate and provide tours for visitors. For much of its history, Johnson has been quite generous about allowing visitors access to the house. In addition to his weekend salons for architecture students, he would often accommodate occasional visitors: "I let anybody in—as long as they were friendly," he remarked recently.[109] However, as he has spent more time at the compound, and especially since he has now relocated from Manhattan to New Canaan, visitor access has been more limited.

The design for the Visitors Pavilion that was built was preceded by two very different designs. The initial one, drawn in 1986, was a shingled structure with a pitched roof and an immense circular window in the center of the facade (fig. 353). Obviously related closely to the House/Study project for Ronald Lauder of that same year, it included an octagonal viewing tower, like a wooden lighthouse.

The second design, from 1992, owed at least a part of its conception to the Slat House project. Like that project, a rigid right-angle wall system is a foil for a curving wall element (fig. 352). A separate roof canopy is held above the pavilion by a series of metal stanchions. Exterior ramps lead to interior stairs, allowing access to all three levels of the pavilion. The stair from the second to the roof levels actually moves out of the pavilion and attaches to a brick wall as it climbs to the roof, recalling the Lincoln Kirstein Tower.

Johnson's final design for the Visitors' Pavilion acquired the moniker "Monsta" during its construction (figs. 354–55). It is contemporaneous with the final design of the Starfish House, the 1992 project for the Lewis compound near Cleveland, and was thus nicknamed because it has the same sense of being a living organism. There are elements of Expressionism in the plan of the pavilion. Three separate programmatic elements merge: an entry and reception space, a small theater, and a service facilities area. The volumes of the spaces transform as one moves through the pavilion; from the exterior, a sense of scalelessness predominates, giving what is in reality a very small pavilion a much larger presence. The walls were constructed using a sprayed concrete system, and the forms of the few openings for door or windows are tied to the local circumstances immediately around them.

Visitors Pavilion
352 (above)   Second scheme, model photograph
353 (below)   First scheme, elevation

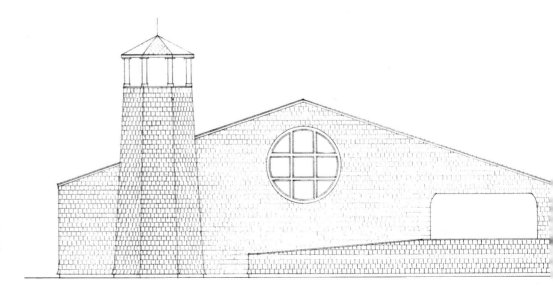

Yet Johnson also related this major pavilion, perhaps the last on the estate, to the first: the Glass House. Even though the Visitors Pavilion is largely composed of solid walls, its colors—red and black—resonate with the colors and tones Johnson used for the brick and bronze in the Glass House. The pavilion reads as a cave, the place from which human beings emerged to discover architecture; at the New Canaan compound, a visitor will emerge from the Visitors' Pavilion and make that same discovery when he finds the Glass House.[110]

Johnson's continual investigation into architecture on his estate is noteworthy for several reasons. By examining the series of New Canaan pavilion designs in the context of his other domestic work, we are privileged to glimpse the workings of his private laboratory, in which the pavilion projects were experiments for his new investigations into form and material. Just as significant is a reappraisal of the Glass House in the context of the half-century evolution of the compound. For all its iconic qualities, Johnson is continually altering the perception of the original Glass House by changing the context in which it is examined. This point extends not just to the varied structures which have been added to the estate since the Glass House was finished, but also to the way Johnson has used these pavilions to shape the landscape in between them. These relationships between architecture and nature distinguish Johnson's sense of proportion, one of his most profound gifts.

The New Canaan compound incorporates the best in American architecture of the last half-century. From the rich variety of forms which have been used to make architecture

to the timeless relation between a building and its land, Philip Johnson's Glass House and its sibling buildings represent a singular contribution to our architectural heritage. They represent the largest part of his ongoing investigation into American residential life in the twentieth century—and yet, we hope, not the only representation. For all the richness we find in the varied ways he has resolved the challenges of domestic architecture through the Glass House and its New Canaan siblings, this book also has attempted to show how much broader Johnson's efforts were. His extended family of houses, descendants in many cases of the Glass House yet reflecting his willingness to explore the entire range of architectural history, from its distant past to its present, is perhaps his greatest accomplishment as an architect.

Visitors Pavilion
354 (above) View of Visitors Pavilion
355 (pages 264–65) View of Visitors Pavilion, looking north

Notes

1. Philip Johnson, "100 Years, Frank Lloyd Wright, and Us" (speech to the Washington State Chapter of A.I.A.), *Pacific Architect and Builder* 13 (March 1957), 35–36; reprinted in Philip Johnson, *Writings: Philip Johnson* (New York: Oxford University Press, 1979), 196.

2. Franz Schulze, *Philip Johnson: Life and Work* (New York: Alfred A. Knopf, 1994), 224.

3. Kurt Andersen, "Philip the Great," *Vanity Fair*, June 1993.

4. Philip Johnson, interview with authors, New York City, 29 June 1993.

5. Schulze, *Johnson: Life and Work*, 151, 160.

6. Philip Johnson, interview with authors, New York City, 19 July 1993.

7. Schulze, *Johnson: Life and Work*, 149.

8. Johnson interview, 19 July 1993.

9. Ibid.

10. Ibid.

11. Schulze, *Johnson: Life and Work*, 151.

12. Johnson interview, 19 July 1993.

13. Ibid.

14. Johnson interview, 29 June 1993.

15. Ibid.

16. Ibid.

17. Ibid.

18. Ibid.

19. Schulze, *Johnson: Life and Work*, 187.

20. "Houses," *Architectural Forum* 79, no. 6 (December 1943), 91.

21. Schulze, *Johnson: Life and Work*, 171.

22. Philip Johnson, interview with authors, New York City, 7 July 1993.

23. Henry-Russell Hitchcock, *Philip Johnson: Architecture 1949–1965* (London: Thames and Hudson, 1966), 9.

24. Landis Gores, unpublished memoirs.

25. Johnson interview, 29 June 1993.

26. Ibid.

27. Richard Pratt, "As Simple as That," *Ladies' Home Journal*, July 1945, 118.

28. Johnson interview, 7 July 1993.

29. Ibid.

30. Ibid.

31. Schulze, *Johnson: Life and Work*, 156.

32. Johnson, interview, 7 July 1993.

33. Philip Johnson, "House at New Canaan, Connecticut. Philip Johnson: Architect," *Architectural Review* 108 (September 1950), 154.

34. Robert A.M. Stern, "The Evolution of Philip Johnson's Glass House, 1947–1948," *Oppositions* (fall 1977), 56–67.

35. Kenneth Frampton, "The Glass House Revisited," *Catalogue* 9 (September/October 1978), 38–51. Publication of The Institute for Architecture and Urban Studies, New York.

36. Schulze, *Johnson: Life and Work*, 191.

37. Philip Johnson, interview with the authors, New York City, 17 August 1993.

38. Philip Johnson, interview with the Stover Jenkins, New York City, 16 November 2000.

39. Schulze, *Johnson: Life and Work*, 187.

40. Philip Johnson, interview with the authors, New York City, 17 July 1993.

41. Philip Johnson, interview with the authors, New York City, 4 August 1993.

42. Kenneth Frampton, "The Glass House Revisited," in *Philip Johnson: The Glass House*, David Whitney and Jeffrey Kipnis, eds. (New York: Pantheon Books, 1993), 98.

43. Johnson interview, 19 July 1993.

44. Johnson interview, 17 August 1993.

45. Gores, unpublished memoirs.

46. Project description, 1948. Department of Architecture and Design, The Museum of Modern Art, New York.

47. Ibid.

48. Schulze, *Johnson: Life and Work*, 203.

49. Bernard Rudofsky, "New-World Xanadu of Steel and Glass: Pavilion and Swimming Pool," *Interiors* 108 (January 1949), 114–15.

50. Schulze, *Johnson: Life and Work*, 203.

51. Philip Johnson, interview with the authors, New York City, 18 August 1993.

52. Ibid.

53. The dimensions of the interior spaces match those of Mies's Tugendhat House almost exactly.

54. Gores, unpublished memoirs.

55. Johnson interview, 18 August 1993.

56. Ibid.

57. Ibid.

58. The teams of architects and artists were: Adolph Gottlieb with Marcel Breuer, David Hare with Frederick Kiesler, Hans Hoffman with José Luis Sert and Paul Wiener, Robert Motherwell with TAC, and William Baziotes with Philip Johnson. A small catalog was printed, regrettably without illustrations.

59. Kootz Gallery exhibition catalog, 1950.

60. Richard Meier, "Philip Johnson Festschrift," *Any: Architecture New York,* no. 90 (July 1996), 24.

61. Colin Rowe, "Neo-classicism and Modern Architecture I" (1956–57), in *The Mathematics of the Ideal Villa and Other Essays* (Cambridge, Mass.: MIT Press, 1976), 120.

62. Johnson interview, 18 August 1993.

63. Johnson often developed close relationships with his clients. Hodgson values his friendship with his architect, which has lasted for nearly half a century. And Johnson certainly looked after clients who had more interest in good architecture than resources to support it in their younger lives. For a number of years after the first

phase of the house was complete, Hodgson tended to the lawn and gardens himself—no small task for a five-acre spread. He recalled that one day, while he was mowing his lawn, a car turned off Ponus Ridge Road and drove directly over an area Hodgson had just seeded with grass. Shaking a rake, he ran across the yard to confront the driver, who instantly pulled the car back out onto the road and drove off. Just a few days later, at a dinner party at the Glass House, Hodgson was introduced to Mies van der Rohe. Mies informed Hodgson that he was pleased to meet him, had heard a great deal about his house, and was anxious to see it. In fact, said Mies, he had stopped by unannounced a few days before to see the house, but "Your gardener chased me off!"

64. Philip Johnson, Wadsworth Atheneum Fiftieth Anniversary Address, Hartford, Conn., 25 February 1984.

65. Johnson interview, 18 August 1993.

66. Schulze, *Johnson: Life and Work*, 214.

67. John Manley, interview with the authors, 30 September 1993.

68. Philip Johnson, "Wiley House, New Canaan, Connecticut, 1943," *Architectural Review* 127, no. 700 (April 1955), 241–42.

69. Robert Venturi, *Complexity and Contradiction in Architecture* (New York: The Museum of Modern Art, 1966), 25.

70. Johnson interview, 18 August 1993.

71. Arthur Drexler, "Town House Remodeled for an Art Collector,"

Interiors 116 (December 1950), 80–85.

72. Schulze, *Johnson: Life and Work*, 243.

73. Manley interview, 30 September 1993.

74. Schulze, *Johnson: Life and Work*, 250.

75. Manley, interview, 30 September 1993.

76. Schulze, *Johnson: Life and Work*, 220.

77. Johnson, "100 Years, Frank Lloyd Wright, and Us," in *Writings*, 196.

78. Philip Johnson, letter to I. M. Pei, 26 January 1954.

79. Harry Weese, "Publisher's Notebook," *Inland Architect* (March/April 1984), 59–60.

80. Philip Johnson, interview with the authors, New York City, 14 November 1993.

81. Philip Johnson, interview with the authors, New York City, 21 December 1993.

82. Ibid.

83. Ibid.

84. Ibid.

85. Schulze, *Johnson: Life and Work*, 216.

86. Philip Johnson, interview with the authors, New Canaan, 11 June 1994.

87. Philip Johnson, "Where Are We At?" (review of *Architecture, Nineteenth and Twentieth Centuries*, by Henry-Russell Hitchcock, and *Theory and Design in the First Machine Age*, by Reyner Banham), *Architectural Review* 128 (September 1960), 173–75.

88. Henry-Russell Hitchcock and Philip Johnson, *The International Style: Architecture Since 1922* (New York: W. W. Norton and Co., 1932), 119.

89. Johnson interview, 11 June 1994.

90. Manley interview, 30 September 1993.

91. Schulze, *Johnson: Life and Work*, 310.

92. Venturi, *Complexity and Contradiction in Architecture*, 22.

93. Johnson's office started another project about this time, which did not go very far, a house in Cleveland for real estate developer Richard Jacobs. The style of the project derived from the work of Karl Friedrich Schinkel; indeed, the drawings take their inspiration from Schinkel's to the extent that his rendering of vegetation is copied. Johnson's participation in the development of this design seems to have been minimal. In all likelihood, the project was sketched out by his staff and then reviewed by Johnson, who considered it to be "too formal in its plan and appearance," according to Christian Bjone, an architect with the firm at the time.

94. Philip Johnson and Mark Wigley, *Deconstructivist Architecture* (New York: The Museum of Modern Art, 1988), 7.

95. Ibid.

96. Philip Johnson, *Mies van der Rohe* (New York: The Museum of Modern Art, 1947), 21.

97. Manley interview, 5 December 2000.

98. Philip Johnson, interview with Stover Jenkins, New York City, 9 June 2000.

99. Rosamond Bernier, "Improving his View," *House and Garden* 158, no. 6 (June 1986), 120.

100. Ibid.

101. One keen-eyed observer has noted the resemblance between the gate with two circles and Johnson's trademark glasses.

102. Johnson interview, 11 June 1994.

103. Kenneth Frampton, *Architectural Design* (1963), reprinted in Frampton, "The Glass House Revisited," 93.

104. Philip Johnson, *Show Magazine* (1963), reprinted in Frampton, "The Glass House Revisited," 93.

105. Robert Hughes, "The Duke of Xanadu at Home," in *Philip Johnson: The Glass House*, 57.

106. Philip Johnson, *L'Architecture d'aujourd-hui*, 1978.

107. Jeffrey Kipnis, "Introduction: Throwing Stones—The Incidental Effects of a Glass House," in *Philip Johnson: The Glass House*, xxiv–xxv.

108. With its split gable, pipe-frame outline, and chain-link fencing, the Gehry Ghost House refers as much if not more to the work of Robert Venturi than to that of Frank Gehry.

109. Johnson interview, 17 August 1993.

110. The idea of the cave originated with Neil Levine during a visit to the compound in 1994, just after the Visitors Pavilion was completed.

Afterword

Philip Johnson's Glass House:
When Modernism Became History
Neil Levine

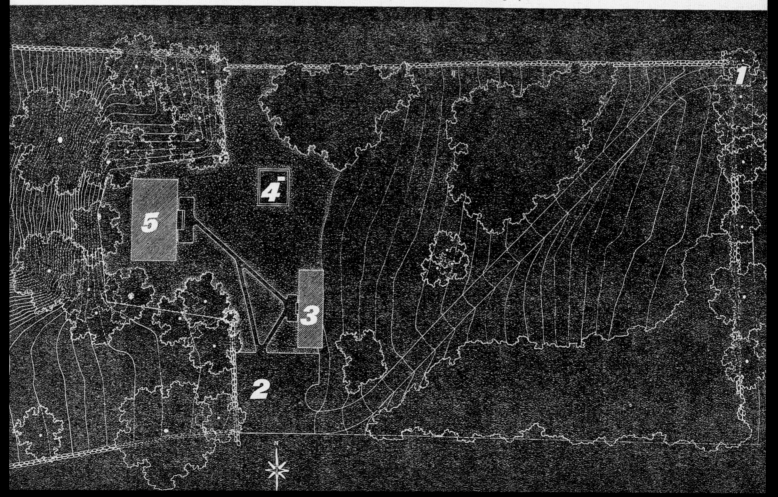

HOUSE AT NEW CANAAN, CONNECTICUT

PHILIP JOHNSON: ARCHITECT

The latest development in 'skin and bones' architecture* is Philip Johnson's glass house, which he has designed for his own occupation. Since the work is proclaimed by the architect as frankly derivative, in this publication of it and the adjacent guest building, Mr. Johnson has followed the unusual and, it should be granted, praiseworthy expedient of revealing the sources of his inspiration. These are presented in consecutive order, and precede the illustrations of the two houses. The commentary is Philip Johnson's own.

key to site plan 1. entrance to site. 2. car park. 3. guest house. 4. sculpture. 5. glass house.

* A phrase once used by Mies van der Rohe to describe the structural system of which he is the leading exponent.

It is almost impossible to think of modern architecture without thinking of Philip Johnson. For nearly three quarters of a century, he has played an instrumental role in its development. As a writer, critic, and museum curator in the 1930s, he helped to define and articulate for the American public the main outlines and characteristic features of the avant-garde work done in Europe by the generation that included Mies van der Rohe and Le Corbusier. After turning to the practice of architecture itself in the mid-1940s, he became a leading figure in the postwar institutionalization of modern design in American domestic life and corporate culture. From the mid-1970s on, he has served as a public spokesman and advocate for a succession of movements and debates that have shaped the course of recent architectural history, this in addition to producing some of the most notable buildings of the era.

Because of his extraordinary significance as a tastemaker and patron of the arts—whether through the agency of New York's Museum of Modern Art, the lecture halls and studios of America's major architecture schools, or a clientele that has included the Rockefellers, Henry Ford II, the de Menils and Schlumbergers, Walter Chrysler, Gerald Hines, Ronald Lauder, and Donald Trump—the subject of Johnson's actual accomplishments as an architect has often taken second place to an interest in his biography and his impact on contemporary intellectual and cultural history. While his influence can be compared with that of Lord Burlington in eighteenth-century England, Johnson should in no way be thought of as merely a critic or amateur. His architectural output has been enormous, and from the moment his Glass House in New Canaan, Connecticut, was completed in 1949, his buildings have attracted a great deal of interest and study.

The many transformations Johnson's architecture has undergone since the first house he built for himself, in Cambridge, Massachusetts, in 1941–42, have led observers to describe his work as eclectic, at best, and at worst as revealing a "quick-change artist," a "harlequin who forever changed the masks of style."[1] Most descriptions of his evolution consequently stress jarring and even inexplicable discontinuities rather than progressive and integral development. Johnson began his career as an architect as a devoted follower of Mies van der Rohe—so devoted to the German émigré's elegant minimalism that he referred to himself in his early years as "Mies van der Johnson." Not everyone is in agreement on when Johnson began to stray from the strictly Miesian line, but, because Mies's work seemed so rigorous and pure, Johnson's divagations have almost invariably been viewed as flagrant, senseless, and even immoral.

Johnson's biographer Franz Schulze points to the historically-derived, blatantly decorative arches and canopied vaults used in the redecoration of the Guest House (1952–53) on the New Canaan property as being the first sign of his apostasy. Shortly thereafter the same devices were publicly deployed in the Kneses Tifereth Israel Synagogue in Port Chester, New York (1954–56).[2] Johnson's close friend Henry-Russell Hitchcock, however, noting the doctrinaire Miesianism of buildings like the Leonhardt House in Lloyd's Neck, New York (1954–56), and the Auditorium and Classroom Buildings for the University of St. Thomas in Houston (1957), dates the definitive end of Johnson's "period of Miesian apprenticeship" to the years 1956–58 when, ironically enough, Johnson collaborated with the master on the Seagram Building in New York City.[3] Others, following the publication of his design for the AT&T Building in 1978, heralding a slew of corporate structures in ever-varying historicizing garb, associate Johnson's reneging on modernism with the postmodern fashion of the late 1970s and 1980s.[4] And though he ostensibly returned to the modernist fold in his designs of the 1990s, they no longer reflect Mies, but rather a theatrical Expressionism.

Regardless of when the break is said to have occurred, the supposed inconsistency and incoherence in Johnson's development is almost always seen as deriving from a historicism on his part that calls into question the fundamental principles of modernism. However, a study of Johnson's designs for private houses gives us a new perspective on the architect's career. Grouped mainly in the years 1945–65—the critical period in his struggle with the Miesian legacy—they reveal an architect intensely engaged with the problems that arise in planning the modern living environment who discovers ever more subtle and elegant structural and compositional solutions. His adaptation of multiple residential types, ranging

(opposite)
**"House at New Canaan, Connecticut
Philip Johnson: Architect"**
Architectural Review 108 (September 1950)
Title page of the article showing a site plan of the New Canaan compound. The article comprised a sequence of 22 numbered images, 21 of which are reproduced beginning on page 272.

from the Miesian court-house and the more traditional atrium model to the zoned, binuclear, and walled or village compound types, suggests a complex pattern of thought involving references to the architecture not only of Mies, but of Wright, Breuer, and Gropius, as well as many of Johnson's peers. Most importantly, we are able to see in Johnson's houses, and especially the ones he designed for himself, more precisely than in any other group of his buildings, how Johnson worked, deliberately and progressively, initially to revise and ultimately to radically alter the very conception of modern architecture he had once set out to promote.

During the first two decades of Johnson's practice, domestic commissions outnumbered all others by about four to one. That figure was more than reversed in the early 1960s when he began receiving commissions for museums, university buildings, theaters, libraries, and the like. That change not only reflects the typical career of a young architect growing into maturity but also characterizes the trajectory of modern architecture as a whole as it moved toward general acceptance in the later 1950s. When Walter Curt Behrendt declared "the victory of the new building style" in his 1927 book of that title, he was naively optimistic. The buildings in Johnson and Hitchcock's International Style exhibition held at New York's Museum of Modern Art in 1932 perforce included almost no significant civic or corporate structures. There were apartment houses and clubhouses of different sorts, but the majority of the principal examples were single-family houses for the upper-middle or upper class. In the MoMA exhibition *Built in USA: Post-war Architecture*, organized by Hitchcock, at Johnson's invitation, on the twentieth anniversary of the 1932 show, single-family houses, more often than not of a rather expensive sort, still far outnumbered any other type. Indeed, both Vincent Scully and William Jordy have convincingly described the immediate prewar and postwar years, when suburbanization took hold of the country, as a period during which domestic architecture attracted the most serious attention from modern architects. For Jordy, who was more positive about the trend than Scully, the focus on the single-family house was so definitive that he felt one could even speak of the "domestication of the International Style" as one of the consequences.[5]

For many obvious reasons, ranging from the political to the economic and cultural, America led the world in this domestication of modern architecture. Professional publications on the subject of the modern house proliferated as never before.[6] In 1956, *Architectural Record* instituted a separate annual issue of the journal, entitled *Record Houses*, entirely devoted to new domestic designs by leading architects. Jordy noted the tremendous outpouring of creative thought and energy in the area. "In the creation of new house types, no previous decade and a half in American architectural history can compare in inventiveness with that from roughly 1935–50," he wrote.[7] There were the Breuer binuclear type, the Wright Usonian house, the Bay Region Style, the Los Angeles Case Study Houses, and the Miesian "skin and bones" pavilion and court-house types. When Johnson entered the Graduate School of Design at Harvard in 1940, the neo-Bauhaus curriculum instituted by Walter Gropius and Marcel Breuer put great emphasis on domestic architecture and the suburban, community-oriented issues related to it. Although only half of Johnson's known studio projects were for residential structures, it is significant that, in a recent interview, he recalled all of them as having been for houses of one sort or another.[8] The most important of these was the design of the house he actually built for himself on Ash Street in Cambridge, which he submitted as his final thesis project in 1943 after being drafted into the army.

In many ways domestic architecture represented for the modern movement an ideal basis for the reform and total redesign of the living environment. In the transplanted American version of the Bauhaus, the privately-owned single-family house came to occupy the prominent position that government-sponsored collective housing had represented in the thought of European architects in the twenties and early thirties. In fact, one of the first things that both Gropius and Breuer did upon taking up their posts at Harvard in 1937 was design houses for themselves in the well-to-do Boston suburb of Lincoln. Their decision to showcase the new architecture in this way also forms part of a larger and peculiarly American phenomenon. Given the relative conservatism of the client base, along with the vagaries of popular taste, it is hardly surprising that the architect's own house became an especially favored place for experimentation, self-representation, and self-promotion.

The tradition of architects designing their own houses as a combined form of advertising and self-expression is fundamentally modern, originating largely in Anglo-American culture. A precocious and rather eccentric instance is the small, picturesque, mock-medieval "castle" that John Vanbrugh built for himself in the London suburb of Greenwich in the early eighteenth century. Although amateurs like Lord Burlington at Chiswick (working in collaboration with William Kent) and Thomas Jefferson at Monticello followed suit, it was not until John Soane began designing his house in London at the very end of the eighteenth century that the type really became established in the historical record. Used as a studio and a "teaching museum" as well as a residence, the Soane house was intended not only to be a sign of its designer's creative genius during his lifetime but also a lasting monument to him through his bequest of it to the nation. Opposite to Soane in almost every way, and viciously critical of his architecture, Augustus Welby Pugin nevertheless understood the image-value of his predecessor's house (which he caustically referred to as "the professor's own house") and constructed his own residence-cum-studio on the outskirts of Ramsgate on the English Channel coast in the mid-1840s, shortly after Soane died.[9] Composed of a Gothic villa with workshops and private chapel appended, Pugin's monastery-like grouping established the type's suburban or rural version, which would become the preferred one in the twentieth century.

Although some continental European architects, like Viollet-le-Duc and Otto Wagner, made the design of their combined residences and studios a significant aspect of their professional profile, it was only with Frank Lloyd Wright that the domestic type became fully identified once again, as it had been with Soane and Pugin, with the architect's design philosophy and approach to life. Wright's first significant building was, in fact, the Oak Park house he designed for himself and his family in 1889. Less than ten years later, he added to this modest Shingle Style structure a studio that was more radical in design and that also announced to the public the removal of his practice to the more bucolic setting of the suburbs. But it is only with the house and studio he began building in 1911 in rural south-central Wisconsin that Wright consolidated the model of the architect's residence as laboratory and showcase that would prove to be so compelling for successive modern architects. Taliesin expressed in its form and in its relationship to the landscape Wright's conception of a "natural architecture." As the place where prospective clients would be introduced to his work, and where journalists, critics (including Johnson in 1932), professional colleagues, and friends would be entertained, Taliesin functioned as a prototype of Wright's architecture, almost the way a "model home" would serve a real-estate developer.

By 1938, when Wright began construction in Arizona of Taliesin West, the desert dwelling that would serve as his winter headquarters for the rest of his life, other architects had followed his example. Two of the most notable are Rudolf Schindler and Richard Neutra, both of whom had emigrated from Vienna and worked for Wright while living at Taliesin. Schindler designed and built his King's Road House in West Hollywood in 1921–22 as an experiment in communal living and working that can be traced both in its ideology and style to his experiences with Wright. After leaving Taliesin, Neutra and his family shared the King's Road House with the Schindlers for about five years before eventually building their own house in the Silverlake district of Los Angeles, beginning in 1932. The VDL Research House, as it was called after the Dutch industrialist C. H. Van der Leeuw who helped finance it, was explicitly meant to show how new materials and new technologies could be incorporated into the construction of the modern dwelling.

It was not only in the orbit of Wright that the architect's own house became an issue of importance. As mentioned, both Gropius and Breuer began building their houses almost as soon as they arrived at Harvard, thus providing American students and enthusiasts of European modernism with authentic examples of how the International Style might be locally interpreted. Within the same Lincoln development at about the same time, the Swiss-born Walter Bogner, another of Johnson's teachers at the Graduate School of Design, also constructed a house for himself. The exemplary status of these designs in the school's curriculum is attested to by the fact that one of the studio problems Johnson was assigned in 1941 was, precisely, "A House in Lincoln [Massachusetts]" (fig. 18). In a curriculum dominated by Gropius and Breuer, it was as abnormal for Johnson to rely on Mies's example in designing his own Cambridge house as it was for him to offer a real building as his thesis project. Nevertheless, the choice of the architect's house as a type was clearly in line with the pedagogical imperatives of the modern movement in America. Indeed, by the time Johnson completed the second house he designed for himself and the one for which he is most famous, the Glass House, his former teacher Marcel Breuer had built himself a new house (1947) in the same town of New Canaan, and Johnson's former Harvard schoolmate John Johansen was in the process of designing his own house next door to Johnson's (1949–50). And almost exactly paralleling the nearly five-year design and construction period of the Glass House was Charles and Ray Eames's nearly equally celebrated steel and glass house in Pacific Palisades, California, begun in 1945 and completed in 1949.

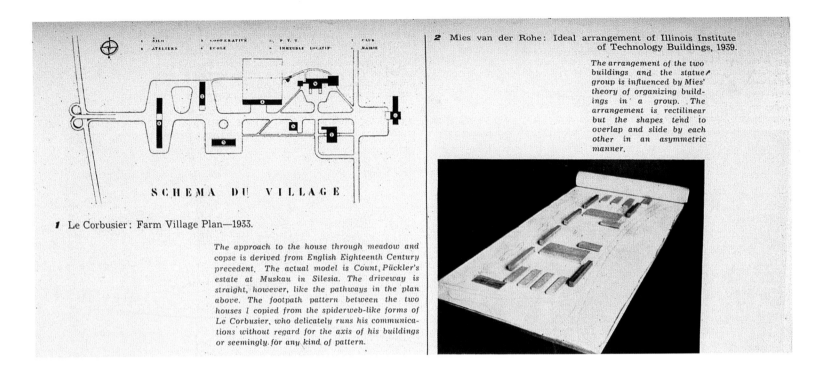

1 Le Corbusier: Farm Village Plan—1933.

The approach to the house through meadow and copse is derived from English Eighteenth Century precedent. The actual model is Count Pückler's estate at Muskau in Silesia. The driveway is straight, however, like the pathways in the plan above. The footpath pattern between the two houses I copied from the spiderweb-like forms of Le Corbusier, who delicately runs his communications without regard for the axis of his buildings or seemingly for any kind of pattern.

2 Mies van der Rohe: Ideal arrangement of Illinois Institute of Technology Buildings, 1939.

The arrangement of the two buildings and the statue group is influenced by Mies' theory of organizing buildings in a group. The arrangement is rectilinear but the shapes tend to overlap and slide by each other in an asymmetric manner.

Johnson's two houses differ from earlier and contemporaneous architects' houses by their willful formal clarity and purity. They are polemical and speculative rather than simply experimental or self-expressive. The schematic realization of an ideal Miesian court-house in the first one and the dynamic juxtaposition of two prismatic pavilions—one glass and transparent, the other brick and opaque—in the second both affirm the notion of architecture as an autonomous discipline. In the Ash Street House, the context of the Brattle Street neighborhood is entirely foreclosed by the high blank wall that enforces the self-contained character of the roofed and unroofed living spaces (fig. 26). The two discrete volumes on the grassy ledge of the New Canaan property barely reveal how they might be inhabited, even though the more prominent of them is conspicuously open to view (fig. 112). When Johnson's Cambridge house was published in late 1943, the editor for *Architectural Forum* remarked on the characteristics that make the design quintessentially modern, namely, the "tendency to simplify, through standardization and repetition, and through elimination of every element which might possibly be left out" and a "flexibility" resulting from "the structural system, which creates a roof on isolated posts" that allows "partitions, exterior walls, closets, etc., [to be] positioned with complete freedom." Although "many elements" of the house "have been popular and will become more so," the writer emphasized that this was no "model home" in the conventional meaning of the words: "For an average U. S. family this house would be almost totally unlivable." Noting the "complete formality of the basic design," the writer elaborated: "Nothing is casual; nothing is accidental. Few people would be at ease in so disciplined a background for everyday living. But the architect . . . was not concerned with the requirements of anybody except himself."[10]

To assume, as readers at the time might, that the "requirements" that concerned Johnson were practical rather than aesthetic would be to miss the polemical and speculative point of the design. So when it came to his later New Canaan house, Johnson made sure that he controlled the public reception of the work. The English *Architectural Review* had been publishing houses by American architects at a steady rate during the later 1940s and early 1950s. As was true in comparable American publications, the articles, normally about five pages long, were composed mainly of photographs accompanied by two or three paragraphs of text. The descriptive text was invariably unsigned and written by one of the magazine's editors. The publication of Johnson's "House at New Canaan, Connecticut" in the September 1950 issue was highly unusual in a variety of ways. Aside from its length, which is eight pages, the article is laid out horizontally rather than vertically. Following a full-page site plan, it is organized in a sequence of twenty-two numbered images accompanied by captions and brief texts. Two of the images occupy a full page, with the accompanying captions and text found on the opposite page; the rest are quarter-page frames,

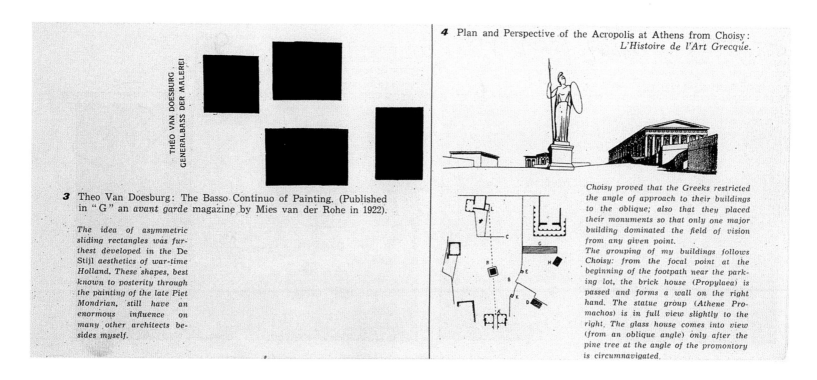

3 Theo Van Doesburg: The Basso-Continuo of Painting. (Published in "G" an *avant garde* magazine by Mies van der Rohe in 1922).

The idea of asymmetric sliding rectangles was furthest developed in the De Stijl aesthetics of war-time Holland. These shapes, best known to posterity through the painting of the late Piet Mondrian, still have an enormous influence on many other architects besides myself.

4 Plan and Perspective of the Acropolis at Athens from Choisy: *L'Histoire de l'Art Grecque.*

Choisy proved that the Greeks restricted the angle of approach to their buildings to the oblique; also that they placed their monuments so that only one major building dominated the field of vision from any given point.
The grouping of my buildings follows Choisy: from the focal point at the beginning of the footpath near the parking lot, the brick house (Propylaea) is passed and forms a wall on the right hand. The statue group (Athene Promachos) is in full view slightly to the right. The glass house comes into view (from an oblique angle) only after the pine tree at the angle of the promontory is circumnavigated.

separated by vertical and horizontal rules. Most importantly, the text was written by Johnson himself. To signal the uniqueness of the presentation, while justifying its own editorial abdication, the *Review* noted, in an introductory paragraph:

> Since the work [the Glass House] is proclaimed by the architect as frankly derivative, in this publication of it and the adjacent guest building, Mr. Johnson has followed the unusual and, it should be granted, praiseworthy expedient of revealing the sources of his inspiration. . . . The commentary is Philip Johnson's own.[11]

The article, whose text and illustrations are reproduced on these pages, begins on a verso so that the whole piece can be perceived and read as four double-page spreads. Each of the four is composed as an integral unit; and from the first to the last there is a visual and narrative progression from exterior to interior, from plan to realization. The opening site plan (page 268) is printed as a negative, white on black. More than half the space of the page is taken up by the diagonal access road crossing a sloping terrain from the top right corner to the bottom center. The positive and negative shapes of the car park, Guest House, sculpture garden, and Glass House pinwheel over to the edge of the page and the ledge. Opposite the site plan are the first four boxes of images and text, reproduced above.

Instead of showing more detailed aspects of the site plan itself or sketches by the architect clarifying how he arrived at the final idea, these frames contain images of plans and drawings by other architects and artists accompanied by extended captions that explain their relevance to Johnson's design. Functioning in a way analogous to footnotes, they are used by Johnson in the "self-annotative manner of T. S. Eliot's *The Waste Land*," as Robert Stern has noted.[12]

Frame 1 shows a plan of Le Corbusier's relatively little-known Cooperative Farm Village project of the mid-1930s, a loose arrangement of structures along a linear cul-de-sac. Johnson first notes that his own site plan "is derived from English Eighteenth Century precedent," although "the actual model is Count Pückler's estate at Muskau in Silesia" (Hermann Fürst von Pückler-Muskau was a friend and disciple of the landscape architect Peter Joseph Lenné and a member of the Schinkel circle). Assuming that the professional or academic reader would know of Le Corbusier's debt to eighteenth-century English ideas of the picturesque and thus logically see him in a mediating role, Johnson skips over the connection to point to the similarity between the straightness of the driveway at the New Canaan property and the pathways in the Corbusier plan. "The footpath pattern between the two houses [the Guest and Glass Houses]," he adds, "I copied from the spider-web-like forms of Le Corbusier, who delicately runs his communications without regard for the axis of his buildings or seemingly for any kind of pattern."[13]

5 Karl Friedrich Schinkel: Casino in Glienicke Park near Potsdam c. 1830. Entrance façade.

The site relation of my house is pure Neo-Classic Romantic—more specifically, Schinkelesque. Like his Casino my house is approached on dead-level and, like his, faces its principal (rear) façade toward a sharp bluff.

6 Karl Friedrich Schinkel: Casino in Glienicke Park near Potsdam c. 1830. Terrace overlooking the Havel.

The Eighteenth Century preferred more regular sites than this and the Post-Romantic Revivalists preferred hill tops to the cliff edges or shelves of the Romantics (Frank Lloyd Wright, that great Romantic. prefers shelves or hillsides).

Frame 2 continues the dialogue about what was then called group planning but refers to a better-known though perhaps still unexpected precedent, given its vastly different scale and program. The image is of one of the preliminary site models Mies did in 1939 for the campus of the Illinois (then Armour) Institute of Technology. When it was published in his book on Mies that accompanied the exhibition of the architect's work he organized at MoMA in 1947, Johnson noted how "the buildings are . . . grouped around a central plaza in such a way that they create a continuous interchange of open and closed spaces. This interwoven effect is achieved by the simple but highly original device of sliding adjacent units past one another, rather than placing them side by side. The plazas thus defined, without being closed, combine the intimacy of the courts, say, at Oxford, with the clarity of a classically arranged campus such as Jefferson's University of Virginia."[14] In the text of the *Review*, Johnson condensed the analysis mainly to affirm that his "arrangement of the two buildings and the statue group [in New Canaan] is influenced by Mies' theory of organizing buildings" so that "the shapes tend to overlap and slide by each other in an asymmetric manner."

The succeeding two frames expand on the artistic and perceptual ramifications of the Miesian and Corbusian planning techniques. Frame 3 links Mies to the De Stijl movement through a work by Theo Van Doesburg published in 1923 (not 1922) in *G,* a magazine with which Mies

was closely associated. The asymmetric composition of four differently-sized rectangles in the Van Doesburg mirrors the composition of car park, Guest House, sculpture garden, and Glass House in the plan of the Johnson property on the opposite page and, by Johnson's own admission, represents the "enormous influence" of the De Stijl aesthetic on all of modern architecture. The final frame in this series shows the plan and perspective of the Athenian Acropolis, from Auguste Choisy's *Histoire de l'architecture* (1899), that Le Corbusier made famous in his *Vers une architecture* of 1923. Johnson remarks that "the grouping of [his own] buildings follows Choisy" in the latter's analysis of the way the Greeks planned their sacred sites so that the approach to a building was always at an oblique angle and "only one major building dominated the field of vision from any given point." Johnson describes how the Corbusier/Choisy method is applied to create a continuous spatio-temporal pattern of movement (what Johnson would later call "the processional element in architecture") in New Canaan.[15]

The double-page spread containing frames 5 through 12 focuses on the siting, planning, and construction of the two main buildings, pairing three-dimensional images of sources for ideas on the verso with two-dimensional ones on the recto. Frames 5 and 6, above, are both photographs of the Romantic-Classical Casino built in Schloss Glienicke Park by Karl Friedrich Schinkel in 1824–25. The first shows the small two-story building head-on, from the entrance side; the second shows it at an angle from

Claude Nicholas Ledoux: Maison des Gardes Agricoles, at Maupertuis
c. 1780.

*The cubic, "absolute" form of my glass house, and the separa-
tion of functional units into two absolute shapes rather than a
major and minor massing of parts comes directly from Ledoux,
the Eighteenth Century father of modern architecture. (See Emil
Kaufmann's excellent study Von Ledoux bis Le Corbusier.)
The cube and the sphere, the pure mathematical shapes, were
dear to the hearts of those intellectual revolutionaries from the
Baroque, and we are their descendants.*

8 Mies van der Rohe: Farnsworth House, 1947. (Now under construction
near Chicago).

*The idea of a glass house comes from Mies van der Rohe. Mies
had mentioned to me as early as 1945 how easy it would be to
build a house entirely of large sheets of glass. I was sceptical
at the time, and it was not until I had seen the sketches of the
Farnsworth House that I started the three-year work of designing my glass house. My debt is therefore clear, in spite of
obvious difference in composition and relation to the ground.*

below the terrace overlooking the Havel River. Johnson remarks that his own Glass House is sited "in a pure Neo-Classic Romantic—more specifically, Schinkelesque" manner. "Like his Casino, my house is approached on dead-level and . . . faces its principal (rear) facade toward a sharp bluff." To reinforce the affinity, Johnson notes how pre-Romantic architects of the eighteenth century preferred flat "regular sites," while post-Romantics "preferred hill tops to the cliff edges or shelves of the Romantics." He acknowledges that, like Schinkel, "Frank Lloyd Wright, that great Romantic, prefers shelves or hillsides," but does so only parenthetically and without reference to Taliesin, the example that was most relevant in this case and surely not far from his mind.

The next two images (above) shift gears abruptly. The perspective of Claude Nicolas Ledoux's late eighteenth-century project for a spherical House of the Agricultural Guards of Maupertuis and the model of Mies's Farnsworth House in Plano, Illinois, conceived in 1945 and built in 1949–51, become exemplars for a modernist architecture of pure geometric shapes. Johnson states that "the cubic, 'absolute' form of my glass house, and the separation of [the] functional units" of Glass House and Guest House "into two absolute shapes . . . comes directly from Ledoux." Once again, Le Corbusier is the mediator. Johnson refers to Emil Kaufmann's 1933 book *Von Ledoux bis Le Corbusier* to justify his reference to Ledoux as "the Eighteenth Century father of modern architecture" in his invention of an

architecture of "pure mathematical shapes." The model of Mies's Farnsworth House, on the other hand, which Johnson had included in his Mies exhibition of three years before, takes the abstract idea of pure geometry and gives it a material and structural basis in International Style modernism. Johnson acknowledges forthrightly that "the idea of a glass house comes from Mies," who "had mentioned to me as early as 1945 how easy it would be to build a house entirely of large sheets of glass." Though "skeptical at the time," Johnson says that when he saw the "sketches of the Farnsworth House" he "started the three-year work of designing [his own] glass house." He concludes this tribute by noting that his "debt is therefore clear, in spite of obvious differences in composition and relation to the ground."

A horizontal section of the corner detail of the Glass House comes next (page 276), directly opposite the Ledoux project and diagonally across from the Farnsworth House. Although it is the first of the framed images to reflect Johnson's own designs, he immediately gives credit to Mies once again in stating that "many details of the [Glass] house are adapted from Mies' work, especially the corner treatment and the relation of the column to the window frames." He adds that the typically Miesian use of "standard steel sections" provides "a strong and at the same time decorative finish to the façade" that may well prove to be the only appropriate kind of "'decoration'" for modern architecture—while wondering aloud if such "manipulation" of structural elements might not also soon lead to mannerism.

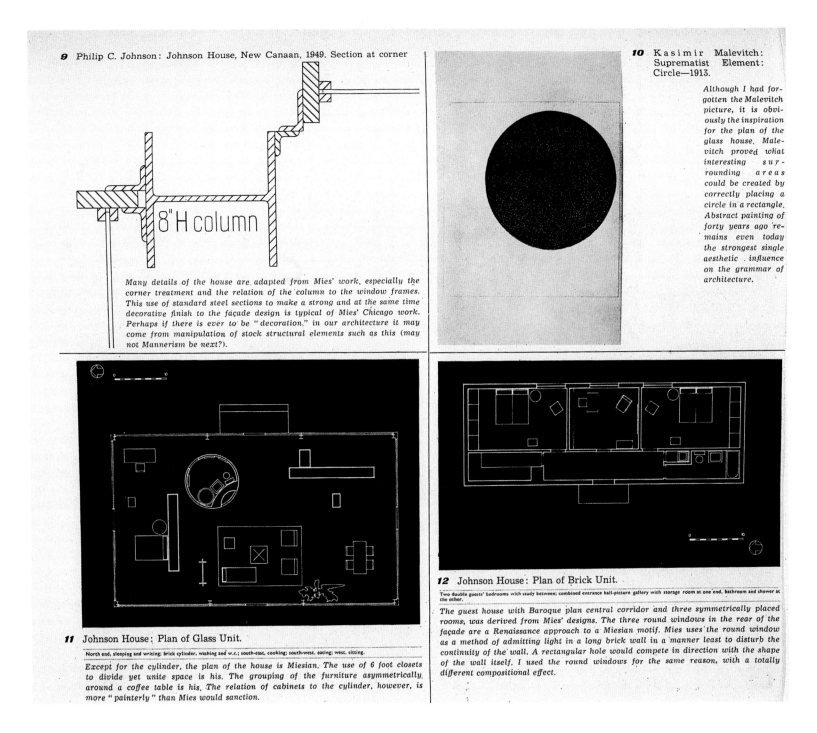

9 Philip C. Johnson: Johnson House, New Canaan, 1949. Section at corner

8" H column

Many details of the house are adapted from Mies' work, especially the corner treatment and the relation of the column to the window frames. This use of standard steel sections to make a strong and at the same time decorative finish to the façade design is typical of Mies' Chicago work. Perhaps if there is ever to be "decoration" in our architecture it may come from manipulation of stock structural elements such as this (may not Mannerism be next?).

10 Kasimir Malevitch: Suprematist Element: Circle—1913.

Although I had forgotten the Malevitch picture, it is obviously the inspiration for the plan of the glass house. Malevitch proved what interesting surrounding areas could be created by correctly placing a circle in a rectangle. Abstract painting of forty years ago remains even today the strongest single aesthetic influence on the grammar of architecture.

11 Johnson House: Plan of Glass Unit.

North end, sleeping and writing; brick cylinder, washing and w.c.; south-east, cooking; south-west, eating; west, sitting.

Except for the cylinder, the plan of the house is Miesian. The use of 6 foot closets to divide yet unite space is his. The grouping of the furniture asymmetrically, around a coffee table is his. The relation of cabinets to the cylinder, however, is more "painterly" than Mies would sanction.

12 Johnson House: Plan of Brick Unit.

Two double guests' bedrooms with study between; combined entrance hall-picture gallery with storage room at one end, bathroom and shower at the other.

The guest house with Baroque plan central corridor and three symmetrically placed rooms, was derived from Mies' designs. The three round windows in the rear of the façade are a Renaissance approach to a Miesian motif. Mies uses the round window as a method of admitting light in a long brick wall in a manner least to disturb the continuity of the wall. A rectangular hole would compete in direction with the shape of the wall itself. I used the round windows for the same reason, with a totally different compositional effect.

The next image, in frame 10 (above), presented in the original layout so that it is juxtaposed with the Farnsworth House and the Ledoux project, is the Suprematist painting *Black Circle* by Kasimir Malevich, done around 1923 though dated by the artist (and Johnson) much earlier. Like the Van Doesburg, it affirms abstract painting's role in the development of modern architecture. In the accompanying text, Johnson claims: "Abstract painting of forty years ago remains even today the strongest single aesthetic influence on the grammar of architecture." But in contrast to the Van Doesburg, which bears a close historiographic connection to Mies, the Malevich stands on its own as a non-Miesian, even anti-Miesian, source for the Glass House plan. In a phrase pregnant with psychological implications as well as chronological questions, Johnson states that, "although I had forgotten the Malevich picture, it is obviously the inspiration for the plan of the glass house." Is Johnson saying that he only remembered the painting after completing the design—which would be a strange way of putting it—or is he saying that the significance of the Malevich was pointed out to him by someone else? Just as strange is the fact that the reference precedes the first image the reader is given of the plan itself.

No doubt for reasons of comparison, the plans of the "Glass Unit" and the "Brick Unit" are placed side by side in frames 11 and 12 (opposite, below). In describing the first, Johnson amends the absoluteness of his reference to Malevich by saying that, "except for the cylinder [containing the fireplace and bathroom] the plan of the [Glass] house is Miesian." In fact, not only is the basic idea of the plan owed to Mies, but "the use of 6 foot closets to divide yet unite space is his" and "the grouping of the furniture asymmetrically around the coffee table [also] is his." Malevich's offset circle marks the only deviation. "The relation of cabinets to the cylinder," Johnson avers, "is more 'painterly' than Mies would sanction." The plan of the brick Guest House is likewise credited almost entirely to Mies's influence, albeit with certain modifications that may well be attributable to the more traditional masonry structure of the building. Johnson states that "the guest house with Baroque plan central corridor and three symmetrically placed rooms was derived from Mies' designs," while "the three round windows in the rear of the facade are a Renaissance approach to a Miesian motif," explaining that Mies used round windows so as not "to disturb the continuity of the wall."

The next double-page spread, containing images 13–17 (page 278), begins the photographic coverage of the property and dispenses with images of influences and sources, though not with textual references to them. Entirely devoted to exterior views of the buildings, the sequence starts with a full-page image of the north end of the west wall taken by Arnold Newman (not reproduced). At the base of the picture is Philip Johnson himself, seen from the back and in silhouette, sitting in a Mies chair at his desk, with a book in his hands. The interior scene is overlaid with reflections of trees on the glass wall in the foreground and on the wall in front of Johnson that opens onto a view of the landscape to the east. Transparency, reflectivity, and opacity combine to create a collage-like picture of ambiguous, shifting meanings. Despite the very personal implications of the image, Johnson once again credits Mies as the source for the idea of using reflections to "give glass a type of solidity," and he quotes Mies's remarks on the Friedrichstrasse glass skyscraper project of the early 1920s to this effect.

The Newman photograph of Johnson at his desk in the Glass House functions as a lens to bring into focus the following sequence of exterior views, and thereby reinforce the fact that it is Johnson himself who is analyzing and explaining their design. Frames 14 and 16 illustrate the relationship between the Glass House and the Guest House as seen from opposite directions. Frames 15 and 17 zoom in on the Glass House in the daytime and at night in what amount to inversions of the view in frame 16. The photographs of the actual buildings prompt Johnson to emphasize the classical aspects of their design as much as the purely modernist, Miesian ones. He notes that "the bi-axial symmetry of each façade of the glass house is as absolute as Ledoux and much purer than any Baroque example," although the placement of the front door in the long elevation could be considered a "slight leftover of [the] Baroque." On the other hand, "the guest house with central door and severely axial plan is jointly descended from the Baroque and from designs by Mies."

The image of the Glass House at night in frame 17 terminates the discussion of the exterior on a quite different note. The brick cylinder takes on a powerful and foreboding appearance in silhouette, which offers Johnson the occasion to expand even further on the idiosyncrasy of its use. Revisiting the earlier non-Miesian reference to Malevich, Johnson states that "the cylinder, . . . forming the main motif of the house, was not derived from Mies, but rather from a burnt wooden village I saw once where nothing was left but foundations and chimneys of brick." Without elaborating any further on where or when this vision occurred, or why he thought its memory had a place in this design, Johnson dispassionately remarks: "Over the chimney I slipped a steel cage with a glass skin. The chimney forms the anchor." The reference to the ruined village is the only one to the vernacular and the only anonymous one in the article.

The cylindrical fireplace-bathroom core barely appears in any of the five photographs of the interior that make up the final double-page spread. Frame 18 (page 279, top left), a single full-page image on the verso, a light and airy wide-angled view from a relatively low point of view, shows the main space of the Glass House looking south across the living room area toward the dining table and the kitchen. A candelabra designed by Johnson, which goes unattributed in the text, borders the view on the left. A grouping of Mies furniture from the Tugendhat House and the Barcelona Pavilion completely fills the foreground and mid-ground of the picture. Aside from the small Giacometti plaster figure, titled *Place* (1950), on the coffee table, the large papier-mâché sculpture *Two Circus Women* (c. 1930)

13 Johnson House: North End of West Wall.

The multiple reflections on the 18′ pieces of plate glass, which seem superimposed on the view through the house, help give the glass a type of solidity; a direct Miesian aim which he expressed twenty-five years ago: "I discovered by working with actual glass models that the important thing is the play of reflections and not the effect of light and shadow as in ordinary buildings."

14 Johnson House: General View of Brick and Glass Units.

The bi-axial symmetry of each façade of the glass house is as absolute as Ledoux and much purer than any Baroque example. Opposite sides of my house are identical and the "minor" axis is almost as developed as the "major". (Is there a slight left-over of Baroque in the fact that the front door is in the long elevation?)

15 Johnson House: Entrance Façade of Glass Unit.

16 Johnson House: Entrance Façade of Brick Unit.

The guest house with central door and severely axial plan is jointly descended from the Baroque and from designs by Mies. (See 12.)

17 Johnson House: Glass Unit at Night.

The cylinder, made of the same brick as the platform from which it springs, forming the main motif of the house, was not derived from Mies, but rather from a burnt wooden village I saw once where nothing was left but foundations and chimneys of brick. Over the chimney I slipped a steel cage with a glass skin. The chimney forms the anchor.

by Elie Nadelman between the kitchen bar and the dining table, and an equally fulsome rubber plant on the right, the focus is on the continuous glass wall that frames the island of Mies furniture. The furniture acts as a kind of artistic signature. "Mies van der Rohe," Johnson explains, "has not only influenced the concept of the house. He has designed all of the furniture—some of it a quarter century ago, none of it later than 1930."

A close-up image of the Nadelman sculpture in frame 19 is used to justify another credit line to Mies (opposite, below left). Noting that the figurative sculpture provides "the type of foil which this kind of building needs," Johnson adds that "Mies again established the precedent in his Barcelona Pavilion." In describing the view in frame 20 looking west from the living area to the valley below, however, Johnson returns to the classical Baroque. Without mentioning the seventeenth-century painting of *The Burial of Phocion,* sometimes attributed to Poussin himself, that can just be seen on

20 Johnson House: Interior looking west.

The view of the valley, with its repoussoir of giant trees, is contrived with the aid of many Baroque landscapes. A view without a frame seems impossible after the Seventeenth Century.

18 Johnson House: Interior looking south.

Mies van der Rohe has not only influenced the concept of the house. He has designed all of the furniture—some of it a quarter century ago, none of it later than 1930.

19 Johnson House: Sculpture Group.

The papier-mache sculpture by Nadelman provides the type of foil which this kind of building needs (Mies again established the precedent in his Barcelona Pavilion).

its Johnson-designed stand in front of the glass wall to the far right, the architect observes that his own use of the trees in the near distance to form a *repoussoir* for the view of the valley is based on Baroque landscape paintings, to which he adds the assertion, "a view without a frame seems impossible after the Seventeenth Century."

The final two photographs in frames 21 and 22 (page 280) come as a kind of anticlimax, dealing as they do with functional issues and making no reference to historical sources. The view of the kitchen in frame 21 shows a waiter about to serve drinks. Of its minimalist design, Johnson has this to say: "The kitchen I reduced to a simple bar so that it would not close off any space. I have no idea what precedent I followed on that." As for the view of the bedroom in frame 22 that shows the east-facing window wall screened for privacy, Johnson simply notes that "strips of pandanus cloth hanging from the ceiling [were] the only screening I felt to be necessary." The desk where Johnson is sitting in the Newman photograph that opened the sequence of pictures of the Glass House is here empty, and the view through the window as well as the reflections on it are absent. In their bland straightforwardness, the final two frames bring the reader back to the instrumental rationality and pragmatic concerns of more typical architectural journalism of the period.

Johnson's house in New Canaan has been the subject of much debate and interpretation since his presentation of it appeared in the pages of *Architectural Review*. In one way or another, consciously or not, positively or negatively, most writers have been influenced by the architect's own description of his motivations. Some have stressed the likeness of the property to an eighteenth-century English landscape garden; others have focused on its use by Johnson as a kind of sketchbook or laboratory for ideas; many have emphasized its standing as a monument to Miesian modernism in its classic phase and, ultimately, as a misprision of it; some have seen the work as an expression of the American myth of the country house as established by Thomas Jefferson at Monticello; a few have taken a more psychological tack and interpreted it in terms of Johnson's

21 Johnson House: Cooking Unit.

The kitchen I reduced to a simple bar so that it would not close off any space. I have no idea what precedent I followed on that.

22
Johnson House: Interior, north-east corner.

Bed and writing desk, with strips of pandanus cloth hanging from the ceiling—the only screening I felt to be necessary.

politics and wartime experience or his homosexuality. Almost all have seen the house, through the article accompanying it, as epitomizing Johnson's views on architecture and as an index to his later architectural thought and production.[16]

The Johnson article can tell us something more, however, about his architecture and its significance for the later history of modernism. Critical to this, and clearly the most striking thing about the article, is that it presents the architect himself "revealing the sources of his inspiration." Not only was this "unusual," as the magazine's editor pointed out in his brief introduction; it is still almost unheard-of for an architect to structure the explanation of a building almost entirely around a description of influences, parallels, and sources. Imagine, for instance, Le Corbusier explaining the Villa Savoye or Mies the Barcelona Pavilion by reference to ideas gleaned from other people's work. Even so dedicated and diehard a revivalist as Pugin in the nineteenth century or Ralph Adams Cram in the twentieth would only speak of a historical model as an exemplar to be transformed in terms of contemporary materials and needs.

As a result of the extraordinary exegetical strategy Johnson adopted, later commentators have almost naturally been led to question his motives and motivations. The first question usually asked is whether Johnson was completely candid in his "revelations" and, if not, whether there are sources and purposes he specifically avoided referring to. Obvious precedents in the long history of metal and glass construction going back to the Crystal Palace have been cited as has the architect's silence on his reasons for splitting the program into two separate units, the one light and transparent, the other solid and opaque.[17] As a corollary to this question, one might also wonder whether all the acknowledged influences were equal in importance and whether the decision to list them in numbered frames was made to obscure an actual hierarchy. A contrast between Mies's Farnsworth House and Malevich's painting immediately comes to mind. The apparent lack of hierarchy has also led some to wonder whether there is a systematic historical method to Johnson's citing of past examples or, indeed, any coherence to the way the multiple frames of reference follow from one another. Peter Eisenman, for instance, has suggested that Johnson was essentially creating a "patrimony" for himself, whereas Craig Owens has characterized his heterogeneous approach as "genealogy" rather than history.[18] Central to all discussions of the article has been the nagging question of authenticity. How could one produce such an ostensibly original and integral work of modern architecture as the Glass House while maintaining a posture of copyist, imitator, even source-monger in accounting for the creative process that led to it? The answer here being that whatever latent eclecticism and antimodern historicism there may have been in Johnson's thinking at the time, it was effectively repressed until two years later, at the very earliest, when the Guest House renovation was first contemplated, or until the mid-1970s, at the very latest, when the AT&T Building was designed.

But what if one takes Johnson at his word—at face value, so to speak—in order to focus on the precedent-based structure of his explanation as a meaningful thing in itself? One would then seek not to agree or to disagree with his purported sources and parallels but to articulate a framework for analyzing the very terms of his argument. This is what I would like to try to do by way of conclusion. To begin with, one should remember that the images and text in the *Review* article are not scattershot but conform to a coherent historical pattern and that they are organized in a deliberate and progressive sequence. While certain types or figures in the development of modern architecture are downplayed or left out, such as Paxton's Crystal Palace or Frank Lloyd Wright, all the references included form part of the history of modernism as it had been constructed by Hitchcock, Giedion, Johnson himself, and others since the later 1920s. Whether it be the picturesque eighteenth-century English garden, the abstract painting of De Stijl and Suprematism, Choisy's analysis of Greek site planning, or the Romantic-Classicism of Ledoux and Schinkel, all had been filtered through the lens of Mies and Le Corbusier to become established elements in the historical lineage of modern architecture. Johnson's enumeration of these precedents and parallels is arranged not according to how his own design came into being but how it would be perceived in reality.[19] The comparisons begin with issues of overall site and group planning before moving on to questions involved with the form of the Glass House itself. After being introduced to the structural system employed and the plans of the two separate living units, the reader/visitor is shown around the outside of the buildings before finally being taken into the Glass House, where the means for relating interior to exterior are recapitulated and the reader/visitor's attention is drawn to a renewed appreciation of the site.

One can find precedents for Johnson's "processional" treatment of the New Canaan house in other modern architects' descriptions of their own work, but not the insistent, almost obsessive linkage of the description to a model or historical source (and, in this sense, Mies or Le Corbusier would be as "historical" as Schinkel or Ledoux). The insistence and obsessiveness are reinforced by the experiential framework adopted. We always see the building "after the fact," never in the process of creation. Unlike Wright, for instance, in his discussion of Unity Temple in *An Autobiography* (1932) or Louis Kahn in his oft-repeated account of the Unitarian Church in Rochester, Johnson never refers to the process of design. One would have no idea that it took more than two and a half years for it to coalesce and that it went through at least twenty-seven different schemes. No sketches or studies are illustrated, just the historical precedents and parallels which, as the reader in 1950 would have had to assume, autonomously predetermined the results that are shown.

The unqualified identity between formal source and material solution in Johnson's description of the New Canaan design takes on added clarity and meaning when it is considered in the light of what was normative in the discourse of the period. As noted above, *Architectural Review* published houses by American architects on a regular basis during the late 1940s and 1950s. These articles follow a typical pattern of description and analysis that has its roots in the philosophical foundations of the modern movement. Site and climate are often first adduced to account for major planning and structural decisions. For the Tremaine House by Richard Neutra in Santa Barbara, California, for instance, the first sentence of a May 1950 article reads: "The threat of forest fires necessitated a reinforced concrete structure for this house, which is surrounded by extensive woods."[20] And for the Revere Quality House for Siesta Key, Florida, by Ralph Twitchell and Paul Rudolph, published in June 1949, the writer notes in his second sentence that the house "is particularly suited for tropical weather conditions, and is designed to be proof against hurricane-shock, mildew, fire, and insects (notably white ants)—all of which present local building problems." "The main rooms," the text goes on, "face south and south-west to catch prevailing breezes; [while] the patio is sheltered from strong north winds by a long wall, an important amenity in Florida."[21]

Economic considerations follow close behind those of site and climate. For the Twitchell and Rudolph design, the writer notes that "construction is of monolithic concrete slab, poured in steel moulds, thus eliminating beams and framing and reducing cost."[22] In an article on Marcel Breuer's own house in New Canaan, published the same year as the one on Johnson's, the author remarks that what would appear to be the very Wrightian cantilevering of the upper floor was done almost solely "for economic reasons," despite its necessitating all sorts of structural expedients such as steel cable supports. It is explained that the deep overhangs are simply the result of the fact that "the lower floor was kept as small in area as possible" to stay within the budget.[23] Function and use were intimately tied to cost and ultimately played the most significant role in explaining planning decisions: "All main living functions are placed on one level on the upper floor, with bedrooms and living-rooms next to the kitchen, which is regarded as the centre of the house, and to which there is ready access from all other rooms." No mention, of course, is made of Wright's Usonian houses that pioneered this idea in the previous decade. Functional considerations are shown to affect exterior design decisions as well as those involving interior furnishings: in the Revere Quality House, "the wide eaves prevent rain streaks on the fascia, and give added shade from the rain"; in the Tremaine House, "a wide, low couch can be divided into a dozen low cubic ottomans" for greater "flexibility," while "a service trolley . . . can circulate through all living rooms and over all terraces to bring food and drink to guests."[24]

Aside from an occasional reference to the way some aspect of a building might reflect its natural surroundings—as when the text on the Tremaine House notes that "the pool has been designed to mirror the impressive skyline"[25]—description is limited to what I have previously called instrumental rationality. All aspects of design are, in effect, seen as direct responses to conditions imposed by site, locality, program, client needs, materials, methods of construction, and budget. No formal intermediary, be it historical or contemporary, is recognized. Though a vulgarization and reduction of the concept of functionalism that underpinned modernist theory of the 1920s and 1930s, such instrumental rationality kept alive the idea of originality that high modernism had proposed. Originality, in this sense, was the direct consequence of the solution to a problem by means newly arrived at and peculiarly appropriate to the times.

"If we feel the need of a new architecture," Le Corbusier wrote in *Vers une architecture*, "it is because . . . *things no longer respond to a need*." "The problem of the house has not yet been stated," and it is "only when a problem is properly stated, in our epoch, [that] it inevitably finds its solution." In order to take that initial step, we must first "shut our eyes to what exists." Then, and only then, can we arrive at the following kind of statement, which implies its own original solution: "*A house*: a shelter against heat, cold, rain, thieves and the inquisitive. A receptacle for light and sun. A certain number of cells appropriated to cooking, work, and personal life." The solution, of course, would not merely read as a checklist of responses, but "if it does not fulfil the very first conditions . . . it is not possible that the higher factors of harmony and beauty should enter in."[26]

Johnson's mentor and prime model, Mies van der Rohe, agreed with Le Corbusier in all fundamental respects when it came to defining the source of originality. He never failed to refer to the spiritual goals of architecture and to the fact that "beauty in architecture . . . can only be attained if in building we have more than the immediate purpose in mind."[27] But he also cautioned that, to avoid simply copying the past, one had to meet "the demands of the time for realism and functionality." "The purposes of our tasks are for the most part very simple and clear," he stated. "One only has to recognize them and formulate them, then they will lead of themselves to significant building solutions." "The site, the exposure to the sun, the program of rooms, and the building materials are the essential factors for the design of a residence," he concluded. "The building is to be formed in response to these conditions. Old familiar pictures may disappear, but in their place residences will arise that are functional in all respects. The world did not become poorer when the stagecoach was replaced by the automobile."[28] The worst offense in Mies's view was to preconceive buildings in terms of form. Only formalism could result. "We know no forms, only building problems," he wrote in *G* in 1923,

> Form is not the goal but the result of our work.
> There is no form in and for itself.
> The truly formal is conditional, fused with the task, yes, the most elementary expression of its solution.
> Form as a goal is formalism; and that we reject.[29]

At the time Johnson republished the above statement in his Mies monograph of 1947 (in a slightly different translation), he was designing the New Canaan house. As we have seen, in both that building and the *Architectural Review* article accompanying it, he appears to contradict Mies, not to speak of Le Corbusier, on almost every score. The article, in particular, makes it clear that Johnson approached the design of his house as a matter of form. Function, cost, materials, climate—none of these factors are acknowledged as having had the least effect on form. Only historical precedent, both very recent and more remote in time, are claimed to have played a role. The recurrence of phrases like "derived from," "copied from," "influenced by," "adapted from," "typical of," and "descended from" to describe the dependence of his chosen forms on those of the past leads us to assume a complete lack of originality on Johnson's part at the same time as the explicitness of the admission suggests another kind of originality, one quite different from the sort that high modernism held as ideal.

In the article, Johnson equates contemporary and historical precedent. Imitating Mies or Le Corbusier is no different from copying Ledoux or Schinkel. But in the actual building, he follows a different course. Schinkel, Ledoux, and the Athenian Acropolis appear only abstractly, theoretically. Mies, however, is there in full material form. And because of the transparency of the relationship to the functionalist subtext of Mies's own architecture, one is allowed to maintain the fiction that the Glass House is equally original in design. But Johnson's explanation of his motivations reveals something else. Where the high modernist buildings of the 1920s and 1930s were generated from a set of practical conditions that in no way predetermined the final "look" of the designs, the Glass House started with a preconceived notion of form, if not in fact a "look." For the modern architect of the generation preceding Johnson's, building was always a direct and immediate response to the new conditions and spirit of the times, therefore always original, unprecedented, and continually in the process of forming the style to put an end to the reign of "the styles." The historically mediated form of the New Canaan house, by contrast, is self-consciously retrospective, preconceived, and in a chosen, classifiable style.

Johnson's critique of the functionalist subtext of modern architecture and its implications for ideas about originality and historicism can certainly be traced back to his earliest writings on the subject. But when he and Hitchcock dismissed the hard-line functionalist position in their book *The International Style* of 1932, that could be seen as a rather hermetic connoisseur's take on the subject. By 1950 times were about to catch up with him. Architects and critics of all persuasions now seemed to agree on one thing, namely, that functionalism as a doctrine had run its course and needed to be replaced by something more flexible and more expansive. Some of the remedies stressed the social and psychological dimensions of the problem, but one of the most powerful and long-lasting of the new approaches focused on the autonomous nature of the discipline of architecture as such and, by extension, its historical roots in the recent as well as the not-so-recent past. In this new "formalism," as it was often called, Johnson, and most particularly the Glass House, played a signal and exemplary role.[30] Louis Kahn's emergence in the mid-fifties as a figure of major importance reinforced the growing historicist component of the formalist mix. Writers like Vincent Scully and Colin Rowe became leading voices in a discourse that would have been unthinkable in the pre–World War II years and just as unthinkable without the trenchant reformulation of modernism offered by Johnson's Glass House. Robert Venturi's precedent-based analysis of architectural form, first articulated in his 1966 book *Complexity and Contradiction in Architecture,* and Peter Eisenman's theorization of a "postfunctionalist" modernism, beginning in the mid-1970s, can both be seen as direct descendants of this evolution in architectural thought.[31]

In the end, Johnson's design of the Glass House and explication of it in the most important architectural journal of the period should surely be considered as significant for the history of modern architecture as was his earlier role in promoting the idea of an International Style. If the International Style exhibition and book gave a name to a movement and brought it to public attention, the Glass House and its publication turned what was a set of universal stylistic principles into a historical phenomenon. In the later example, modernism and historicism were no longer two diametrically opposed positions. Rather, modernism itself was seen in historicist terms and thus became, like any other system of forms, open to historical reference. Where in the 1930s it would have been Mies *or* history, by 1950 it was Mies *as* history. By dismantling the prop of instrumental rationality that ensured high modernism's originality and uniqueness, in the article on his New Canaan property, while maintaining the full-blown appearance of its modernist effects in the Glass House itself, Johnson was able to perform an act of architectural legerdemain that still stuns by its subtlety. As the tensions in that opposition have come to manifest themselves in discrete and often ambiguous ways over the course of his remaining career, not to speak of those influenced by it, the Glass House serves to remind us of the complexity of modernist thinking at the very core of Johnson's oeuvre at the same time as it reveals the central role he has played in the construction and deconstruction of its meanings. One might go so far as to say that, with the design and publication of the Glass House, Philip Johnson defined the moment when modernism became history.

Notes

1. Open letter from Robin Middleton to Philip Johnson, *Architectural Design* 37 (March 1967), 107; and Franz Schulze, *Philip Johnson: Life and Work* (New York: Alfred A. Knopf, 1994), 194, 4.

2. Ibid., 235-40.

3. Introduction by Henry-Russell Hitchcock, in *Philip Johnson: Architecture, 1949–1965* (New York: Holt, Rinehart and Winston, 1966), 10–13.

4. Richard Pommer, "Philip Johnson and History, *Artforum* 17 (October 1978), 26–29; Marc M. Angélil and Sarah R. Graham, "'Man kann nicht die Geschichte nicht kennen': Philip Johnsons Architektur, eine Frage des Stils," *Werk, Bauen + Wohnen* 74 (September 1987), 4–9, 76; and Craig Owens, "Philip Johnson: History, Genealogy, Historicism," in David Whitney and Jeffrey Kipnis, eds., *Philip Johnson: The Glass House* (New York: Pantheon Books, 1993), 89.

5. Vincent J. Scully, Jr., "Doldrums in the Suburbs," *Journal of the Society of Architectural Historians* 24 (March 1965), 36–47; and William H. Jordy, *American Buildings and Their Architects*, vol. 4: *The Impact of European Modernism in the Mid-Twentieth Century* (New York: Doubleday & Company, 1972), 165–219. The phrase "domestication of the International Style" was earlier used by Alfred H. Barr in "What Is Happening to Modern Architecture?: A Symposium at The Museum of Modern Art," *The Museum of Modern Art Bulletin* 15 (spring 1948), 8.

6. Some of the most well-known are Henry Wright and George Nelson's *Tomorrow's House* (1945), Frederick Gutheim's *Houses for Family Living* (1948), Elizabeth B. Mock's *If You Want to Build a House* (1946), Katherine Morrow Ford and Thomas H. Creighton's *The American House Today* (1951), Robert Woods Kennedy's *The House and the Art of Its Design* (1953), and Frank Lloyd Wright's *The Natural House* (1954).

7. Jordy, *American Buildings,* vol. 4, 168.

8. See above, p. 18.

9. The reference by Pugin is in the caption to the illustration of the Soane House in the first edition of *Contrasts,* published in 1836.

10. "Houses: House in Cambridge, Mass., Philip Johnson, Architect, S. Clements Horsley, Assoc." *Architectural Forum* 79 (December 1943), 91–92.

11. "House at New Canaan, Connecticut. Philip Johnson: Architect," *Architectural Review* 108 (September 1950), 152.

12. Commentary by Robert A. M. Stern, in Philip Johnson, *Writings* (New York: Oxford University Press, 1979), 212.

13. "House at New Canaan," 153. All succeeding quotations from Johnson, unless otherwise noted, are from this publication.

14. Philip C. Johnson, *Mies van der Rohe* (1947; 2d ed. rev., New York: The Museum of Modern Art, 1953), 131, 137.

15. Philip Johnson, "Whence and Whither: The Processional Element in Architecture" (1965) in Johnson, *Writings,* 151–55.

16. Whitney and Kipnis, *Philip Johnson;* Christine S. E. Magar, "Project Manual for the Glass House," in Debra Colemen, Elizabeth Danze, and Carol Henderson, eds., *Architecture and Feminism* (New York: Princeton Architectural Press, 1996), 72–108; and Alice T. Friedman, *Women and the Making of the Modern House: A Social and Architectural History* (New York: Harry N. Abrams, 1998), 147–59.

17. Jeffrey Kipnis, "Introduction: Throwing Stones—The Incidental Effects of a Glass House," in Whitney and Kipnis, *Philip Johnson*, xiv-xv; and Friedman, *Women and the Making of the Modern House*, 149–54.

18. Peter Eisenman, "Introduction," in Johnson, *Writings*, 10–25; and Owens, "Philip Johnson," in Whitney and Kipnis, *Philip Johnson*, 81–90.

19. This is noted in ibid., 82.

20. "House at Santa Barbara. Richard Neutra: Architect," *Architectural Review* 107 (May 1950), 325.

21. "House in Florida. R. S. Twitchell and P. M. Rudolph: Architects," *Architectural Review* 105 (June 1949), 287.

22. Ibid., 287.

23. "Marcel Breuer's Own House. Marcel Breuer: Architect," *Architectural Review* 105 (January 1949), 11–12.

24. Ibid., 11; "House in Florida," 288; and "House at Santa Barbara," 329.

25. Ibid., 326.

26. Le Corbusier, *Towards a New Architecture*, trans. Frederick Etchells (1927; New York: Holt, Rinehart and Winston,1960),102–6.

27. Ludwig Mies van der Rohe, "Build Beautifully and Practically! Stop this Cold Functionality" (1930), in Fritz Neumeyer, *The Artless Word: Mies van der Rohe on the Building Art*, trans. Mark Jarzombek (Cambridge, Massachusetts, and London: MIT Press, 1991), 307.

28. Mies van der Rohe, "Solved Tasks: A Challenge for Our Building Industry" (1924), in Neumeyer, *The Artless Word*, 246–47.

29. Mies van der Rohe, "Building" (1923), in Neumeyer, *The Artless Word*, 242.

30. An early account of the development is Vincent J. Scully, Jr., "Archetype and Order in Recent American Architecture," *Art in America* 42 (December 1954), 250–61. See also William H. Jordy, "The Formal Image: USA," *Architectural Review* 157 (March 1960), 157–65; and Jürgen Joedicke, *Architecture Since 1945: Sources and Directions* (New York and Washington: Frederick A. Praeger, 1969), 138–53.

31. For a polemical statement of his position, see Peter Eisenman, "Post-Functionalism," *Oppositions* 6 (fall 1976), editorial.

Acknowledgments

Compiling nearly sixty years of Philip Johnson's residential designs has been an enthralling process, which has extended over much of the past decade. Our efforts would have been impossible without the assistance of a great number of people. They include the following individuals whose working relationships with Johnson, taken all together, span his entire career: Christian Bjone, Renny Booth, Barbara Hartmann, Hugh Jacobsen, Joe Katanik, Maurine Knorr, John Manley, Aron McDonald, Elizabeth Murrell, Sherida Paulsen, Alan Ritchie, Joe Santaeramo, Robert Walker, Barbara Wolf, and Ivan Zaknik.

As this book was being researched, Johnson's archive was relocated to the Getty Research Institute in Los Angeles. Wim deWit, Director of Special Collections, was most helpful in providing access to the collection, as were Getty staff members Ken Brown, Beth Guynn, Charlie Rossow, and Ted Walbye. Janet Parks at Columbia University's Avery Architectural and Fine Arts identified a number of Johnson's projects and provided essential assistance in locating illustration materials. In the Department of Architecture and Design at The Museum of Modern Art, New York, Pierre Adler and Christopher Mount helped to find archival photographs and drawings for the Glass House. *The Architectural Review* graciously permitted reproduction of the article by Philip Johnson discussed by Neil Levine in the afterword; we are grateful to Lynne Jackson, on the *Review* staff, for her timely help.

Additional assistance came from Jim Quigel and Tom Weprich at the Special Collections Library at Penn State University; Sara Brown and Sharon Turo at the New Canaan Historical Society; Mary Daniels at the Special Collections Library, the Harvard Graduate School of Design; Brian Sullivan at Harvard University Archives; Martin Durrant at the Victoria and Albert Museum; Patricia Crosby, Archivist for the Ford Motor Company; Libby Oldham at the Nantucket Historical Society; and Judy Greenberg, Director of the Kreeger Museum. In addition to the new photography by Steven Brooke, archival images from a number of noted photographers are used; we are especially grateful to Louis Checkman, Christine Cordazzo at ESTO, Nancy Crampton, Elsie Cyr and Judy Cyr, Robert Damora, Richard Payne, and Robert Walker.

Present owners of Johnson's houses were consistently gracious in providing access to their homes. We thank these original owners: Henry Beck, Patricia Beck, and their daughter Colita McCarthy; Sylvie and Eric Boissonnas; James A. D. Geier; and Richard and Geraldine Hodgson. We are also grateful to Joan and Bugs Baer (Tremaine Estate) and to Kathleen Housley, biographer of the Tremaine family; Monsieur and Madame Bober (Tourre House); Jeane and Ordway Burden; Mr. and Mrs. Robert Damora (Booth House); Frank Gallipoli (Wiley House); Robert Heimann and Robert Heimann Jr. (Geier House); Peter and Donna Hurwitz (Oneto House); Gay and Clif Leonhardt; Bill Matassoni and Pamela Valentine (Boissonnas House in New Canaan); Vance Muse and Elsian Cozens of the Menil Collection; Liza Ozkural (Wolf House); Janet Phypers (Ball House); Mark and Pearl Rabin (Paine House); and Michael and Penny Winton (Davis House).

Friends and associates provided timely help and guidance. They include Albert M. and Wanda June Jenkins, Bentley and Karen Jenkins, Alexander Roesle, Joe Fung, Henry Myerberg, Daryl Barnes, Alice Yang, Cara Berman Marks, Gil and Bill Stott, Gerhard Kallman, Jennifer Luce, Doris Latino, Richard Shaffer, Fred Schwartz, and David Thall. Thanks also go to Maria Dallerba-Ricci, Sarah Whiting and Ron Witte, Evelyn Jacobs Calvert, Mark Royse, Dana Cox, Virginia Miller, and Faith Harders. Special assistance came from David Whitney, Hilary Lewis, Mabel Lamb, Carter Manny, Olga Hirshhorn, Wylie Tuttle, I. M. Pei, John Johansen, Vinnie de Simone, Edward Smith, and Pam Gores. Louis Blanc, Mike Soriano, and Sarah Heller assisted with new renderings. At Abbeville Press, thanks are due to Jackie Decter, Nancy Grubb, Mary Christian, Ashley Benning, and especially Mark Magowan and Christopher Lyon, for starting and completing this project, respectively. Neil Levine and Steven Brooke have remained engaged fellow travelers throughout this process.

Above all, our appreciation must go to Philip Johnson, who has made not just his documents and records available to us but, much more importantly, his thoughts and memories of these projects. We thank him for a commitment to architecture at the highest level, extending back over nearly three-quarters of the twentieth century, and continuing now into the twenty-first.

Stover Jenkins and David Mohney
New York and Lexington, April 30, 2001

Selected Bibliography

Writings by Philip Johnson

1932 Johnson, Philip and Henry-Russell Hitchcock. *The International Style: Architecture Since 1922*. With an introduction by Alfred H. Barr. New York: W. W. Norton & Company, 1932. Reprint, with a foreword by Henry-Russell Hitchcock and a foreword by Philip Johnson, New York: W. W. Norton & Company, 1995.

1932 Johnson, Philip, Alfred H. Barr, Henry-Russell Hitchcock, and Lewis Mumford. *Modern Architects* (exh. cat.). New York: The Museum of Modern Art, 1932.

1934 *Machine Art* (exh. cat.). With a foreword by Alfred H. Barr. New York: The Museum of Modern Art, 1934. Reprint, with a foreword by Philip Johnson, New York: The Museum of Modern Art, 1995.

1947 *Mies van der Rohe*. New York: Museum of Modern Art, 1947.

1949 "Frontiersman: FLW." *Architectural Record* 106 (August 1949): 105–10.

1950 "House at New Caanan, Connecticut, Architect: Philip Johnson." *Architectural Review* 108 (September 1950): 152–60.

"Preface" and "Comments." In *Postwar Architecture*. Edited by Henry-Russell Hitchcock and Arthur Drexler. New York: The Museum of Modern Art, 1952.

1953 "Correct and Magnificent Play." Review of *Le Corbusier, Oeuvre complète: Volume 5, 1946–1952*, edited by W. Boesiger. *Art News* 52 (September 1953): 16–17, 52–53. Reprinted in *Philip Johnson: Writings*, with a foreword by Vincent Scully, introduction by Peter Eisenman, and commentary by Robert A.M. Stern (New York: Oxford University Press, 1979).

1954 "Remarks from an informal talk to students of Architectural Design at Harvard, December 1954." *Perspecta: The Yale Architectural Journal* 3 (1955): 40–44. Lecture originally titled "The Seven Crutches of Modern Architecture." Reprinted in *Philip Johnson: Writings*.

1955 "Style and the International Style." Speech at Barnard College, 30 April 1955. Reprinted in *Philip Johnson: Writings*.

1955 "The Wiley House." *Perspecta: The Yale Architectural Journal* 3 (1955): 45.

1957 "100 Years, Frank Lloyd Wright and Us." *Pacific Architect and Builder* 63 (March 1957): 13, 35–36.

1959 "Whither Away-Non Miesian Directions." Lecture at Yale University, New Haven, Connecticut, 5 February 1959. Reprinted in *Philip Johnson: Writings*.

1960 "Informal Talk, Architectural Association." Lecture at the Architectural Association of the School of Architecture, London, 28 November 1960. Reprinted in *Philip Johnson: Writings*.

1960 "Where Are We At?" Review of *Architecture, Nineteenth and Twentieth Centuries*, by Henry-Russell Hitchcock, and *Theory and Design in the First Machine Age*, by Reyner Banham. *Architectural Review* 128 (September 1960): 173–75.

1961 Johnson, Philip. Letter to Jurgen Joedicke, 1961. In *Philip Johnson*, by John Jacobus, 120–22. New York: George Braziller, 1962. Reprinted in *Philip Johnson: Writings*.

1961 "Johnson." *Perspecta: The Yale Architectural Journal* 7 (1961): 3–8.

1961 "Speech Honoring Mies van der Rohe on His Seventy-Fifth Birthday." Speech in Chicago, 7 February 1961. Reprinted in *Philip Johnson: Writings*.

1962 "The Seven Shibboleths of Our Profession." Speech at the 11th Annual Northeast Regional A.I.A. Conference, Oceanlake, Oregon, 12, October 1962. Reprinted in *Philip Johnson: Writings*.

1963 "Full Scale False Scale." Show III, June 1963. Reprinted in *Philip Johnson: Writings*.

1965 "Whence and Whither: The Processional Element in Architecture." *Perspecta: The Yale Journal of Architecture* 9/10 (1965): 167–78. Reprinted in *Philip Johnson: Writings*.

1966 *Philip Johnson: Architecture 1949–1965*. With an introduction by Henry-Russell Hitchcock. New York: Holt, Rinehart, and Winston, 1966.

1975 "What Makes Me Tick." Lecture at Columbia University, 24 September 1975. Reprinted in *Philip Johnson: Writings*.

1979 *Philip Johnson: Writings*. With a foreword by Vincent Scully, introduction by Peter Eisenman, and commentary by Robert A.M. Stern. New York: Oxford University Press, 1979.

1988 Johnson, Philip and Mark Wigley. *Deconstructivist Architecture*. With a foreword by Stuart Wrede. New York: The Museum of Modern Art, 1988.

Writings about Philip Johnson, his Architecture, or Related Material

1943 "Cambridge House for Philip Johnson." *Architectural Forum* 79 (December 1943): 89–93.

1945 Platt, Richard. "As Simple As That." *Ladies' Home Journal*, July 1945, 118.

1946 Platt, Richard. "House for a Millionaire with No Servants." *Ladies' Home Journal*, April 1946, 227.

1948 Haeberly, Mabel. "This New House in Connecticut Needs No Windows." *New York Times*, 12 December 1948, Real Estate section.

1949 "New-World Xanadu of Steel and Glass: Pavilion and Swimming Pool." *Interiors* 108 (January 1949): 114–15.

1949 Roche, Mary. "Living in a Glass House." *New York Times*, 14 August 1949, section 6, p. 34.

1949 "Modern Guest House of J.D. Rockefeller 3d Nearing Completion on East Fifty-second Street." *New York Times*, 2 September 1949, p.30.

1949 "Glass House." *Life Magazine*, 26 September 1949, 94–96.

1949 "A Glass House in Connecticut." *House and Garden*, October 1949.

1949 "New Canaan: Architecture Opaque and Transparent: Johnson's Glass and Brick House." *Interiors* 109 (October 1949): 90–101.

1949 "New Canaan: Glass House Permits Its Owner to Live in a Room in Nature." *Architectural Forum* 91 (November 1949): 74–79.

1950 "New Canaan: Le pavilion de verre, maison de week-end." *Architecture d'aujour-d'hui* 20 (July 1950): 48–50.

1950 "House at New Caanan, Connecticut, Architect: Philip Johnson." *Architectural Review* 108 (September 1950): 152–60.

1950 Drexler, Arthur. "Town House." *Interiors* 110 (December 1950): 80–85.

1950 "Guest House." *Architectural Forum* 93, no. 2 (August 1950): 84–87.

1953 Hitchcock, Henry-Russell and Arthur Drexler, eds. *Built in USA: Post-War Architecture* (exh. cat.). With a preface by Philip Johnson. New York: Museum of Modern Art, 1952.

1953 "New Canaan House for R. Hodgson." *Architectural Record* 113 (March 1953): 156–61.

1953 "Maison à New Canaan." *Architecture d'aujourd'hui* 24 (December 1953): 116–17.

1954 Gueft, Olga. "Home For A Collector's Double Life: Philip Johnson Bends the Minnesota Climate to His Will" and "Pavilion in the Desert: Philip Johnson Isolates a Domed Sanctuary from Time and Place." *Interiors* 113 (July 1954): 62–67, 70–71.

1954 "Indoor Gardens Can Be a Source of Light." *House and Home* 6 (August 1954): 110–15.

1954 Hess, Thomas B. "New York Salon." *Art News*, no. 52 (1954): 24–25.

1954 "How to Turn an Old Barn Into a Modern House, Madison, Connecticut." *House and Home* 6 (October 1954): 148–49.

1955 "Clearcut Expression of the Double Life: Wiley House, New Canaan." *Architectural Record* 117 (June 1955): 167–72.

1955 "Connecticut House for Wiley Development Corp." *Architectural Record* 118 (November 1955): 176–79.

1955 Johnson, Philip. "The Wiley House." *Perspecta: The Yale Architectural Journal* 3 (1955): 45.

1959 Jordy, W. H. "Mies-less Johnson." *Architectural Forum* 111 (September 1959): 114–23.

1961 Hitchcock, Henry-Russell "Current Work of Philip Johnson." *Zodiac* 8 (1961): 64–81.

1962 Jacobus, John M., Jr. *Philip Johnson*. New York: George Braziller, 1962.

1962 "Philip Johnson." *Architecture d'aujourd'hui* 6 (February 1962): 64–75.

1962 "Glass Living Pavilion Tops Views: Residence on Lloyds Neck, Long Island." *Architectural Record* 31 (May 1962): 110–13.

1962 "Recent Work of Philip Johnson." *Architectural Record* 132 (July 1962): 113–28.

1962 "Maison de vacances au Cap Bénat, Côte d' Azur." *Architecture d'aujourd'hui* 33 (September 1962): 54.

1965 "Villa Becomes an Acropolis: Riviera Vacation House." *Interiors* 125 (December 1965): 68–72.

1966 "Connecticut Bunker: Philip Johnson Has Completed an Underground Museum to House His Growing Art Collection." *Architectural Forum* 124 (May 1966): 57.

1966 "Philip Johnson Goes Underground." *Art in America* 54 (July–August 1966): 88–97.

1967 "Johnson Underground." *Progressive Architecture* 48 (April 1967): 146.

1967 "Three Projects by Philip Johnson, Each Designed for a Hill." *Architectural Record* 141 (June 1967): 139–50.

1967 "Boissonnas, France." *House and Garden*, August 1967.

1968 MacPherson, Myra. "The Great Hall: A Mansion Is Attached." *New York Times*, 8 September 1968, sec. 1, p. 88.

1968 "The Kreeger House." *Time*, 13 September 1968.

1970 Dixon, J. M. "Sculpture Under Glass: Philip Johnson's Personal Sculpture Collection in New Canaan, Conn." *Architectural Forum* 133 (December 1970): 22–25.

1973 Goldberger, Paul and Philip Johnson. *Philip Johnson: The Architectural Forum* 138, no. 1 (January–February 1973).

1977 "Geier House, Cincinnati." *Landscape Architecture* 67 (May 1977): 247–49.

1977 Stern, Robert A.M. "The Evolution of Philip Johnson's Glass House, 1947–1948." *Oppositions* (fall 1977): 10.

1983 Wagner, Walter. "Johnson Study/Library, New Canaan, CT." *Architectural Record* 171 (July 1983): 114–19.

1986 Scully, Vincent. "Architecture: Philip Johnson, the Glass House Revisited." *Architectural Digest*, November 1986.

1987 Giovannini, Joseph. "Johnson and His Glass House: Reflections." *New York Times*, 16 July 1987, sec. 3.

1993 Whitney, David and Jeffrey Kipnis, eds. *Philip Johnson: The Glass House*. New York: Pantheon Books, 1993.

1994 Lewis, Hilary and John O'Connor. *Philip Johnson: The Architect in His Own Words*. New York: Rizzoli, 1994.

1994 Schulze, Franz. *Philip Johnson: Life and Work*. New York: Alfred A. Knopf, 1994.

1996 Kipnis, Jeffrey. *Philip Johnson: Recent Work*. Architectural Monograph Series, no. 44. London: Academy Editions, 1996.

1999 Viladas, Pilar. "They Did it Their Way: Whatever the Conventional Wisdom, the de Menils Defied It—Especially at Home." *New York Times Magazine*, 10 October 1999, 85–93.

2000 Welch, Frank D. *Philip Johnson and Texas*. With a foreword by Philip Johnson. Austin: University of Texas Press, 2000.

2001 Goldberger, Paul. "Philip Johnson: The Architect's Daring New Residential Projects." *Architectural Digest*, March 2001.

Archival Collections

Philip Johnson Papers, Archival Accession # 980060, Getty Research Institute, Special Collections/Photo Study Collection, Los Angeles.

Philip Johnson Papers, The Department of Architecture and Design, The Museum of Modern Art, New York.

F. S. Lincoln Photograph Collection, Historical Collections and Labor Archives, Special Collections Library, Penn. State University, Philadelphia.

Index

Photography Credits

Unless otherwise indicated, all color photographs are by Steven Brooke. Additional photographers and sources of drawings and photographic material are as follows:

The Architectural Review (London): pp. 268, 272-76, 278-80; Louie Blanc: fig. 272; Bon Hui: fig. 268; Renny Booth: fig. 353; © Louis Checkman (model by Joe Santeramo): fig. 216; Chicago Historical Society, Prints & Photographs Department: fig. 214; Columbia University, Avery Architectural and Fine Arts Library, Drawings and Archives Department: figs. 39-43, 51-53, 58, 67, 68, 157, 158, 185, 187-89, 195, 196, 204, 206-10, 228, 239, 240, 241, 243, 244, 247; Nancy Crampton: fig. 338; © C. J. Cyr. (courtesy of Elsie Cyr and Judy Cyr): fig. 131; Robert Damora: fig. 34; Fondation Le Corbusier, © FLC L2 (19)15: fig. 19; Joe Fung: fig. 76; Frank O. Gehry & Associates, Inc.: fig. 284; Getty Research Institute, Special Collections/Photo Study Collection (Philip Johnson Papers, Archival Accession No. 980060): page 4; figs. 11-18, 20, 21, 25, 26, 30, 31, 36, 38, 46, 48, 50, 54-56, 59, 63-65, 77-91, 93-102, 105 (above and below), 106-10, 111 (above), 114, 115, 119-22, 127-29, 132, 133, 136, 139, 145, 147, 152, 154-57, 162, 166, 169, 174-76, 178, 182-84, 191, 192, 198, 202, 205, 212, 215, 217,

218-21, 226, 227, 230, 231, 233, 242, 245, 246, 252, 256, 258, 262, 312, 315-19, 322-24, 329, 331, 333, 337, 340-42, 344, 346; Bill Hedrich, Hedrich-Blessing Studio (courtesy Chicago Historical Society): figs. 75, 203; Sarah Heller: figs. 5, 6, 45, 269, 270, 326, 327; Stover Jenkins: figs. 37, 76, 103, 229; Philip Johnson/Alan Ritchie Architects: figs. 267, 273, 274, 280, 282, 293, 297, 301 (model by Ken Lin): 303, 305, 306, 334, 335, 349; Ladies' Home Journal: figs. 32, 33; George Lewis: fig. 10; Ken Lin: fig. 309, 310; F. S. Lincoln (courtesy of the Historical Collections and Labor Archives, Special Collections Library, Penn State University): figs. 35, 47, 49, 92; John Manley: figs. 276-79, 281, 283, 285-88, 291, 295, 298, 299, 304, 307, 308, 350; Merit Studios (courtesy Getty Research Institute, Special Collections/Photo Study Collection): fig. 153; Elizabeth Murrell: fig. 300; Elizabeth Murrell, Ken Lin, and Pietro Filardo: fig. 302; © 2001 The Museum of Modern Art, New York: figs. 2-4, 7, 8, 104, 118, 186; Paul Parker (courtesy The Museum of Modern Art, New York): fig. 1; Sherida Paulsen: fig. 271; Richard Payne: figs. 60-62, 321, 347, 348; Mike Soriano: figs. 22, 23, 24, 194; Ezra Stoller, © Esto: figs. 29, 44, 57, 110, 111 (below), 134, 140-142, 167, 173, 177, 179, 180, 211, 213, 314, 325; The Victoria and Albert Museum, The Victoria and Albert Picture Library: fig. 248; © Robert Walker: figs. 275, 289, 290, 292, 294, 296, 351, 352.